Prince of Wales

Dr. Bhau Daji

Mount Stuart Elphinstone who presented Divinia Commedia to the Asiatic Society

Dhyani Buddha from Borobudur

Plate IV

Victoria & Albert Museum

Bust of Birdwood in the Library,
University of Mumbai

Sir Bartle Frere, Governor of Bombay

Juggonath Sunkersett

Plate V

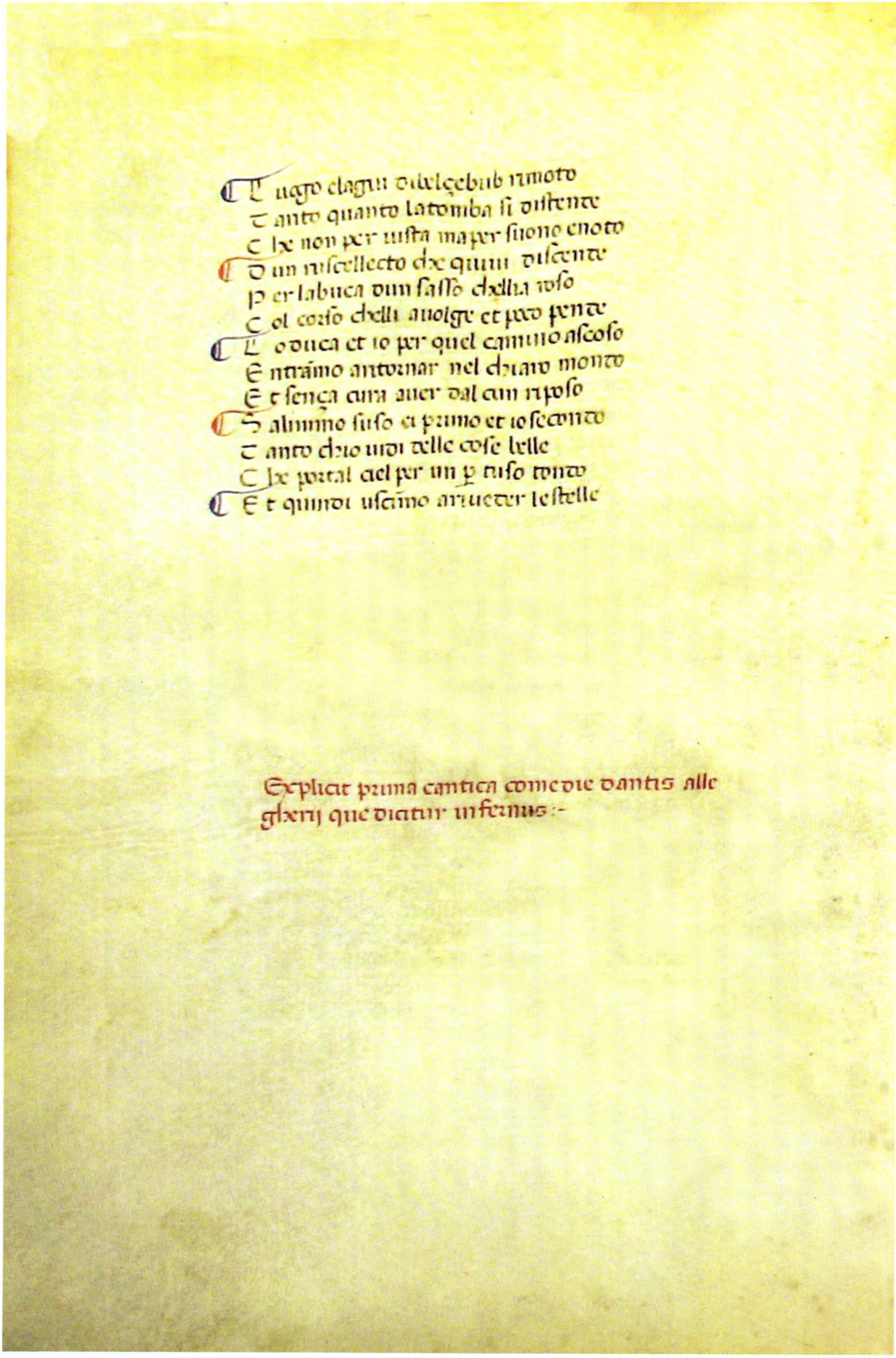

L uogo elagiu dibelçebub rimoto
T anto quanto latomba si distende
C he non per uista ma per suono e noto
D un ruscellecto che quiui discende
P er labuca dun sasso chellia roso
C ol corso chelli auolge et poco pende
L o duca et io per quel camino ascoso
E ntrámo antornar nel chiaro mondo
E t sença cura auer dalcun riposo
S alimmo suso ei primo et io secondo
T anto chio uidi delle cose belle
C he portal ciel per un p tuso tondo
E t quindi uscimo ariueder lestelle

Explicit prima cantica comedie dantis alle
ghierij que dicitur infernus :-

Plate VI

Dante's Divinia Commedia, discovered by Dr. Birdwood

Incomincia il primo canto della seconda can-
tica della comedia di dante allighieri da firen-
ce nel quale canto lautore prohemiçça singu-
larmente questa seconda parte dicta purga-
torio: Et tracta qui della honestate ponendo
che il primo che trovo uscendo dinferno fu cato
lo quale significa lonestate. pero che fue homo
molto honesto et molto virtuoso: Et pero trac-
ta delle quactro virtu cardinali deli illi fu illu-
minato cioe prudentia iustitia temperança,
et fortitudo: Et da questo canto tracta della
nime punite fuor del purgatorio: In dugia-
ro tentrare a purgarsi in quello per che i
dulgiarono a pentirsi in Questa vi-
ta de peccati :-

Per correr miglior
acqua alça le vele
Omai la navicella
del mio ingegno
Che lassa dietro a
se mar si crudele
Et cantero di quel
secondo regno
Doue lumano spi-
rito si purga
Et di salire al ciel
diventa degno
Ma qui la morta poesi resurga
O sancte muse poi che vostro sono
Et qui calliope alquanto surga
Seguitando il mio verso con quel suono
Di cui le piche misere sentiro
Lo colpo tal che disperar perdono

Plate VII

suitable public building at his disposal for its accommodation, and a sum of Rs. 6,000 for the necessary expenses and appointed Dr. Impey its in charge.[5]

The committee appointed by the Government, consisting of Dr. Impey, President, Dr. Buist, Professor Sinclair, W.F. Hunter, Esq., and Professor Alex Garden Fraser, met in September 1855 and elected Dr. Buist as Secretary, and Curator.[6]

The committee, on examining the premises, found it in a state of disrepair. They realized that the building would not be ready for use until New Year's Day, 1856.[7]

Meanwhile the Curator, Dr. Buist was instructed by the committee to acquire necessary articles to set up the Museum.[8]

The committee also published a Memorandum explaining the objects of Government in establishing the Museum.[9]

"The Museum is proposed to be at once Educational and Economical,"10 they declared in their *Directions for Contributions to the Bombay Central Museum.*

As Lord Elphinstone said in Bombay, it was established "for the illustration of general economic processes and the development of the commercial and Industrial resources of Western India."[11]

At first the museum was housed in the mess-room and adjoining rooms of the Town Barracks in Bombay. In 1857, due to the uprising in Bengal, the Brigadier General gave urgent orders for the museum to be removed in order to house European regiments arriving in Bombay on their way to Bengal.[12] There was such a rush and haste in moving the exhibits, that the labour employed, indiscriminately threw exhibits from the windows and many exhibits were lost. It is also said that the same fate was met by the office of the Society. Some of the exhibits that were saved from this holocaust were kept in the Town Hall.[13]

The entire museum was then shifted and re-arranged in the Town Hall.

Consequently, under Government instructions, new committees were formed in the Bombay Presidency for the express purpose of raising the requisite collections for the new Government Central Museum.[14]

---

5 *GD,* vol. 73 of 1856, p. 370.

6 *Ibid.*, p. 371.

7 *Ibid.*

8 *Ibid.*, p. 372.

9 *Ibid.*

10 *GD,* vol. 73 of 1856, p. 19

11 *Gazetteer of the Bombay City and Island,* (henceforth *GBCI*) vol. III, p. 379.

12 *GBCI,* vol. III, p. 380.

13 Priyolkar, A.K., *Dr. Bhau Daji: Vyakti, Kaal va Kartrutva, Mumbai Marathi Sahitya Sangh,* Mumbai, p. 379.

14 *GD,* vol. 73 of 1856, p. 373.

Dr. Buist, an erudite scholar, lacked the patience necessary to cultivate human relations. He disagreed with the various committees on several points and they in turn pointed out his mistakes.

Dr. Buist, much to the chagrin of Lord Elphinstone, was asked to resign. Rev. Dr. Alex Garden Fraser succeeded Dr. Buist in the Curatorship.[15]

Dr. Fraser suggested the founding of a self-sufficient museum. The suggestion was taken up in earnestness by leading citizens of Bombay such as Messrs. Framjee Nusserwanjee, Cursetjee Nusserwanjee Cama, Munguldas Nathoobhoy, Dr. Bhau Daji, Dhunjeebhoy Nusserwanjee Cama, Dr. George Birdwood and all the friends of the Museum, which led to the formation of a committee. However, Sir Jamsetjee Jeejeebhoy was unable to join due to ill health.[16] The new Museum Committee was comprised of eminent citizens of Bombay, Parsis, Sethias and Europeans.[17]

Dr. Fraser handed over charge to Dr. Birdwood and, in 1858, Lord Elphinstone appointed him Curator and Secretary of the museum.[18]

When organising the museum in the Town Hall, Dr. Birdwood had to pack away certain items like woods and Aden corals till such time as a suitable building was provided for the museum.[19]

Dr. Birdwood made use of his numerous contacts for the furtherance of his cause—developing the museum. One of his contacts was the Agri-Horticultural Society, set up in 1830 in Bombay as a branch of the Agricultural and Horticultural Society of Bengal established ten years earlier. The Society aimed to promote commercial agriculture, improve agricultural techniques and introduce new crops into Western India.[20]

Dr. Birdwood, by dent of his vision, and by making use of the facilities provided to him by the Agri-Horticultural Society, put the museum in correspondence with Aden, the Cape, Australia, USA, Singapore and Hong Kong for the exchange of natural products.[21] He was interested in natural products as well as manufactured goods.[22]

It was Dr. Birdwood who brought to the notice of the Government and the mercantile community that so many European and Asiatic manufactures made their way overland into

15 Birdwood, *Report,* p. 48.

16 *Ibid.*

17 Dossal, Mariam, *"The Hall of Wonder Within the Garden of Delight"* in *Bombay to Mumbai,* pp. 208-19., Marg Publication, 1997.

18 Birdwood, *Report,* p.48

19 *GD,* vol. vii of 1861, p.18

20 Dossal, Mariam, art.cit., pp. 208-19

21 *GD,* vol. vii of 1861, p. 25

22 *Ibid.,* pp.24-25

Central Asia, although the ocean and the Indus were in British hands. He suggested placing Bombay in regular communication with the Persian Gulf to economise exchange of trade.[23]

Dr. Birdwood's efforts towards collection of specimens for the museum can be gleaned from the widespread correspondence of the Financial Commissioner for the Punjab to the Commissioner in Sind. The latter, H.B.E. Frere was prompted to write to Dr. Birdwood on 28 January 1859. Expressing his views in favour of the outlay for the Central Museum in Bombay, he wrote, "I think it would be desirable to have the larger sized collection, and that Rupees 2,000 (two thousand), would be [a] very moderate sum to pay for—judging from the specimens sent to Kurachee, it would be found of the highest value both to mercantile and scientific inquiries and in its way, quite unique."[24]

The Government Resolution No. 324 dated 5 February 1859 sanctioned a smaller collection of economic products. This Resolution also stated that the collection could be enlarged later when permanent quarters were provided for the Bombay (Central) Museum.[25]

In the meantime, the Honourable A. Malet strongly voted for a separate building in favour of the Victoria Museum, as it was regrettable that the Museum continued to be housed in the Town Hall, while the Government intended to institute a Central Museum in Calcutta.[26]

Again it was Dr. Birdwood's persuasive power, reasoning and personality that encouraged the philanthropist Munguldas Nathoobhoy to donate an elaborately carved screen in black wood, a specimen of native skill from Bombay, costing nearly five hundred rupees, which was "well worthy of a place in the Central Economic Museum." Dr, Birdwood, informing the Secretary to the Government, General Department, sought permission to display it in the Council Room of the Town Hall.[27] Further, Nathoobhoy presented a model of a Hindu temple in sandalwood, the work of a Malabar carver, a very handsome and costly piece of art.[28]

Dr. Birdwood was constantly thinking of enhancing the Museum collection as is seen in

23 *Ibid.*

24 *GD,* vol. 38 of 1859, p. 39. True copy signed and attested by G.C.M. Birdwood, Secretary, and Curator of the Central Museum. Also see Letter of D.F. McLeod Esquire, C.S. Financial Commissioner of the Punjab, Amritsar, 21 December 1858, & others, *Ibid.,* pp. 11-19.

25 *GD,* vol. 38 of 1859, p. 41.

26 *GD,* vol. 38 of 1859, p. 33, Also, p. 35, Letter from the Bombay Castle, dated 10 February 1859, No. 370 of 1859. (Authur Malet [1806-1888) was a member of the Indian Civil Service, Chief Secretary of the Bombay Government from 1847-1854, a member of the Legislative Council and Chief Judge of the 'sadr diwani adalat' and 'sadr foujdari adalat' in 1857. Before he retired in 1860, he devised a scheme for Bombay harbour.') article: http://www.oxfordnb.com

27 *Ibid.,* p. 45, 14 February 1859.

28 *Ibid.,* p. 109, No 65 dated 9 March 1859.

his letter to the Secretary to Government, General Department. "It is of utmost importance," he wrote, "that an ample collection of Raw Products should be forwarded to the Museum as simultaneously as possible, otherwise their arrangement will be injuriously delayed, as has been the case with respect to the few Geological specimens received by me."[29]

Dr. Birdwood's clear thinking and logical division of the Raw Products of the Bombay Presidency is seen in the Circular No. 31 of 1859, addressed to the Secretary to the Government Central Museum District Committee. He delineated two divisions of Raw Products: the *First,* including all the substances used by man as *food* and the *Second,* all animal and vegetable products used by man *in manufacture.* He made it clear that only imperishable specimens should be sent to the Museum. This circular was signed by George Birdwood and attested as a True Copy.[30]

Dr. Birdwood had specified, "Exhaustive Collections should be attempted only by Committees located in the Sudder town of any Collectorate. Committees at minor towns should forward to the Museum such Raw Products alone as they believe are confined in habitat or in some unusual economic application to their immediate neighbourhood."[31]

Thinking on the same lines, Dr. Birdwood felt that it was highly desirable that the Central Museum should possess a series of specimens illustrating the preparation of Opium.[32] Dr. Birdwood outlined 24 stages of the preparation of opium; he mentioned points right from the sample of opium soil to the native drawings of the manufacturer.

He felt that it would be desirable to obtain from the independent states of Central India specimens illustrating the manufacture of opium. He indicated that it would be invaluable to the Government to apply to the Home authorities for *authenticated specimens* of Smyrna, Constantinople, Trebizond and Egyptian opiums.[33]

On 1 March 1859, Dr. Birdwood wrote to the Secretary to Government, General Department, suggesting that the Bengal Government should be applied to for Dried Indigo plants pasted on paper from the Benares, Tirhoot, Bengal and Oudh plantations, emphasising the various stages of production of Indigo. However, unlike Opium, which was not under the control of the Government, the application for Indigo, he said, should be made through an official channel as it was impossible to distinguish between the various India Indigos once they had passed through the Custom house. Indeed, the difference between Indian Indigos

29 *Ibid.,* p. 49.

30 *Ibid.,* pp. 50-53.

31 *Ibid.,* p. 53. (Please refer to footnote 26 of Chapter 1).

32 *Ibid.,* Letter to the Secretary to Government, General Department, pp. 71-74.

33 *GD,* vol. 38 of 1859, pp. 73-74. The Empire of Trebizond founded in April 1204, was one of the three Byzantine successor states of the Byzantine Empire. Geographically, the Empire of Trebizond never consisted of much more than the Southern coast of the Black Sea.

and others from Philippines, Java, Sumatra and Central America was difficult.[34]

As for Madras Indigo, he himself would apply to the Curator of the Central Museum in that Government.

About the same time Bombay Government recommended that certain Portuguese inscribed stones at Alibagh, proposed to be acquired by Dr. Birdwood,[35] and a marble slab at the Revdanda Fort commemorating the arrival of the Jesuit Francis Xavier be forwarded by the Sub-Collector of Colaba to the Central Museum.

However, the Governor in Council did not consider it advisable to remove from the Revdanda Fort the marble slab.[36]

Dr. Birdwood must certainly have appreciated from the historical perspective the thoughts of the Governor.

Dr. Birdwood continued to receive interesting articles for the museum collection. We learn from his letter of 11 January 1862, that Mr. Cursetjee Rustomjee Cama presented an authentic model of a Parsi *Dokhma* or Tower of Silence. It had been prepared under the immediate superintendence of the donor, who had devoted himself for years to the study of the history and customs of his race. Besides kindling the interest of observers, this exhibit would instigate research and study of the Parsis.[37]

Dr. Birdwood's ability to facilitate deals is brought out when we look at the case of the Sattara Native Library. To understand the story we have to go back in time.

On the 6 January 1862, Mr. M.M. Mackenzee, Secretary of the Sattara Native Library wrote to Dr. Birdwood explaining the history of a valuable collection in the Library's possession.

Mr. Mackenzee wrote that the Sattara Native Library received, in 1854 or thereabouts, a very large and valuable collection of Fossils, Minerals and Shells from London. It was packed in well-made Mahogany cases or drawers. They were all neatly marked and catalogued. On their arrival in Sattara, the Library Committee had a handsome standing glass case made for their exhibition. The case and contents were in perfect order when they were received.

The committee rightly thought it a pity that such a valuable collection should lie in Sattara utterly useless. The Committee, therefore, felt that the collection should be offered for sale. Mr. Mackenzee suggested that if the Central Museum in Bombay did not already possess such a collection, it should think of investing money and purchasing it.

He stated that the purchase of the articles alone cost the Committee Rs. 379, the boxes Rs. 26 and standing glass case Rs. 40. This did not include the freight from England.

He felt that it was but right that the Government Central Museum should have the first

34 *Ibid.*, pp. 75-77.
35 *Ibid.*, p. 103.
36 *Ibid.*, p. 105.
37 *GD*, vol. 21 of 1862-64, p. 233.

priority over the collection. However, if the collection was not purchased by the Government Central Museum, He requested Dr. Birdwood to send it to other parties who may be desirous of procuring it. Mackenzee suggested the Poona Institute and requested that the three catalogues be sent to the Secretary of that institute; if the Secretary did not desire to have the collection he was to inform Mr. Mackenzee and return the catalogue.[38]

Dr. Birdwood's tour de force is evident in his prompt letter of 10 January 1862 to the Secretary to Government, General Department, Bombay, when on receiving the letter from Sattara, he forwarded the letter and catalogues to Mr. Cowasjee Jehanghier. This gentleman at once presented Dr. Birdwood with a cheque of Rs. 475 for the purchase of the collection and its transport to Bombay.[39]

Birdwood ended his letter to the Government by assuming that it would direct him to communicate the thanks of the Government to Mr. Cowasjee Jehanghier.

Dr. Birdwood spread his net wide and collected rare products for the Museum as can be seen from his Report of Donations to the Museum.[40]

On 10 January 1862,[41] Dr. Birdwood informed the Government of a sizeable presentation to the Museum by a Parsi gentleman, who chose to remain anonymous, of 16 packages (quarter catts) of tea, 12 kegs of fruits, and samples of musk, rhubarb, ginseng root and *chandoo* (extract of opium that can be smoked), and a complete opium smoking apparatus, all from Canton.

This incidentally, was the first instalment of economic products that this gentleman was collecting at Dr. Birdwood's request, at the ports of the eastern archipelago, China, and Japan with which he was commercially connected.

This gentleman had also ordered Dr. Birdwood to have a set of Museum cases made (in the first instance six) according to a pattern fixed by Dr. Birdwood himself, and without any limitation as to the cost. In fact, the gentleman was desirous that they should at once be suitable cases, as the best possible illustration of Bombay blackwood carved work.

Dr. Birdwood emphasized that the donation, especially that of the items stated at the beginning, was an instance of the facility with which a museum in Bombay might be filled without any expense to Government, with the rarest and most interesting economic products by merchants who have the intelligence and goodwill to take advantage, as in this case, of their commercial connections for public good.

It is, however, a matter of regret that Dr. Birdwood had to report that he could not fully accommodate the present donation, obviously due to lack of space. He could only avail of this

38 *GD,* vol. 21 of 1862-64, pp. 237.-238.

39 *Ibid.,* pp. 233-234, No. 2 of 1862.,

40 *Ibid.,* pp. 263-264 – No. 1279 EXTRACT from the Proceedings of the Government of Bombay, in the General Department, 25 July, 1862.

41 *Ibid.,* pp.241-243.

when the Victoria Museum was near completion.[42]

Further, Dr. Birdwood had received from the Government of the Cape of Good Hope, an instructive collection of the woods, grains, and valuable drugs of that colony, named and catalogued by the well-known botanist Dr. Pappe.

From Aden, through the kind exertions of Captain Playfair, he had received samples of many of the interesting products of Arabia and the Troglodyte Coast.[43] These included, among others, the *korarima* cardamom of Abyssinia, and a large collection of gums and gum resins.

Dr. Birdwood had keen interest in promoting the products of local manufacturers. He was greatly disappointed to note that a large bulk of exhibits sent to the 1862 Exhibition in London had to be purchased by the Government and even the most intelligent manufacturers in Bombay did not send any exhibits on their own account, chiefly because the exhibition was held far away in London. He proposed to the Government that a local exhibition should be held in Bombay, which would probably draw bona fide exhibitors from the city as well as from Ceylon, Singapore, Madras, Calcutta and perhaps even Australia. He further proposed that the exhibition be opened in November 1863, with the Government needing no expense beyond setting and fitting up the shed, which would be reimbursed through the ground rent and entrance money.[44]

Dr. Birdwood thought, "the exhibition should be a really great event for British India," and that it should be opened on 1 November 1863, the Anniversary of the Queen's Proclamation, and be closed on 15 February the year after.[45]

These are but a few examples illustrating Dr. Birdwood's zeal and drive that spurred him in setting up the Central Museum in Bombay.

42 *GD,* vol. 21 of 1862-64, p. 263.

43 Coast of Africa from Libya to the Red Sea. (Another explanation) Africa Red Sea Coast, in the area of the "Troglodyte's (ancient Greek denomination of the inhabitants of the Red Sea Coast).

44 *GD,* vol. 21 of 1862-64, pp. 263-264.

45 *Ibid.,* p. 277.

CHAPTER II

The Genesis of a Grandiose Plan: Victoria Museum Phase I Remains a Cliff Hanger

In the nineteenth century the role of museums in India had a manifold effect in widening the curiosity of the people. However, primarily, as has been noted, Lord Elphinstone had said in Bombay, the Government Central Museum was established to display the commercial and material assets of Western India.

Recent historians have viewed the functions of the museum in another light, suggesting that the museums were a source of maintaining British supremacy and sustaining British rule in India, Asia and other colonies.[46]

Although this may have been a direct consequence of the thinking of some bureaucrats, not all Englishmen were insincere about their objectives, and were concerned about the fruits that the 'natives' would reap. Dr. Birdwood was among this gallant group of Englishmen. He was indeed a nature aficionado, who believed that the "Museum and Gardens were to be powerful instruments of recreation."[47]

Dr. Birdwood hoped that the museum would be "a source of inciting among the masses habits of observation and taste for rational pleasures."[48] He thought, "It would be a means of bringing Europeans and Natives more frequently together."[49]

From the point of view of Indians, it would have an egalitarian effect on all classes of people high and low; rich and poor would be able to meet in the "enjoyment of innocent and ennobling pleasures."[50]

---

46 Mitter, Partha and Clunas, Craig, *A Grand Design, A history of the Victoria and Albert Museum, pp.1-14;* http://www.vam.ac.uk/vastatic/microsites//1159_grand design/essay-the-empire-of-things new.html

47 *GD,* vol. vii of 1861, p. 141.

48 *Ibid.*

49 *Ibid.*

50 *Ibid.*, pp. 141-142.

Dr. Birdwood's administrative skills at the macrocosmic as well as microcosmic level, balancing feelings of the Indians while satisfying his European superiors in the difficult times following the uprising of 1857 are aptly borne out when we view the case of the Museum.

On 15 December 1858, the Sheriff of Bombay, E. Heycock, some Europeans and inhabitants of the city met in the Town Hall, for the purpose of initiating measures for the establishment of an Economic Museum with Natural History and Pleasure Gardens. As a tribute of the citizens of Bombay to Her Majesty the Queen, and with her permission, the Museum was to be named Victoria Museum and Gardens.[51] The object of the project was the evidence of the citizens' loyalty to the Queen.[52]

Although Lord Elphinstone, the Governor, had been asked to preside at the Public Meeting, he sent a letter through his Private Secretary, E. Bates, that he would be unable to preside over the first meeting, as he considered it would be better, in every respect, that "the undertaking should owe its first success to private exertion solely, without the participation in it by Government."[53]

It is significant to note that later Lord Elphinstone said, "The amount of the Government contribution should be considered and determined. I think that if the Government were to subscribe a sum equal to the contributions of the people it would be very handsome. At the same time Government ought to pay for the accommodation it requires for the office of the Director."[54]

Also in minutes of a meeting dated 26 April 1859, Lord Elphinstone proposed to appropriate a site on the Esplanade for the Victoria Museum and Garden Committee.[55]

By a Government Resolution of 1 June 1859, the Civil Architect, the Director of Public Instruction, the Secretary and Curator of the Government Central Museum, and the Victoria Museum and Gardens Committee were informed that the plans of the ground, then occupied by marines, and the space intervening them and the Back Bay be forwarded to the Secretary of State, with a request that His Lordship invite architects to send in designs for the projected edifice.[56]

Originally, Captain Wilkins, Executive Engineer on Special Duty, Poona, was appointed to design a cluster of buildings that would form one harmonious design on the Esplanade adjoining Back Bay. These were the Victoria Museum, Elphinstone College, Elphinstone Institution, Bombay University, the Director of Public Instructions' offices, and the Jamsetjee School of Art.[57]

51 *Ibid.*, pp. 97-98.
52 *Ibid.*, p. 100.
53 *GD,* vol. vii of 1861, p. 98.
54 *Ibid.*, pp. 167-168.
55 *Ibid.*, p. 41.
56 *Ibid.*, pp. 41-42.
57 *PWD,* vol. 10 of 1861, No. 1097 of 1860; also *Ibid.*, p. 1.

After much deliberation, Captain Wilkins envisaged a Gothic building without much ornamentation, bearing in mind the funds available. He proposed that the Museum be built either entirely of rubble masonry with cut stone dressings, or with rubble, faced with ashlar on one or both ends. He suggested that three different coloured stones be employed, namely Coorla which is reddish brown, Porebunder, which is yellowish white and Waree bunder or Doongarsee, which is bluish grey.[58] The use of many coloured stones, which lends itself to the Neo-Gothic style of architecture, and its relatively easy accessibility to Mumbai, was one of the reasons why there was a boom of this style of architecture in Bombay in the 19th century.[59]

The Government Plan of the Museum by Captain Wilkins was submitted to the Victoria Museum and Gardens Committee in January 1861. It was for a building of the dimensions recommended by the Committee earlier but it was in the Venetian-Gothic style instead of the Doric style suggested by the Committee.[60]

It may be noted that on 8 September 1860, the General Department of the Government informed the Victoria Museum and Gardens Committee that in consideration of the various objections that exist to the provision of a site on the Esplanade for the Victoria Museum and Gardens, the Government would propose a site on a portion of the Mount Estate.[61]

It is to the credit of Dr. Birdwood that he along with his joint secretary Bhau Daji put forward to his superiors the advantages of having the Museum on the Esplanade.

Indeed, Dr. Bhau Daji did not by any manner of means make a sudden appearance in the role of joint secretary. He had avidly supported establishing the Government Central Museum. The Museum itself was established in September 1855, but before that on 13 January 1855, the English newspaper *Lancet* writing about Dr. Bhau Daji said:

"To his exertions, Bombay will owe the Economic Museum and Zoological Gardens and the various Galleries of Science and Art now in the process of organisation."[62]

Dr. Birdwood lucidly spelt out the advantages of having the Museum on the Esplanade. He strongly pleaded for the Esplanade stating *inter alia* that it was the site mentioned at the time of raising the subscription from the people of Bombay, that it was especially convenient for all office-goers, and that it was convenient for students from colleges and for school-going children inside and outside the Fort.[63] Furthermore, it was a fine open site on which

58 *PWD,* vol. 10 of 1861, p. 13. Also *Ibid.*, p. 8.

59 Gupchup, Vijaya, *St. Thomas' Cathedral Bombay, A Witness to History,* Eminence Designs Pvt. Ltd. Bombay, 2005, p. 77.

60 *GD,* vol., vii of 1861, pp. 45-46.

61 *GD,* vol. vii of 1861, p. 42.

62 *Lancet, 13 January 1855,* p. 48, cited in Priyolkar, A. K., *Dr. Bhau Daji: Vyakti, kaal va Kartrutva,* published by Mumbai Marathi Sahitya Sangh., Mumbai, 1971, p. 278.

63 *GD,* vol. vii of 1861, pp. 145-146; also p. 173.

a handsome building would present an imposing *coup d'oeil,* and be an ornament to the city and a conspicuous monument of loyalty to Her Majesty.

He also indicated that at the Esplanade there was a space in which the college, schools, university, etc., may be added at any future time, thereby increasing the convenience to the people and enhancing the architectural effect of the whole.[64]

In fairness, Dr. Birdwood also pointed out the disadvantages of the Esplanade. He wrote that it was unsuited for gardens of a horticultural or botanical nature, and that there may be bad smells from the beach.

He conceded that Mount Estate, on the other hand, which was a site being considered by the Government, had the following advantages:

1) The soil and climate were suitable for botanical gardens.
2) The air was sure to be pure and free of smells.

He enumerated the disadvantages of Mount Estate, saying that:

1) The site was not central and the distance prohibitive for Colaba people.
2) There could be no architectural *coup d'oeil* and the institution would not be a "conspicuous" monument of loyalty as intended.
3) It would be inconvenient for students and business people from the Fort area.
4) The Museum and Gardens would be separated by a lane and the slope of the ground would not be suited for a well-laid out garden.
5) The entire Institution, Gardens as well as Museum would not fulfil any of the objects for which it was designed.[65]

Dr. Birdwood said, "I feel confident myself that unless the Esplanade is given up to the Committee, or formally appropriated for the Museum by Government, not another rupee will be received from the general public, and that under no circumstances will more than half of the money required by Captain Wilkins be forthcoming. There will be no difficulty however about this moiety, and it could be collected within the Committee without a general appeal, if the members were sure of seeing the Museum built in their day, and on the scale, and in the style proposed by the Government."[66]

So far the Committee had collected only Rs. 88,000 to meet Captain Wilkins' estimate of Rs. 3,54,853.[67]

Again Dr. Birdwood wrote, undoubtedly with a view to please his superiors, "I feel pretty confident, that means might be expected not only to erect the Victoria Museum in the

64 *Ibid.*, p. 174.
65 *GD,* vol. vii of 1861, p. 174 and p. 147.
66 *Ibid.*, pp. 50-51.
67 *Ibid.*, p. 47.

style estimated by Captain Wilkins, but with such embellishments of detail and richness of material as should make it the great architectural work of British India."[68]

And then from the point of view of his Indian friends he wrote, "With the style I have no concern *ex-officio*, but as one of the public I should not like to see Bombay miss the chance of such a structure, in suitable material, although in my opinion, the tower, the gabled windows on the highest story and the porches require slight retouching."[69]

While the Museum Committee disapproved the locality of Mount Estate, the Agri-Horticultural Society "most warmly" accepted it for their gardens. It must be noted that the Agri-Horticultural Society was set up earlier on 11 February 1830. The Museum Committee comprising of eminent citizens of Bombay, Parsis, Sethias and Europeans, decided albeit reluctantly, that the new Museum should be placed in the Society's gardens so that they could both work together in furthering their common interests, even though their management could be kept distinct, while the yearly reports on both the Victoria and Albert Museum and the Victoria Gardens were prepared at the same time.[70]

Thus in order to dispel misunderstandings it was agreed that the Victoria Museum and Society's gardens would become separate interests.[71]

On 8 May 1861, Charles Wood, Secretary of State, writing from the India Office in London to His Excellency, the Honourable Governor in Council, Bombay, mentioned that the Esplanade site for the Museum was wisely abandoned as the space that could have been appropriated for the purpose would have been clearly insufficient, and it would have entailed the Bombay Government the heavy expense of removing and reconstructing "the Marine Battalion Lines."[72]

This could be one of the reasons that Dr. Birdwood must have put forward his suggestion to the Committee and the citizens of Bombay, in order to convince them to accept the site on Mount Estate for the Museum.

Charles Wood recognized that if Mount Estate were selected for the site, the uprooting of a village would become necessary, and Rs. 15,000 would have to be awarded as compensation to the inhabitants, and half the value of improvements would become payable to the lessees of Mount Estate though the definite figures were not yet clear and discernible.[73]

He then clearly stated, "Although, therefore, Her Majesty's Government is willing to afford reasonable assistance to a project which is so highly creditable to the inhabitants of

68 *Ibid.*, pp.55-56.

69 *Ibid.*, p. 56, Forwarded 15 May 1861.

70 Birdwood, *Report,* 1864, p. 1.

71 *GD,* vol. vii of 1861, pp. 42-43.

72 *GD,,* vol. vii of 1861, p. 157.

73 *Ibid.*, p. 157.

your Presidency, they cannot become a party to arrangements which are likely to involve an outlay for exceeding what is anticipated by the projectors of the Museum and gardens."[74]

In a letter written by the General Department to Her Majesty's Principal Secretary of State for India in Council, London, dated 12 September 1861, and written from the Bombay Castle, it was stated:

We beg to forward a plan and design prepared by Captain H. St. C. Wilkins, of the Bombay Engineers, and fully approved of by the Committee of the Museum [sic, on the Esplanade site].... If Captain Wilkins' design were carried out completely, including the Tower and Porch, the cost would be Rupees 3,37,000, but he has shown that if these additions be omitted, and every part be constructed in a plain and economical manner, all these essential parts of the building can be secured for Rupees 2,47,000. Considering the immense increase of prices in Bombay, we doubt whether it would be possible to construct a building of the required dimensions for less money. But supposing that the work be performed for two lakh, the question remains whether any portion of this sum is to be contributed by the Government.[75]

Earlier there had been no proper commitment on the part of the Government to contribute a moiety of the total cost of the building. The first mention of a contribution was made in a meeting by the Honourable Mr. Malet dated 3 March 1860, suggesting that the Government ought to contribute to a building for the Central Museum and for the Sir Jamsetjee Jeejeebhoy School of Art and Industry one and a half lakh rupees.

Lord Elphinstone had earlier made a statement that the Government contribution should be considered and determined and had suggested a sum equal to the contribution of the people. It appears therefore to have been generally understood by the public that Government would double the people's contribution, or contribute about a lakh. Accordingly, in the Minute of His Excellency the Governor, dated 11 September 1860, a sum of one lakh was entered in list IV appended to the Minute.[76]

Charles Wood, writing from the India Office on 18 June 1861, said, "I infer from your letter of 15th idem, that your Government are prepared to make a grant of half the cost estimated at no less that Rs. 3,37,000, the Committee stating that 'with the Government donation of a sum equal to that which may be raised by the public, they confidently expect the realization of the money necessary for carrying out in its integrity the design of Captain Wilkins'."

"If the plan of Captain Wilkins provides only for the Museum," he cynically continued, "I must withhold my approval from the proposed grant of public money. For not to mention

74 *Ibid.*

75 *GD,*, vol. vii of 1861, p. 175.

76 *Ibid.*, p. 175.

financial considerations, I am of the opinion that the character of the projected Museum as an enduring testimony of the loyal devotion of the inhabitants of Bombay to 'Her Most Gracious Majesty,' would be entirely destroyed, if a moiety of the cost of the building, in addition to the whole cost of the permanent maintenance of the Museum, were to be defrayed out of Her Majesty's Indian revenues."[77] His asperity would have unnerved any Government official, let alone the Museum Committee.

He concluded by almost admonishing the Governor. He complained that the correspondence in this case had been recorded in a very incomplete and irregular manner. He advised greater care to be taken to present a clear view of the proceedings on all subjects considered worthy of record, and to secure their entry in the relevant books in a regular and consecutive order.[78]

On 16 January 1862, however, in Paragraph 2 of a Despatch from Her Majesty's Principal Secretary of State for India, he writes, "I conclude that the extra allowance mentioned in No. 726, of Rupees 200 a month granted to Captain H. Wilkins while engaged in preparing a Design for the Victoria Museum, will be included in the lakh of Rupees which you have already authorised to be expended on this object."[79]

Later a Resolution was passed by the Acting Chief Secretary to the Bombay Government, on 25 January 1862, that an extract of paragraph 4 of the Despatch from Her Majesty's Principal Secretary of State for India in Council be transferred to several Departments of the Secretariat for information and guidance.

Actually, paragraph 4 reads, "It is with much regret that I have noticed the irregularity which has marked your proceedings in this matter, and I trust that Her Majesty's Government may not on future occasion, from the want of a previous reference for their sanction, be forced to the alternative of either authorising an expenditure which they disapprove, or of withholding their support from your Government in a matter in which your faith appears to have been pledged."[80]

Accordingly, J.B. Piele, Acting Under-Secretary to the Government, gave orders from Bombay Castle in February 1862 that the Civil Paymaster communicate with the Chief Engineer of the Presidency and the auditor of Public Works Accounts and include the amount paid to Captain Wilkins in the lakh of rupees which the Bombay Government had already authorised to be expended against the Victoria Museum and Gardens.[81]

77 *Ibid.*, pp. 161-162.
78 *Ibid.*, p. 162.
79 *PWD*, vol. 38 of 1862, p. 168.
80 *PWD*, vol. 38 of 1862, p. 165.
81 *Ibid.*, p. 167.

Sir Charles Wood's orders were also communicated to the Victoria Museum and Gardens Committee on 25 January 1862.[82]

On 22 March 1862, the price of the ground (Rs. $1\frac{1}{4}$ per square yard), granted for the Museum on Mount Estate, was ordered by a Government resolution to be deducted from the lakh rupees sanctioned by the Secretary of State.

It was not until 2 May 1862 that things were finally resolved. At first Lots No. 16 and 17 were made over to the Museum Committee, but subsequently Government allowed an exchange to be made between the Agri-Horticultural Society and the Museum Committee of Lots Nos. 1 and 2 for Nos. 16 and 17. From a rough tracing submitted by Dr. Birdwood it appeared that Lots Nos. 1 and 2 measured 7435 and 9681 square yards respectively.[83]

Besides the site for the museum, the name also changed slightly for, on the death of the Prince Consort, to mark respect for his memory, it was designated "The Victoria and Albert Museum".[84]

The cornerstone of the Victoria and Albert Museum was laid by His Excellency Sir Bartle Frere, K.C.B., before the people of Bombay on 19 November 1862. On the same day, Lady Frere opened the Victoria Gardens, which had been commenced on the 27th day of July the same year.[85]

Jugonnath Sunkersett, the President of the Committee, speaking on this occasion stated that a lakh of rupees had been subscribed by the people of this Presidency to the project.[86]

The Committee then wanted to know in what form they should draw the sums required from time to time from the Government grant of one lakh rupees. An arrangement was suggested by W.S.D. Birch, whereby the Museum Committee were permitted to draw month by month on the Government donation from the Oriental Bank, which had been authorised to meet cheques drawn by the Committee's President and the two joint Secretaries conjointly—that is, in the same manner as they had done with reference to the citizens' deposit in the Oriental Bank. They were to state an amount equal to so much as they might certify to have expended in the preceding month from the private funds. They could draw on the General Treasury Bank of Bombay, and forward the document to the Deputy Auditor and Accountant General's office for countersignature before it were presented for payment.[87]

The bureaucracy was stifling and suffocating! No wonder then that it was justifiably said, "The chief feature of the administration of Mr. Birdwood was the conversion into a

82 *GD*, vol. I of 1866, p. 291.
83 *GD*, vol. I of 1866, p. 291.
84 Birdwood, *Report*, p. 49.
85 *Ibid.*, p. 2, para 5. Also GD, vol. I of 1866, p. 291.
86 *GD*, vol. I of 1866, pp. 291-292
87 *GD*, vol. I of 1866, pp. 292-293.

garden and pleasure-ground of certain useless and low-lying land known as Mount Estate in Mazagon, now regarded as forming part of Byculla."[88]

Dr. Birdwood's resilience to trying situations is aptly borne out by his settingt aside temporarily the nitty-gritty of bureaucratic procedures and eagerly spelling out the object of building a museum. He said, "It will afford the most perfect means and the best opportunities for prosecuting original research in Indian and Eastern natural history, with the special object of aiding the economic progress of the country."[89]

"It will be a standing agency for the organisation of periodical exhibitions of the Industries of India,"[90] he was quick to add, "as the museum is not to be a mere exhibition but a *college of inquiry.*"

Dr. Birdwood himself set an example of prompt action when in late July 1862, he wrote his report that plants were being transferred from Sewri, where the gardens of the Agri-Horticultural Society originally stood from 1842, under the joint secretary-ship of Dr. George Buist and Dr. F. Giraud.[91] Birdwood wrote that work had also commenced on laying and planning the Victoria Gardens.

His practical approach is seen in his remarks regarding the layout of the Victoria Gardens. "The chief hand implements are the *yila* or sickle, and the *koita* or bill-hook, and the *kudal, kudli* or pick; and so perfectly adapted are the forms of these implements to the work to be done with them, and so true the steel used in their fashioning, that in the work of the Victoria Gardens, Bombay, I preferred them to the best American and English-made gardening tools."[92]

The architect of the Museum building changed. Captain H. Wilkins was replaced by William Tracey. Tracey's name appears in a message engraved on the inside of the lid of a copper box embedded under the cornerstone. Tracey was assisted by George Wilkins Terry, Superintendent of the Jamsetjee Jeejeebhoy School of Art.[93]

William Tracey (1831-1864) designed the Victoria Gardens (now Veer Mata Jijabai Udyan) and the Victoria and Albert Museum (now Bhau Daji Lad Museum). The laying out of the Victoria Gardens at Byculla by the Agri-Horticultural Society began in 1862, as we have seen. However, the Society ceased to exist in 1873 and the gardens were handed over to the Bombay Municipality. William Tracey died young at the age of 33. The building was then

88 *GBCI,* vol. III p. 377.

89 Birdwood, *Report,* p. 3, para 9.

90 *Ibid.*

91 Dossal, Mariam, *"The Hall of Wonder Within the Garden of Delight,"* in *Bombay to Mumbai,* Marg Publication, 1997, pp. 208-219.

92 Birdwood, *Sva, 'The Mahratta Plough.'* p. 71.

93 Dossal, *art.cit.* Also Birdwood, *Report,* pp. 55 and 57.

modified by Scott McClelland and Company. William Tracey had designed the building in Palladian style, sometimes referred to as the Italian Renaissance style.[94]

TRIALS AND TRIBULATIONS OF THE FULFILMENT OF A DREAM MUSEUM: PHASE II

The Victoria and Albert Museum, as we have said, was built in the Palladian style of Architecture, named after the Venetian architect Andrea Palladio (1508-1580). Palladio's work was strongly based on symmetry, perspective and values of formal classical temple architecture of the Ancient Greeks and Romans.

Architectural styles evolve and change with each individual client. In England around 1746 when the Duke of Bedford, decided to rebuild Woburn Abbey 'Palladian' was the most fashionable style of the era. Henry Flitcroft was the architect of Woburn Abbey. His style though Palladian in nature, would not be recognized by Palladio himself. The central block is small with only three bays; the temple-like portico is merely suggested and it is in fact closed.[95] It may be noted that the three bays is what the Victoria and Albert Museum Committee settled for. However, this development of style would be repeated in countless houses and town halls in Britain over hundred years. But it fell out of favour during the Victorian era and was only revived by Sir Aston Webb for his refacing of Buckingham Palace in 1913.

The Victoria and Albert Museum can be visually compared to Stourhead House, South façade, designed by Colen Campbell and completed in 1720. (Picture under "Palladian architecture," in Wikipedia online.)

Alternately, we can also compare Tracey's monument in the St. Thomas' Cathedral in Bombay to the Palladian or Serlian arch or window as interpreted by Palladio. , (picture of Palladian arch or window—Wikipedia.)

This style continued to be popular in Europe throughout the 19th and 20th centuries where it was employed in the design of public and municipal buildings. From the latter half of the 19th century it was rivalled by the Gothic revival.

---

94 Gupchup, Vijaya, *"St. Thomas' Cathedr*al, *A Witness to History*, p. 142. It is interesting to note that a memorial to Tracey exists in the St. Thomas' Cathedral. It is a becoming piece worked in contrasts—white marble framed by brownish-grey stone. On either side of the epitaph are two pairs of green marble pillars with their bases and capitals in brown stone. It is a unique monument in the shape of a Transitional arch. Also refer to *The Bombay Builder,*vol. I, No. I, 5 July 1865, pp. 11 & 14 for *The David Sassoon Clock Tower, Victoria Gardens; Ibid.,*No. 3, 5 Sept. 1865, pp. 49 & 53, for *Lady Frere's Temple-Victora Gardens;* and *Ibid.,* No. 7, 5 Jan. 1866, p. 142, *The Triumphal Arch Screen-Victoria Gardens.*

95 Wikipedia: Palladian architecture.

Why then did the Victoria and Albert Museum Committee members choose the Palladian style over the Gothic?

Perhaps they believed that the total cost of the building would amount to less than the Gothic plan designed by Captain H. Wilkins for the Victoria Museum formerly intended to be erected on the Esplanade.

The story of several buildings planned in the 1860s in Bombay, be it the St. Thomas' Cathedral or the Victoria and Albert Museum, to speak only of two, was marked by vicissitudes. This compelled persons closely connected with it to appeal to the Government in Bombay for more funds.

How did these building projects suffer from the same plight?

In order to answer this question we have to look at the economic scenario, financial upheavals and their social impact of that time.

Bombay had become the largest exporter (80%) of Indian cotton in the late 17th century, a situation facilitated due to the increasing importance of the Bombay port. After the Industrial Revolution, from 1764 to 1868, Great Britain remained the most important consumer of Indian raw cotton.[96] India along with the cotton-producing countries of the world competed in assuaging this appetite for cotton. But with the invention of the ginning machine by Ely Whitney in 1793, the market for raw cotton was revolutionised and America took the lead as exporter.[97] All efforts by the East India Company and Manchester, to augment the cultivation and export of Indian cotton were nullified by the dominance of American cotton. Even in China, which had been an important buyer, Indian cotton faced competition from cheaper American yarns and goods.[98]

The saving grace for the Indian cotton Industry came with the commencement of the American Civil War in 1861. This cut off the supply of American cotton to Great Britain. India benefited and its cotton sales rose phenomenally. This resulted in wealth and speculation to an inordinate degree. But the bubble burst with the ending of the American Civil War in 1865. Share prices suddenly lurched to a depressing low, resulting in bankruptcy and insolvency.[99]

This is when Dr. Birdwood appealed to the Government, on 28 May 1866, for an extra grant to the Museum building, as he could not have raised the funds from the public which was facing a financial crisis.

---

96 Dantawala, M.L., *A Hundred Years of Indian Cotton, Bombay East India Cotton Association Ltd.,* Bombay, 1947., pp.16-18.

97 *Ibid.*, p. 18.

98 *Ibid.*, p. 16.

99 Wacha, D.E., *A Financial Chapter in the History of Bombay,* p. 8. Also Gupchup, Vijaya, *St. Thomas' Cathedral Bombay, A Witness to History,* pp. 46-47.

He explained to the Chief Secretary to Government that it had already given a lakh of rupees towards the building and the public had already subscribed more than the same amount, however, due to improvements suggested in the building and the great cost of building in Bombay, it was found that the building would cost at least one lakh and twenty thousand more than the two lakh collected.

So Birdwood appealed to the Government to subscribe one-half of this excess, that is 60 thousand rupees. He pointed out that the Government had helped in other public buildings and as Secretary and Curator of the Victoria and Albert Museum, he felt he should make this further demand.

He pleaded that the grant should be made without delay; it could be given as a loan, pending supreme sanction.

The reason for this urgency was that although the public had paid Rs. 50,000 towards the completion of the building earlier in February 1866, no payments had yet been made and the Committee already owed its architects Rs. 40,000. As the Committee could not during that time call up for subscriptions, it was necessary to put pressure on the Government. Dr. Birdwood concluded by saying, "If this timely help cannot be acceded, the gravest apprehensions are justifiable as to the uninterrupted completion of the Victoria and Albert Museum. On public grounds, the Committee is precluded from making a strenuous appeal to the public in the face of the present times; decency enforces them to wait until in better times they can quietly complete this monument of the loyalty of Bombay to Her Majesty the Queen and therefore it is that meanwhile they appeal to the assistance of Government."[100]

So sensitive was Dr. Birdwood to the Share-Mania of 1861-65 which was a result of sudden wealth due to the boom in prices of Indian cotton followed by a collapse after the end of the American Civil War in 1865, that writing about Sett Premchund Roychand, the philanthropist merchant of Bombay, he said:

"I was so intimately 'at the back' of the whole private history of 'the Bombay Share Mania of 1861-5,' and so confidentially in the counsels of Mr. Premchund Roychand as a civic benefactor, that I have made it a sacred rule never to publish any of the incidents and circumstances of the time to which, merely through my privileged relations with individual persons and personages, I became privy. There is always a grave wrong, involved in such revelations, toward those of one's fellow-sufferers in misfortune who have meanwhile died, and cannot reply to the injustice directly or indirectly and intentionally or unintentionally done to their good name and fame."[101]

100 *GD* , vol. I of 1866, pp. 275-276.

101 Birdwood, George, *Sva,* p. 89; edited by F.H. Brown, London: Philip Lee Warner. Humphrey Milford, Oxford University Press, Bombay, Melbourne, Toronto, MDCCCCXV (1915).

MONETARY WRANGLES

Dr. Birdwood's efforts of securing an extra grant for the Museum building for Rs. 60,000 met with several bureaucratic hurdles. The Acting Under-Secretary to the Government responded on 28 June 1866 asking Birdwood for a clear statement that showed:

1) How much has been actually received and spent of private subscriptions?
2) How much Government money was used?
3) What sum is now due for work already done and material delivered?
4) What further sum is required to complete the building?[102]

The Under Secretary also wrote to Captain C. Finch, Architect Executive Engineer and Surveyor, (Public Works Department) Bombay, on the same day asking for his opinion on the sufficiency or otherwise of the architect's estimate of the work done and remaining to be done in connection with the building of the Victoria and Albert Museum. Capt. Finch's enquiry with Birdwood resulted in the latter's response on 4 July 1866.[103]

Birdwood informed Capt. Finch that "the Victoria and Albert Museum Committee has paid up to date on account of the actual building of the Victoria and Albert Museum Rupees 1,93,436.9.2 [Rupees, annas and pies] and that Rupees 15,000 is now due on account of work done; and Rupees 60,300 on the iron interiors and roof of the Museum ordered by the Committee and whole invoiced and part arrived."[104]

He added, "There is no contract estimate for the completion of the building. Messrs. Scott McClelland are to be asked to furnish it. There was a contract with Mr. Johnstone, the builder, for building the Museum—but it is no longer binding—as extensive alterations were made in the plans and the sum originally contracted for having been exceeded. I send you the original contract and plans. I estimate that the whole sum required to finish the Museum will be Rupees 1,20,000—of which Rupees 60,000 will probably be subscribed by the public. But I cannot in the present state of Bombay hope that more will be. I must refer you to Messrs. Scott McClelland for the revised plans on which to found your independent estimate of the cost of completion. On the part of the Committee I would only say, that any reductions in the plans you may propose they will cheerfully accept."[105]

Birdwood concluded, "The shell of the Museum is complete—the whole interior and roof is part out and whole invoiced and can be put up in a few months and the only question is how to pay for it, how to get Rupees 1,20,000 or under."[106]

102 *GD,* vol. I of 1866, p. 295, No. 1244 of 1866.
103 *GD,* vol. I of 1866, pp.299-301; No. 22 of 1866.
104 *GD,* vol. I of 1866, p.299.
105 *Ibid.,* pp. 299-300.
106 *Ibid.,* p. 301.

Birdwood was trying his utmost to convince the Government officials to sanction grants for the completion of the Museum building. It is not clear how he estimated the remaining cost of completion of the building to be Rupees 1,20,000.

On 21 July 1866, Capt. Finch submitted a detailed Report to the Acting Under-Secretary to Government elaborating mainly on the design of the Museum building and the work carried out till that date and secondly on the issue of sufficiency of the architect's estimate of the work done and remaining to be done.[107]

He regretted that there was no architect's estimate forthcoming from the Honorary Secretary of the Committee and that the only document furnished was the contractor's accepted tender. He opined that the original design had been almost entirely changed both in elevation and in interior distribution, with the present building being much more highly ornamental than was first. Capt. Finch found fault with the manner in which the original tender was accepted as it did not reflect clearly the items of work to be executed. Further, he commented that the said contract had been made four years earlier in July 1862 and had not been implemented correctly or stopped in a regular manner, hence "such extraordinary action has been taken throughout that it remains no longer a matter of surprise that the first estimate has long since been exceeded."[108]

Capt. Finch stated how the present building, designed in Italian style, differed considerably from the original design and concluded, "Where such alterations have taken place the architect's estimate would be no guide whatever in forming an opinion of the value of work done."[109]

Capt. Finch goes on to note that the completion of the building had then been entrusted to Messrs. Scott McClelland & Co., who had forwarded a copy of the estimate amounting to Rupees 2,60,000 for the work remaining to be done.[110] He found the estimate to be excessive and commented on three points.

Firstly, the estimate included Rupees 85,000 for the ironwork, in columns, girders, roof, etc., which had been ordered from England and a portion of which had already been shipped. With no details of these items available, Capt. Finch did not opine on its sufficiency.

Secondly, an amount of Rupees 57,500 was estimated for fixing and painting the ironwork in Bombay. Again, although Capt. Finch felt that the amount was large, he could not say whether it might be reduced.

107 *GD*, vol. I of 1866, pp.311-320; No. 504 of 1866 (PWD).

108 Ibid., p. 313.

109 Ibid., p. 315.

110 Ibid., pp. 323-324; Copy of Estimate of cost of completion certified as True Copy by George Birdwood, Honorary Secretary, V&A M Committee.

Thirdly, Rupees 20,000 was provided for gilding an extra decoration; Capt. Finch felt that this item might be left out at that time and added later.[111]

Thus Capt. Finch indicated, "The three items I have above noticed amount to Rupees 1,62,000, leaving less than one lac for paving, plastering, woodwork etc., which appears to me quite sufficient for the intended work."[112]

In his Report, Capt. Finch adds, "I have been informed by the Honorary Secretary, Victoria and Albert Museum Committee that the sums already expended and still due for work done amounts to Rupees 2,08,436 which with Messrs. Scott and McClelland's estimate for completion, if sanctioned, will make a total of Rupees 4,68,436 as the cost of the Victoria and Albert Museum—a sum considerably in excess of what it might have been built for, had a properly detailed estimate been prepared in the first instance, and strictly adhered to throughout; but as the committee have been in the habit of sanctioning alterations in any manner their architects advised, without any professional knowledge of the probable cost of such alterations, the present result is not surprising."[113]

As a result of the correspondence initiated by Dr. Birdwood with the Government, his persistent efforts along with those of Dr. Bhau Daji, to convey to the Government the views of the Victoria and Albert Committee, in their capacity as joint Honorary Secretaries, and the Report submitted to the Government by Capt. Finch, a Resolution No. 2103 was passed by the General Department on 19 October 1866, under the signature of the Chief Secretary to Government from the Bombay Castle.[114]

The Resolution stated:

1. It seems that the building on which Rupees 2,08,000 have been spent is at a standstill, and likely to fall into ruin unless immediate steps are taken to secure it from further damage.
2. There are no assets beyond promised subscriptions, amounting to about 60,000 Rupees, and these are not likely to be paid for some time to come.
3. There is no exact estimate for completing the building in a suitable manner.
4. The building has a public object as a Museum and would have been probably provided sooner or later on a more moderate scale by Government. But the loyal inhabitants of Bombay came forward and volunteered to undertake the work as a monument of their gratitude and loyalty to the British Crown. They have failed, not from fickleness or niggardliness on their own part, and might have gone further, yet there seems to be fully $1^3/_4$ lacks [sic] of Rupees worth of work on the ground and it is clear that unless Government resume the work much of what has been already done will be lost and thrown away.

111 Ibid., p. 317.
112 Ibid., p. 318.
113 *Ibid.*, pp. 318-319.
114 *GD*, vol. I of 1866, pp. 337-338. Also *The Bombay Builder*, vol.II, No. 6, 5 December 1866, p. 117.

5. His Excellency the Governor in Council thinks (sic) [that] under these circumstances Government might take charge of the work, provided Government can (sic) [could] be secured against unknown liabilities, either for the past or future.
6. His Excellency the Governor in Council is, therefore, pleased to allow Capt. Finch, the Architectural Executive Engineer, to take charge of the building, and to complete it, so as to be weather-tight, on condition that satisfactory assurance be given that Government shall not thereby be made answerable for any unpaid claims for work already done, or materials already used.
7. If this be done, the Executive Engineer should be instructed to take charge of the building and to take immediate measures for securing it against further damage by the weather.
8. He should then as speedily as possible submit an estimate for completing the building, so as to be perfectly secure and fit for occupation but without any sort of furnishing or ornament (using up and paying for any materials which may be on hand).
9. The Executive Engineer and Dr. Birdwood should be requested to submit a joint report on the liabilities and means of the Museum funds, showing what is owed and what has been promised in the way of subscriptions, etc. This will enable Government to see how the Institution stands as regards work already done and liabilities already incurred.
10. In a separate estimate they should include all that is necessary to fit up the building in such simple style as will render it available for the purpose for which it was designed.
11. If prosperity returns, as Government hope it will, to the people of Bombay, His Excellency the Governor in Council has no doubt their loyalty will induce them to redeem the pledges of themselves and their predecessors by suitable ornamentation. But what Government does now must be strictly limited to what is necessary to render the building useful."[115]

The Public Works Department acted on implementing the directions in the Resolution. The Chief Engineer, Presidency Division, issued Memorandum No. 3114 dated 8 December 1866, forwarding, with certain observations, a letter from the Architectural Executive Engineer. It reported that a careful examination of the Victoria and Albert Museum had shown the building to be in a highly unsatisfactory state, and that it would be necessary to pull down and rebuild certain portions of the building. It recommended that a Committee be appointed to report on the state of the building and to ascertain upon whom the responsibility for the present condition should rest. Resolution No. 2589 of 1866 dated 19 December 1866, of the Public Works Department issued by the Under Secretary to Government, stated that Messrs. Ormiston and Russel Aitkin might be requested to join themselves with the Chief Engineer as a Committee to report on the present condition of the walls, its probable cause, and to suggest a remedy, and that Messrs. Scott & McClelland should be informed and invited to attend the Committee.[116]

115 *Ibid.*

116 *GD,* vol. I of 1866, p.341.

The Public Works Department had swung into action to complete the Victoria and Albert Museum building. Dr. George Birdwood, as Secretary of the Victoria and Albert Museum Committee continued his cooperation with the PWD till 1868, when he left India for England due to ill health. Earlier, Dr. Birdwood's contribution to museum culture among Indians and his knowledge of Indian art was recognized by his being sent by Sir Bartle Frere to the Universal Exhibition In Paris in March 1867.[117]

The Victoria and Albert Museum building was completed in 1872 and the Museum was opened to the public in the month of May at the hands of Sir Seymour Fitzgerald, the Governor of Bombay, and the exhibits of the old Central Museum stored in the Town Hall were brought to this new Museum building. Although the Victoria and Albert Museum Committee had promised 50 per cent contribution of the expenditure involved, they could collect only Rupees 1,10,000. The entire expenditure amounted to Rupees 4,30,000 and the Government had to bear the difference in the expenditure.[118]

It may be noted that the Victoria and Albert Museum was renamed 'Dr. Bhau Daji Lad Museum' in 1975 in honour of the man whose vision and dedication ensured its establishment. Of course, Dr. George Birdwood's part as joint secretary of the Museum was by no means any the less important. Both Dr. Lad and Dr. Birdwood played stellar roles as friends and crusaders towards building a monument, which was to become an institution of great merit and relevance for the city of Bombay.

Unfortunately, the Museum fell into a derelict condition. In February 2003, an agreement was signed between the Municipal Corporation of Greater Mumbai (MCGM), the Jamnalal Bajaj Foundation and the Indian National Trust for Art and Cultural Heritage (INTACH) to restore and revitalise the Dr. Bhau Daji Lad Museum. This public-private partnership established for the Management of a Cultural Institution has carried out the entire restoration work for which the Museum was awarded the UNESCO 2005 Asia-Pacific Award of Excellence for Conservation.

The achievement of INTACH in restoring the building as well as the Museum collection has been highly acclaimed by leading personalities connected with such Institutions as the Victoria and Albert Museum in London, Peabody Essex Museum in Salem U.S.A., and others.[119]

It is a source of pride for Bombay that Dr. Birdwood through all these wrangles, steadfastly forged ahead with his vision of building a museum. He did not as many would have, cast it aside out of exasperation, as an otiose project. Instead, he shared the words of Henry Carter, Secretary of the Central Committee Bombay, who as early as 21 August 1854, pronounced,

117 *JIAI, art. cit.*, p. 45.

118 Priyolkar, A.K. *Dr. Bhau Daji: Vyakti, Kaal va Kartrutva,* (Marathi), p. 304.

119 *Brochure on Dr. Bhau Daji Lad, Museum City Museum* available at the Museum.

CHAPTER III

The Bombay Branch of The Royal Asiatic Society with Birdwood as its Honorary Secretary

The Victoria and Albert Museum espoused itself to the betterment of the 'natives,' exposing them to hitherto unknown pleasures of viewing a vast range of economic products; the Bombay Branch of the Royal Asiatic Society had comparatively, a more esoteric beginning. Its founder was Sir James Mackintosh who came to India in 1803, on his appointment as Chief Judge of Bombay. An enterprising man, he was enthused by the conviction of establishing a Society on the same lines as the Asiatic Society of Bengal, conceived 20 years earlier in September 1783 and founded by the Oriental scholar William Jones in 1784.[126] Mackintosh's object was to bring together in high intellectual purpose and effort the best English talent variously employed in work in the Bombay Presidency.[127]

The first meeting was held on 26 November 1804 at Government House, Parel, where Sir James lived. The meeting was attended by 17 persons, among whom were the Governor, the Hon'ble Jonathan Duncan, and Sir James Mackintosh.[128] Also present were Lord Valentia, Dr. Helinus Scott, Mr. (later Sir) C. Forbes, Sir Jasper Nicolls, Major (later Colonel) Moor, Mr. Erskine and Mr. Salt. While recalling this, the Hon'ble Mr. William Edward Frere,[129] President of the Royal Asiatic Society, could not resist remarking that it was "an array of names, the equal of which, we may I fear, seek for in vain among any seventeen who could now be collected together in Bombay or India."[130]

126 Gupchup, Vijaya, Bombay Social Change:1813-1857, p. 86.

127 *JBBRAS,* The Centenary Memorial Volume, p. 17. (henceforth *CMV*)

128 *BBRAS,* Sardha Satabdi Celebrations, p. 1. Cited in Gupchup, Vijaya, *op.cit.,* p. 86.

129 Hon'ble W.E. Frere became President of the BBRAS in 1854 and retired in 1864.

130 *Times of India* cutting in Minutes of the Royal Asiatic Society, 1860-65, p. 460. The first edition of *The Bombay Times* and *Journal of Commerce* appeared on 3 Nov. 1838 under editor J.E. Brennan. Between 1846-1857 the newspaper changed hands. George Buist, LL.d, F.R.S. became editor of the Times from 1840-57. In 1861 Editor Robert Knight amalgamated *The Bombay Times & Standard* and *Bombay Telegraph & Courier* to form *The Times of India.* These remarks were made in 1864.

It must here be noted, that of the original members of the Society, Governor Duncan was proficient in the Persian tongue, and intimately acquainted with the characters and manners of the natives of India; Major Edward Moor was the author of an interesting narrative of the proceedings of Lieutenant Little's detachment, which threw much light on the habits of the natives of the interior of India and on the geography of parts of the country then little known; Dr. Robert Drummond had published a grammar of the language of Malabar; Major David Price, had distinguished himself by his memoirs of Mohammedan history, besides other valuable works on Oriental subjects, and was known for his acquaintance with Persian. He had made some progress in Mahratta [Marathi] language; Major General Sir Jasper Nicolls was one of the first to promote the views of the Society by his remarks on the temperature of the island of Bombay; Dr. Helinus Scott, was a physician; Lord Valentia later became Earl of Mountnorris, and Mr. Salt who later became Consul-General in Egypt, being then in Bombay were present at the first meeting of the Society and all became its members.[131]

We gather from Sir James Mackintosh's son, who wrote about the life of his father,[132] that before leaving England, Sir James had resolved to do everything in his power to promote the progress of knowledge. It was no easy task, as he was soon to realize, for those who came out to India for the civil and military services, were very early caught up in studies that had a practical direction, and were left with little leisure for literary pursuits and historical investigations. But being an intelligent, clear thinker, Sir James realized that having seen much of a new country and its strange manners they had something to tell. At the same time, few of them had habits of writing, except on official matters, and they were in general unwilling to commit themselves on what to them seemed new and dangerous ground. Even the men pursuing medicine, whose education was necessarily more complete, had left Europe at an early age in order not to lose rank, which depended solely on seniority. As a consequence, few of them possessed leisure or opportunity to pursue collateral branches of study such as chemistry, botany, mineralogy or natural history. Thus Sir James, from the commanding view that he took of the varied subjects of human knowledge, and of their comparative value, from his frank open character, his candour for everyone, was admirably suited to urge forward and direct such an institution.[133] In spite of the difficulties, Sir James, after some previous communication, forged ahead with his plans to gather leading personalities and like-minded persons together and called a meeting at his house at Parel when the Literary Society of Bombay was formed.[134]

131 *Times of India* cutting found in *Minutes of the Asiatic Society,* 1860-65, p. 461.

132 Life of James Mackintosh in *Transactions of the Literary Society of Bombay,* vol. I, p. 236, *Times of India* cutting in *Minutes of the Asiatic Society, 1860-65,* p. 460.

133 *Ibid.,* p. 461.

134 *Ibid.*

A proposal was made to appoint the Governor, Patron of the Society. After some discussion, this was set aside, on the ground that, as a literary body it should preserve a character of perfect independence. Mr. Duncan subscribed to this view very readily, expressing the thought that it was indeed sufficient honour to be a part of a group that forwarded such objects and be an associate on terms of perfect equality.[135]

Thus Sir James Mackintosh was elected the first President, Mr. Charles Forbes, the Treasurer and Mr. William Erskine, the Oriental Scholar and lawyer, became the Secretary. However, it was no doubt the triumvirate comprising the Governor Jonathan Duncan, the President James Mackintosh, and Erskine who gave concrete shape to the Society.[136] The President supplied the ideas and plans, the Governor the support and assistance of authority, while the Secretary provided the industry and labour essential for an organization of this kind. Their wise planning and organizational capacity had such far-reaching results that the structure of the Society has been retained to this day.[137]

One of Sir James Mackintosh's last Acts before leaving Bombay on 5 November 1811, was an attempt to rectify the want that was felt from the Society not possessing a *good* library.[138] The remedy used by the Society was a request to Sir James himself to send out a collection of standard books best fitted to the formation of a Public Library, as well as to order annually the principal new publications as they appeared suitable and affordable with the funds of the Society. But even with this assistance from Sir James, no large Library was formed, for the first catalogue printed in 1817 contained only 1,412 works including those expected from England and a collection of books on Oriental Literature presented to the Society by the Government in 1812.[139]

In 1815, it was agreed on the motion of Captain Basil R.N. to open a museum for receiving antiquities, specimens in Natural History, and the arts and mythology of the east. No records of lists of contents of the Museum for a period more than 30 years suggest that the Museum languished for several years until presents of coins were received from Sir Alexander Burns and minerals from Dr. Malcolmson.[140]

In 1815, Sir James Mackintosh and Sir John Malcolm[141] were appointed to revise the contribution to the Society and, in 1821, the Society published these revised contributions in three Volumes of Transactions, which met with an encouraging reception from all interested

135 *Ibid.*

136 Gupchup, Vijaya, *op. cit.,* p. 87.

137 *BBRAS, Sardha-Satabdi Celebrations,* p. 2.

138 *Times of India* cutting in *Minutes of the Asiatic Society 1860-65,* p. 461.

139 *Ibid.*

140 *Ibid.*

141 *Times of India* cutting in *Minutes of the Asiatic Society, 1860-65,* p. 463. Major Genl. The Hon. Sir John Malcolm was elected to the office of the President on 26 Nov. 1827, and served as President for 3 years.

in Oriental Literature, and became a standard work procurable, but with some difficulty.[142]

In 1827 the Literary Society of Bombay was grafted as a Branch on the Royal Asiatic Society of Great Britain and Ireland and from that time to 1841 all literary communications from the Branch Society were sent to the Parent Society in England, and appeared in the journal of the Society.[143]

In 1841, it was decided to publish a Quarterly Journal of the Bombay Branch with Mr. Orlebar, the accomplished Secretary, as the editor. However, the journal never was what it was originally intended to be, a Quarterly Journal; instead for the next 20 years, six volumes of about 400 to 500 pages each were published and, as stated by the retiring President, the Hon'ble William Edward Frere, in 1864, they had "no reason to be ashamed of the work."[144]

It would be relevant here to mention that in the year 1833 there was a great opposition to the admission of a native as a member of the Society. At that time it was the practice of the Society not to keep on record those who had been proposed as members and blackballed. Suffice it to say that though there were some popular and influential members who tried to get this native admitted, they signally failed.

In sharp contrast, it may be stated that Dr. Birdwood, as Secretary of the Society,[145] meticulously jotted the Minutes in his own hand. One of the early members proposed during his Secretary-ship was Karsondas Madowdass, Esq. The membership was proposed by Dr. Birdwood and seconded by Bhau Daji Lad. Along with him the membership of G. Latham Esq. Civil Engineer, was proposed by W. London, Esq., and seconded by Secretary Dr. Birdwood.[146] This shows that both Indians and Europeans were proposed as members.

To continue with the story of native membership, it was not until 1840, and largely due to the enlightened President-ship of John Wilson, that a Parsi, Mr. Maneckjee Curtsetjee was elected.[147] The President, the Hon'ble Frere, in tracing the history of the Society on his retirement in 1864, could not resist remarking about Mr. Maneckjee Cursetjee, "All honour be to him," he said, "for his characteristic perseverance and indomitable courage on this and all occasions."[148]

142 *Ibid.,* p. 461.

143 *Ibid.,* p. 461.

144 *Ibid.*

145 Dr. Birdwood was elected Secretary, by a motion brought forward by Mr. Horton, and seconded by Mr. Dhunjibhai Framjee on Wednesday, 21 May 1862 on the resignation of Dr. H.J. Carter. He was elected at the June meeting in 1862. Dr. Birdwood formally signed the papers on Thursday 10 July 1862. *Minutes of the Asiatic Society 1862-65,* p. 130.

146 *Minutes of the Bombay Branch of the Royal Asiatic Society, 1862-65,* p. 142. 9 October 1862- Committee of Management.

147 Gupchup, Vijaya, *op.cit.,* pp. 88-89.

148 In 1862, Maneckjee Curtsetjee, presented 2 copies of his work, *"A few passing ideas for the benefit of India and Indians,"* fourth series Presented at the Meeting of 13 Nov. 1862, *Minutes of 1862-65,* p. 145.

After Mr. Maneckjee Curtsetjee was admitted, the Hon'ble Jugonnath Sunkersett, Sir Jamsetjee Jeejeebhoy and other Indian members were admitted. The President the Hon'ble Frere said in 1864, "And good reason have we not only to be proud of our native members, but be grateful to them for the splendid additions they have made to our Library and Museum."[149]

He said, "To whom we are so much indebted for presents of Books, and a large costly collection of coins as to Cowasjee Jehanghier Readymoney, Esq., and the Hon'ble Jagonnath Sunkersett, and have not Bal-Gungadhar Shastree, Dr. Bhow Daji and Dunjeebhaee Framjee been large and useful contributions to our journals. Gifts and contributions such as these may well make the Society proud and grateful to our native members."[150] The President concluded about Indian members on this note.

This approbation of Indians was rightly due when we consider their contribution to the Society. Dr. Bhau Daji Lad, the first Hindu scholar, enriched the work of the Society with his stupendous research. His collection of manuscripts is one of the treasured possessions of the Society to this day.[151]

The admission of Indians to the Society was to prove useful to it, both from the point of view of scholarship as also as a recipient of generous donations. Dr. Birdwood was quick to realize this, for it must be noted that the Indian membership increased during his Secretary-ship.[152]

The President, the Hon'ble William Edward Frere's words amply bear the immense credit that is due to Dr. Birdwood. On the eve of his own retirement he said, "Though it is advisable to select your President sometimes from those who have not Literary powers and accomplishments to recommend them, it is to the Secretaries you must look for the substantial benefits to your Society. The Society is honoured by having such men as those I have named above as its Presidents;[153] but it is nothing new that I should tell you that it is to Mr. Erskine, Colonel Kennedy, Cotton, Money, Orlebar, Malcolmson, Bird and Carter that we owe our material prosperity. You are probably surprised at my finishing the list with Carter and you have good reason to be so. Those I have named have all passed away from us, and have become as it were subjects of history which all may canvass; and I have entirely

149 *Minute Book of the Royal Asiatic Society, 1862-65, Times of India,* Paper cuttings on pp. 461-462, Hon'ble Frere's retirement speech.

150 *Ibid.,* p. 462.

151 *JBBRAS, CMV,* p. 23.

152 *Minutes of the Bombay Branch of the Royal Asiatic Society, 1865-68,* p. 81.

153 *Times of India,* paper cutting in *Minutes of the Bombay Branch of the Royal Asiatic Society,* p.462. Also refer to p. 463 for List of Presidents. Frere said, "I would ask you to look at the annexed list, and bear in mind what your Presidents have done for Oriental and General Literature. When among the names of Presidents appear the names of Mackintosh, Taylor, Money, Elphinstone, Malcolm Vans Kennedy—Wilson, Stevenson, it appears presumptive to have allowed my name to be among them" *Ibid.,* p. 462.

misunderstood our present Secretary Doctor Birdwood, whose ability, research and science, and whose energy and zeal in our service is second to none of his predecessors, is beyond all praise and known to you all."[154]

If one briefly views Dr. Birdwood's career as Secretary it is at once possible to grasp the value of his work.

Dr. Birdwood succeeded Dr. H.J. Carter as Secretary. Dr. Carter resigned as Secretary on taking sick leave and proceeding to England in May 1862 after serving the Society for 15 years. The Society, on his departure, voted him an address and presented him with a Microscope of the value of Rs. 1,000, in testimony of their sense of his long services as Secretary and of his distinguished labours as a Naturalist.[155]

In acknowledging his appreciation, Dr. Carter wrote to Dr. Birdwood and his letter was read at a monthly meeting of the Bombay Branch of the Royal Asiatic Society (BBRAS) on Thursday 11 September 1862. Dr. Carter said he was "deeply sensible of the Sincerity of all kind of expressions"[156] contained in the report regarding his retirement and he only wished he had done more to deserve them.

Regarding the microscope as a parting token of friendship he wrote, "I can state that the instrument will always recall to my mind a delightful remembrance of the Members individually as well as the time I have been with the Society at large, while I trust my health may enable me as kindly anticipated by the Society to turn it to advantage in making further discoveries and thus render the Society's friendly gift, in the end subservient to the advancement of their grand object of scientific research."[157]

Lastly the gift of Honorary Membership ... has crowned me with a wreath which brightening as age advances will only fade when in the course of nature, all that is dear must pass away from the hand of poor mortality."[158]

To take on the Secretary-ship after a much-respected person like Dr. H.J. Carter was perhaps a daunting task, but Dr. Birdwood handled his tenure brilliantly. Even as early as the Annual report of 1861-62, one perceives the change. Recording the number of members,, Dr. Birdwood reported that there were "at present 97 Members on the Register namely 77 Resident and 20 Non-Resident against 78[159] and 20 respectively at the corresponding date

154 *Ibid.,*

155 *Minutes of the Royal Asiatic Society, 1862-1865,* p. 151.

156 *Ibid.,* p. 138. The Minutes of the Asiatic Society were collected from three sources (1) The CD entitled Minutes 1862-1865-This is a scanned copy of the actual hand-written Minutes. (2) Hand written records, entitled Minutes 1860-1865 (3) Hand written records entitled Minutes 1865-1868, all from The Asiatic Society, Mumbai (ASM).

157 *Ibid.,* p. 139.

158 *Ibid.*

159 *Minutes of the Asiatic Society, 1862-65,* p. 148.

last year."[160]—that is one less than the year 1860-61. Dr. Birdwood also states that one has died during the year. In so far as the Library was concerned, he mentions that 147 works in 212 volumes were added; the same periodicals continued to be subscribed. Dr. Birdwood has meticulously noted several points of information.

- A Committee consisting of Sir A. Grant, Bt., Prof. J.P. Hughlings and J. Gibbs appointed Dr. Birdwood to draw up an alphabetical catalogue of the Library.
- Unwanted books were recommended by the Committee to be removed.[161]
- During the year several books were added to the Library Rooms and the books were all newly arranged in accordance with the new catalogue.
- The Book Agent was changed in April from Messrs. Smith Elder and Co. to Mr. Mudie. However, the Committee were displeased with Mr. Mudie, as fewer books had been supplied. Furthermore they were in a defective condition and carelessly selected and like the periodicals were not dispatched with punctuality. Mr. Mudie had been inattentive to the letters sent to him by the Secretary. Therefore the Committee of Management were now considering making other arrangements.
- The Finances of the Society were in a satisfactory state.[162]
- The Society's *Museum* had been removed from the North to the South Room. There had been seven donations of coins and geological specimens.
- On completion of the Library catalogue, the Museum catalogue would commence being made.[163]

Dr. Birdwood was mindful of the Society's economy and all Indian papers were voted to be discontinued. Dr. Birdwood observed that out of Rs. 3,000 a year spent by the Society on books and periodicals, Rs. 869, went to the newspapers and periodicals exclusive of scientific periodicals and magazines of a literary character.[164]

At this meeting it was also proposed by Mr. Walter Cassels, and seconded by Mr. Henelly, that unwanted novels and romances should be removed. The new Committee for 1862-63, appointed to select and arrange for the purchase of suitable books as also disposing off unwanted books, consisted of Sir A. Grant, Bt., the Rev. John Wilson, D.D., and W.R. Cassels, Esq.[165]

160 *Ibid.*, p. 149.
161 *Ibid.*, p. 150.
162 *Ibid.*, p. 151.
163 *Ibid.*, p. 150.
164 *Ibid.*, p. 152.
165 *Ibid.*, p. 153.

In December 1862, Dr. Birdwood recorded that 43 presents were given to the library. They were varied and valuable.[166] There was an interesting piece of marble bearing Hamayaritic Inscriptions from Tibet, presented by Dr. Davidson through Dr. Coles.[167]

An engaging item at the Meeting of the Society on 8 January 1863 is the name of William Tracey, Esq., who was proposed as a member by the Secretary Dr. G. Birdwood and seconded by Sir A. Grant, Bt., and the name of Prof. Candy proposed by Sir A. Grant, Bt., and seconded by the Secretary. They were both elected as is reported in the meeting of 12 Feb. 1863.

William Tracey, it will be recalled, was the Architect of the Victoria and Albert Museum and the Victoria Gardens. He died the next year in 1864. Prof. Candy was the famous Sanskrit scholar whose Dictionary is used even today.[168]

On 12 Feb. 1863 the Secretary announced the publication of the new alphabetical catalogue for the Library, corrected up to 31 December 1862, and laid before the Meeting some copies for their inspection.[169]

The Committee recorded their sense of the care and attention devoted by Sir Alexander Grant, Bt., Prof. Hughlings and Dr. Birdwood to the preparation of the catalogue and their warmest acknowledgement of Sir Alexander's laborious exertions in carrying it through the press. [170]

Dr. Birdwood never forgot the original objectives of the Society as expressed in Dr. Carter's letter to him, quoted earlier. In keeping with this, on 21 February 1863, it was resolved: "That the Society be maintained as a Scientific Society." Also, "That light literature be only admitted when ordered by the Committee appointed on 24 November 1862.[171]

On 21 February 1863, it was also proposed by Sir A. Grant and carried:

"That the Society recognizing the character of the existing Library which assumes a public importance, should petition Government to endow a Librarianship and an Establishment for its due conservation at an expense of Rs. 3,600 per annum."[172]

The Society and its members were certainly taking steps towards establishing it on a permanent status.

---

166 *Ibid.*,p. 157.

167 *Ibid.*, p. 158.

168 Prof. Candy undertook a minute perusal of Prof. Wilson's Sanskrit and English Dictionary and noted many words and terms which had before escaped his observation. He also reversed the Sanskrit part of the excellent English & Marathi Dictionary of Captain Molesworth. Major Candy's English & Marathi Dictionary were well-known.

169 *Ibid.*, p. 163.

170 *Ibid., p. 163.*(CD)

171 *Ibid.*, p. 324

172 *Ibid.*, p. 325.

Dr. Birdwood's leanings towards Indian History, Maratha and Gujarati Literature and culture, and other varied interests, is seen from the encouragement he gave to and thereby the presents he received for the Society. To state an example, the Presents received as recorded on 12 March 1863 were: (1) *History of India, the Hindu and Mahomedan Periods* by the Hon'ble Mountstuart Elphinstone, Translated in Gujarathi from his Marathi version of 1862 by Rao Sahib Vishvanath Narayan Mandlik, one volume presented by the translator. (2) *Report of the Nagdevi Charitable Dispensary* from May 1853 to April 1860 and from May 1860 to 30 April 1861 presented by Bhau Daji, Esq.[173] (3) Monthly notices of the Royal Astronomical Society No, II of vol. XXIII for 12 December 1862 presented by the Society.[174]

To quote another example, Dr. Murray Mitchell, on 9 April 1863, read his paper titled "Specimens of the Marathi Poetry," translated.[175]

Meanwhile, at the same meeting, eminent personalities and an increase of Indian members is noticed, for example Dr. George Buhler,[176] Professor of Sanskrit, Elphinstone College, proposed by Sir Alexander Grant, seconded by the Secretary Dr. Birdwood, Vurjeevumdass Mahadowdass, Esq., proposed by the Secretary and seconded by the Hon'ble Jugonnath Sunkersett, and Rao Bahashir Tirmalrao Venktesh proposed by Rao Sahib Vishvanath Narayan Mandlik and seconded by Rev. Dr. Wilson, Honorary President.[177]

Through all these activities Dr. Birdwood was striving to make arrangements for better Management of the Library and more satisfactory circulation of books.[178]

On 13 August 1863, the Committee of Management recommended to apply to Government for Rs. 300 a month to assist the Society in the promotion of its General objects amongst which were the conservation and enlargement of its Library,[179] particularly of the Oriental and Scientific Department and the publication of Bibliotheca of valuable General Marathi and Sanskrit texts; the latter was Dr. Buhler's plan of a Bibliotheca Orientalis of Bombay.[180]

173 *Ibid.,* p. 334. Dr. Bhau Daji was responsible for tremendous humanitarian service to the dispensary. It may be noted that Dr. Bhau Daji had wide and varied interests. On 12 July 1862, he had submitted Ajanta Cave Inscriptions, with Facsimilies, Transcripts and Translations for the abstract of a paper. *Minutes of the Royal Asiatic Society, 1862-65,*p. 135.

174 It may be noted that this present is in keeping with the resolution of 21 February 1863 that the Society be maintained as a Scientific Society. *Minutes of the Royal Asiatic Society,* p. 324.

175 *Ibid.,* p. 338. For an abstract of this paper see *Times of India,* 23rd and *Bombay Gazette* 24 April 1863.

176 An abstract of his paper '*Early Marriages of the Hindoos*' appeared in the '*Times of India,* of 30 July 1863 and '*Bombay Saturday Review*' of 1 August 1863; p. 353. Also see *Minutes,* 1862-65, p. 336.

177 *Ibid.,* p. 336.

178 *Ibid.,* p. 351.

179 *Ibid.,* p. 363.

180 *Ibid.,* p. 355.

In keeping with the Society's character one reads about an interesting present to the Society on 8 October 1863—the *Marriage of Hindu Widows,* advocated by the Pathare Reform Association of Bombay, with *The Epitome of the History of Bim Raja*—Presented by the Poona Association.[181]

The Society fostered original research and communication as is seen in the Hon'ble Mr. Justice Newton's paper *On the Sa'h Gupta and other Ancient Dynasties of Kathiawar and Goozerat,* "[182] which he read on 10 September 1863[183]

The Government had, in 1858, sent a number of coins of the type on which Mr. Newton had deciphered[184] the word Bhallarabha. The Society, however, even with the help of Vishnu Shastree, remained baffled and requested the Government to send the coins to England. But no better success attended the inquiries in England than in Bombay. The President, the Hon'ble W.E. Frere congratulated the Society that it was reserved to one of its body to decipher this legend and to discover the coins of the Wallabhi dynasty. "Extracts from Mr. Newton's paper ought to be sent to Government," Hon'ble Frere said, and concluded by thanking Mr. Newton for the honour he (Newton) had done the Society. However, the President suggested that at some time Mr. Newton should examine all procurable coins of the Wallabhi type to ascertain whether they were all from one reign, and he trusted that Mr. Newton would carry his research to the very end.[185]

The Annual Report of the Bombay Branch of the Royal Asiatic Society for 1862-63, read by the Secretary at the Anniversary Meeting on 30 November 1863[186] showed sizeable changes in the Library. The Secretary reported that 368 works in 957 volumes, exclusive of periodicals, had been added to the Library by purchase, against 147 works in 212 volumes bought the previous year; 83 works in 103 volumes and 26 pamphlets had been presented to the Society; and 84 in 231 volumes had been re-bound and 88 files of newspapers stitch bound.[187]

A tabular statement with 26 classes and subjects with a total of 368 works in 957 volumes was presented by the Secretary. The subjects were (1) Theology and Ecclesiastical History, (2) Natural Theology, Metaphysics, etc., (3) Logic Rhetoric, and works relating to Education, (4) Classics, Translations etc., (5) Philology, Literary History and Bibliography, (6) History, Historical Memoirs and Chronology, (7) Politics Political Economy and

181 *Ibid.,*p. 373. That the Pathare Reform Association should have got the Society as a platform for its forward-looking ideas was commendable.

182 For abstract of this paper see local papers of 21 September 1863; also 13 October 1863.

183 *Ibid.,* p. 366 and p. 370.

184 *Ibid.,* p. 375.

185 *Ibid.*

186 *Ibid.,* p. 381.

187 *Ibid.,* p. 382.

Statistics, (8) Jurisprudence, (9) Public Records, Statutes and Parliamentary Papers, (10) Biography and Personal Narratives, (11) Antiquities, Numismatics, Heraldry, etc., (12) Voyages, Travels, Geography and Topography, (13) English Poetry and Dramatic Works, (14) Novels, Romances and Tales, (15) Miscellaneous and Works on Several Subjects etc. (16) Foreign Literature, (17) Natural Philosophy, Mathematics, Mechanics, etc., (18) The Fine Arts and Architecture, (19) The Science of War and Works of Military Subjects, (20) Natural History, Mineralogy, Geology, etc., (21) Botany, Agriculture and Horticulture, (22) Medicine, Surgery and Anatomy, (23) Physiology, Dietetics and Medical Jurisprudence, (24) Transactions of Learned Societies, etc., (25) Dictionaries, Lexicons, Vocabularies, etc., (26) Oriental Literature.

The tabular form devised by Dr. Birdwood was indeed very organised and allowed easy access to scholars' needs.

The Alphabetical Catalogue of the Library corrected up to 31 December 1862 and the rules were printed during the past year at an expense of Rs. 2,000 and distributed gratis to Members. A Supplemental Catalogue, alphabetical and classified, of works received during the year was in the press, and proofs of the Alphabetical portion were laid before the meeting.

There were two donations to the Museum during the year, one a large trap rock bearing Canarese characters, forwarded by Dr. Ross from North Canara, through his Excellency the Governor of Bombay, and one slab of marble, bearing Hamayaritic Inscriptions from Jebel presented by Dr. Davidson through Dr. Coles.[188]

At the Anniversary meeting held on 30 November 1863, the Hon'ble President Frere, CS., said that it was his duty to inform the Society how much the Society was indebted to their Secretary for the satisfactory report that the Committee had been able to submit to the Society. He was happy also to inform the Meeting that Mr. Cowasjee Jehanghier had placed a sum of Rs. 5000 with Messrs. Smith, Elder & Co., for the purchase of Oriental Works for the Society, and the Hon'ble Jugonnath Sunkersett had presented an equal sum to be expended on works on Natural History.[189]

The Extraordinary Meeting of the Bombay Branch of the Royal Asiatic Society held on 17 December 1864 was a landmark.[190] It was specially held to read the memorandum prepared by the Committee of Management on Hon'ble W.E. Frere's retirement as President.

It may be recalled that at the first meeting of the Literary Society of Bombay it had been suggested that the Hon'ble Jonathan Duncan, Governor of Bombay, be made Patron of the Society. Although at that time, in 1804, this proposal had been set aside, sixty years later,

188 *Ibid.*, p. 386.
189 *Ibid.*, p. 388.
190 *Ibid.*, p. 495.

in 1864, we find that the name of His Excellency the Hon'ble H.B.E. Frere, K.C.B., was recorded as the Patron of the Society.

Also, at this meeting, a number of ladies graced the scene with their presence and were seated in the gallery. Among them were observed Lady Frere and Misses Frere, Mrs. Dunsterville (wife of Lieut-Colonel J. B. Dunsterville, one of the four Vice-Presidents of the Society), Mrs. Marriot (wife of one of the Members, Colonel W.F. Marriot), Miss Manockjee, and Mrs. Niven (wife of W. Niven, Esq., M.D.).[191]

The Secretary, Dr. Birdwood read the address to the Hon'ble W.E. Frere, ex-President. Among other things, he said, "You have been a member of this Society for thirty-three years, and from your first connection with us [you] were distinguished for your hearty interest in our affairs and the intelligence and sound judgement with which you ever sought to further the objects of the Society."[192]

Dr. Birdwood cited the ex-President's contribution to the Society, and emphatically stated, "Above all, we would most gratefully acknowledge your ready and generous appreciation of the desire of native gentlemen to enter and enrich the Society. To this we owe the strength which we derive from a body of fifty native subscribers and the truly noble benefactions of the Hon'ble Jugonnath Sunkersett and of Messrs. Cowasjee Jehanghier and Premchund Roychund to our Library and Museum. The importance of your appreciation of the native liberality during the present critical period of the history of Bombay cannot be too highly estimated. You have thus helped to give a worthy direction to the wealth, daily pouring into this great and growing city and placed the prosperity of this Society upon a sure because *of (sic)* an indigenous basis."[193]

Dr. Birdwood had thus expressed his thoughts on the invaluable step of encouraging native membership.

Indians had carved out an important place for themselves. In 1865 when the Hon'ble Jugonnath Sunkersett passed away, Dr. John Wilson, the Honorary President of the Society read a most telling eulogy that made a deep impression among natives and Europeans in Bombay. Dr. Wilson aptly brought out the Hon'ble Sunkersett's talents and force of character, his generosity and enlightenment, which stood him in good stead to take part in the social and public affairs of the city of Bombay.[194]

191 *Ibid.,* p. 495.

192 *Ibid.,* The Hon'ble Frere was elected as Secretary of the Society in 1833. In 1835, he had to leave Bombay on public duties. In 1854, on his return to Bombay, he was elected President and held office for 10 years. His membership to the Executive Council of the Government helped the Society as he was able to influence the Government to the Society's advantage.

193 *Ibid.,* p. 495. The ex-President in his reply, speaking about throwing open the doors to native gentlemen said, "I may remark, however that the Society now really is Asiatic, which it hardly was before, but which I trust it will ever continue to be." *Ibid.,* p. 496.

194 Newspaper cuttings in the *Minutes of the Royal Asiatic Society, 1860-65,*p. 511.

It is noteworthy that the first Public Meeting held in the Great Room of the Town Hall on Thursday 12 October 1865 was organised on the occasion of Dr. David Livingstone's Lecture on the Discoveries in Africa.[195]

Dr. Wilson told the gathering that his discoveries had been universally acknowledged to be of the greatest importance. Actually, one of his earliest reviewers in *London Athenaeum* had called him the African Columbus. Dr Livingstone had initially gone to Africa as a medical missionary in 1840, and it was not until 1852 that he undertook his great journeys for which he was so celebrated. In 1856, he had gone to England, where, after fifteen months' labour, he produced his first great work that relates to his movements and observations.[196]

In 1864 he revisited England and again, after about the same period, produced another great volume. He was now (in 1865) in Bombay on his way to Africa on his third exploratory campaign.

Contributions were invited from the Bombay merchants towards Dr. Livingstone's exploratory expeditions.

On 22 November 1865, writing from his Malabar Hill residence in Bombay, Dr. Birdwood enclosed a cheque of Rupees 6,450 on the Bank of Bombay towards Dr. Livingstone's daring adventure.[197]

Dr. Livingstone acknowledging receipt of the cheque from the Asiatic Society said he would deposit the amount with Messrs. Ritchie, Steuart & Co. He elucidated that the objects that he had in view were partly geographical and partly the opening of East Africa to the influences of Christian civilization.

He further wrote to Dr. Birdwood, "Having been a witness of the depopulation and disorganization which have resulted from slave trade, I am thoroughly convinced that if the Bombay merchants should succeed in supplanting it with lawful commerce, they will perform a most acceptable service to the merchants and to their fellow-men."[198]

Dr. Birdwood said he had written to Dr. Livingstone to say that the Bombay subscription to his enterprise was absolutely at his own disposal and he had read this correspondence merely to inform the public that the fund had been disposed of according to the resolution on which it was subscribed.[199]

At the Anniversary Meeting of the *Bombay Branch of the Royal Asiatic Society* on Monday, 27 November 1865, Dr. Birdwood, while reading the Annual Report, read the Benefaction to the Library. He said that Mr. Premchund Roychund had written to him on the 9 February

195 *Minute Book, 1865-68,* p. 3 of Newspaper cutting.
196 *Ibid.*
197 *Ibid.,* p. 10.
198 *Ibid.*
199 *Ibid.*

1865, to fit up the room, resumed by the Society in 1864 from the Geographical Society, with bookcases on the condition of their being used for the works of Oriental Literature and Antiquities and named after the President William Edward Frere.

Mr. Premchund Roychand had sent Rupees 10,000, the estimated cost of the cases with his letter.[200] The Society had thanked him for his generous gift.

It was undoubtedly Birdwood's friendship and influence that had generated funds from Indians.

At the beginning of the next year, on Thursday, 11 January 1866, at a monthly meeting of the Bombay Branch of the Royal Asiatic Society, many members, including Mr. M. Stovell, Esq., M.D.,—Vice-President in the chair—were taken by surprise.[201] Dr. Birdwood tendered his resignation of the office of the Honorary Secretary of the Society as he was going to Mahableshwar for some months and he believed that so distinguished an office should not be occupied by anyone acting for him. Dr. Stovell expressed his feelings of regret and felt the members then present would one and all shared his disposition. He said that until he received the paper convening the meeting he had not the slightest idea that their Secretary had contemplated such a step,, and that he could not help remarking that the reasons urged for taking it, did not convince him of its necessity. He would therefore prevail upon Dr. Birdwood to re-consider the question. He and the members so fully appreciated the very able manner in which Birdwood had, at all times, performed the duties of his office. He referred to the ex-President the Honourable Frere's speech in which he bore graceful testimony to the value of the Secretary's services.[202]

Dr. Stovell suggested a suitable step be adopted which would enable Dr. Birdwood to retain his post. After all Dr. Birdwood was only leaving Bombay for a time for the recovery of his health. He was not going to Europe, but merely to Mahableshwar. He thought, therefore, that the meeting would act wisely in following the example recently set on a somewhat similar occasion by the Agri-Horticultural Society, who succeeded in retaining Dr. Birdwood as Secretary, by providing for the performance of his duties owing to his temporary absence. He suggested the adoption of a similar step and request Dr. Birdwood to retain the post of Secretary.

The Honorary President, Dr. Wilson entirely agreed with the Chairman, Dr. Stovell. He felt that the services of Dr. Birdwood had been of singular value, and should not be dispensed with. While a practical arrangement would be made, he could return to the Society after his

200 *Ibid.*, p. 9.

201 *The Times of India, Minute Book of 1865-1868,* p. 12.

202 *The Times of India, Minute Book 1865-1868,*p. 12.

An edition of the Society's Journal that had appeared during the past year was a really valuable one.[214]

The chronological adjustment of the coinage both of the *Sah* and *Vallabh* coinage of Saurashtra by the President, the Hon'ble Justice Mr. Newton C.S., was an important contribution not only to numismatics but to history. The older coins connected with the same province, which had lately been discovered, would yield results after Mr. Newton completed his research.[215]

Dr. Wilson also touched upon the much-wanted Bibliotheca for words on Maratha History, a part of Dr. Buhler's plan started in 1863.[216]

It may be noted that the Bopp Testimonial Fund was started during the Secretary-ship of Dr. Birdwood. This was to mark the fifteenth anniversary of the commencement of Professor Bopp's career. It was at the instance of Dr. Wilson in July 1866, that the *BBRAS* had created it as a token of its admiration of the labours of Prof. Bopp in the field of Scientific Philology. Taking as his standard reference the Sanskrit language, Prof. Bopp had traced the analogies which associate with it and with each other, the Zend, Greek, Latin, Gothic, German and Sclavonic (sic) [Slavic] languages. He had established a near relationship between the languages of the nations separated by the intervention of centuries and the distance of half the globe, relying upon differences of physical formation and social institutions—between the forms of speech current among the dark-complexioned natives of India and the fair-skinned races of ancient and modern Europe. This was not known fifty years earlier; recently the Sanskrit language had been carefully studied and the principles of alphabetical and syllabic modulation, upon which its grammatical changes are founded, had been applied to its kindred forms of speech by the philologers of Germany.[217]

At this meeting it was agreed that the subscription of thirty guineas should be forwarded to Messrs. Smith Elder & Co., the agents of the Society in London on whom the Berlin Committee should be empowered to draw for the amount.[218]

At the meeting of 26 November 1866, Dr. Birdwood read the letter from Professor Weber of Berlin acknowledging the receipt of the Society's contribution to the Bopp Testimonial.[219]

At the monthly meeting of the *BBRAS* held on 10 January 1867, an interesting item was presented to the Museum. This was the earliest English Rupee coined in Bombay, presented by the Hon'ble Justice Gibbs, C.S. On 7 January 1867, he had written to Dr. Birdwood,

214 *Ibid.*, pp.29-30.

215 *Ibid.*, p. 30.

216 *Minutes of the Royal Asiatic Society, 1862-1865*, p. 363.

217 *Minutes of the Bombay Branch of the Royal Asiatic Society, 1865-1868*, p. 21.

218 *Ibid.*, p. 21.

219 *Ibid.*,p. 30.

informing him that it was the only specimen he had been able to procure, as these were very scarce. It was purchased for Justice Gibbs at a coin sale at Sotheby's in London. "It bears—*Obv.* In centre 'The Rupee of Bombain' and two roses beneath. Round the margin, 'Struck by the authority of Charles the Second'."

"*Rev.* Royal Arms—England, Scotland, France and Ireland-quarterly –Legend continued from Obv. 'King of Great Britaine, France and Ireland'."

There were other particulars that he could not decipher as he did not have a copy of *Ruding's Annals,* which he proposed to buy when he got home (to England).[220]

Justice Gibbs concluded his letter by stating that the Society's collection should not be without the first English Rupee—a very generous and valuable gift that Justice Gibbs parted for the interest of the Society's Museum.

Thursday the 13 August 1868 was a day that would be marked as monumentally regrettable in the history of the Society.

At a meeting of *BBRAS* on that day, Hon'ble Mr. Justice Newton, the President, reported the retirement of Dr. Birdwood. The President recalled that there were many institutions in Bombay that were under obligation to Dr. Birdwood. But perhaps the largest share of his energetic and unceasing labours had been given to the Asiatic Society. He said that the Agri-Horticultural Society might dispute this claim. Further, he added that it could not be overlooked that Bombay was largely indebted to Dr. Birdwood's exertions and for his care for the Victoria Gardens. However,, the President concluded that it was in connection with the *BBRAS* that Dr. Birdwood would feel himself to have earned the best right to be remembered.[221]

More than six years had passed since the President had the pleasure of proposing him as the Secretary, and each successive year had drawn attention to the value of his services. He was elected at a meeting in June 1862 and the Society had progressed considerably since that date.[222]

Comparing the figures with those of an equal number of years immediately preceding, he was able to mark the Society's improvement. During the seven years before Dr. Birdwood's election, the Society had purchased 1,309 works in 1,896 volumes, whereas during the last six and a half, the Society had added to the library 3,505 works in 6,200 volumes, or about three times the former number.[223]

As to the membership, during the earlier seven years, the number of members added to the list was—resident 70 and non-resident 29—total of 99, whereas during Dr. Birdwood's

220 *Ibid.,* p. 32. *Ruding's Annals* was a reference book about the coinage of Great Britain and dependencies.
221 *Minute Book of the Bombay Branch of the Royal Asiatic Society, 1865-68,* Newspaper cutting, p. 80.
222 *Ibid.,* pp. 80-81.
223 *Ibid.,* p. 81.

six and a half years 262 resident members and 77 non-resident members were elected, adding up to a total of 339.[224]

The last balance sheet before Dr. Birdwood succeeded to the office showed the following amounts in Rupees – annas – pies:

Receipts	Rupees 10,568-09-6
Expenditure	Rupees 5,328-15-0
Cash in hand	Rupees 5,239-10-6

The balance sheet of 1867 exhibited:

Receipts	Rupees	34,489	0	7
Expenditure	Rupees	23,390	15	3
Cash in hand	Rupees	11,098	1	4

The receipts were more than treble, the expenditure more than quadruple, and the balance in hand double.[225] The results were laudable.

Besides, the Society owed much to Dr. Birdwood's energetic advocacy of the claims of the Society and to his personal action and influence, which had procured valuable contributions.

In 1864, Government sanctioned a sum of Rupees 300 per month for the general purpose of the Society. Mr. Cowasjee Jehanghier, in 1864, made a donation of Rupees 800 for the purchase of a valuable collection of coins and the fitting up of a room for their custody and exhibition.

The same gentleman most liberally added a sum of Rupees 5,000 for the purchase of works on Oriental Literature.

Mr. Premchund Roychand gave Rupees 10,000 for fitting up the room assigned to Oriental Literature.[226]

The late Mr. Jugonnath Sunkersett presented Rupees 5,000 for the purchase of works on Natural History.

In 1863, during Dr. Birdwood's Secretary-ship, and with his assistance, a complete catalogue of books—the first since 1845—was published, and every year since that time Dr. Birdwood had kept the catalogue complete up to date by supplements both alphabetical and classified according to subjects.[227]

224 *Ibid.*
225 *Ibid.*
226 *Ibid.*
227 *Ibid.*

The 22nd, 23rd, and 24th issues of the Society's Journal had been brought out under Dr. Birdwood's editorship, and No. 25 was in the press in 1868. He himself contributed papers, in these issues, on one of the trees that yields the Luban maitee or Olibanum of commerce, on the Inlaid work of Bombay, and on recent discoveries in Eastern Africa illustrating De Foe's adventures of Captain Singleton.

The latter part of Dr. Birdwood's tenure of office saw the awakening of an interest with respect to the Society's objectives in the minds of the native chiefs, and the higher classes in the mofussil—especially in the most promising part of the Presidency, namely Kathiawar.

Indeed, the meeting of 13 August 1868 alone demonstrated this by the enrolling of names of several of these chieftains and Indians as members of the Society.

Hon'ble Mr. Justice Newton admitted that although Dr. Birdwood was less directly connected with the enrolment of members, he reiterated that he had been encouraged by the never flagging interest of Dr. Birdwood to bring this about.[228]

Dr. Birdwood always had the welfare of the Society in mind. Although several tangible results of his Secretary-ship, many of them material, could be estimated, there were other services of a very special manner that had characterised his term of office.

He was nearly always present in the Society's rooms. He always showed his care for the members' comfort and convenience. His efficient style of management and his pride in the reputation of the Society were conspicuous. It must be appreciated that a Society such as the Asiatic Society, the foremost literary and scientific institution in an important city, had many functions to perform. It had a character to sustain towards the general public in the city, and even towards more distant communities represented not infrequently by visitors—at times by visitors of distinction.[229]

In all these respects, the Society and Bombay had been worthily represented by Dr. Birdwood.

Details were always taken into consideration by him as is evidenced by the thought and taste displayed in effective combinations of colouring the different rooms of the Society.[230]

Justice Newton, as President, found Dr. Birdwood's aid invaluable, enhanced by the excellent spirit in which it was always rendered. The President went on to say that some people perhaps found Dr. Birdwood combative. The President's experience was otherwise. Dr. Birdwood's straight-forwardness and enthusiasm had sometimes been more prominent. However, his transparent candour and thorough earnestness of purpose had always been appreciated by all.[231]

228 *Ibid.*

229 *Ibid.*, p. 81.

230 *Ibid.*, p. 81.

231 *Ibid.*

The Society had achieved excellence due to the service rendered to it by able and earnest honorary secretaries and the name of Dr. Birdwood could justifiably be associated with those of Erskine, Vans Kennedy, Malcolmson and Carter. The high tone and character which the Secretaries had always helped to give the Society was evident. "Those who follow them will be guided by their examples of zeal and high-mindedness," the President said.

The President then proposed that the Committee of Management be requested to draw up and lay before the Society a statement of Dr. Birdwood's services and to consider and report the mode in which these services could be most suitably acknowledged.[232]

The Rev. Dr. Wilson, Honorary President, while seconding the motion of the President commended Dr. Birdwood for the ability, zeal and success with which he had discharged his duties of the Secretary-ship of the Society during the years he had held office. The time he had devoted to the Society's work indicated much self-denial on his part. His courteous attention to distinguished men, from different lands and his instructive exhibition of the numerous objects of curiosity and interest collected in the literary and antiquarian depository were to his credit.

It was through Dr. Birdwood's exertions that benefactors from the community helped to enlarge the library not only in bulk beyond anything yet exemplified in the East, but in value.

Besides the other advantages enumerated by the President, the Society was an educational instrument of no small importance. It united the intelligent people of all classes in the country with Europeans who had founded the Society. The result was most beneficial, for India which had been silent for so long, would soon speak of its own wonders.

Before sitting down Dr. Wilson made another proposal to the Society. He suggested that the name of Dr. Birdwood should be enrolled in the list of its Honorary Members, an arrangement, similar to that adopted in the case of Dr. Carter. This would do honour to the Society in anticipation of what Dr. Birdwood might do for it with the greater leisure, which it was hoped that he might enjoy in Europe where he would find a career of usefulness and happiness.[233]

Rao Saheb Vishwanath N. Mandlik touched upon Dr. Birdwood's role in popularising the Society by making it more accessible to the Indian community as was evident by the list of members.[234]

Mr. James Taylor, whose name had been proposed by the President for the post of Honorary Secretary,[235] said he had been acquainted with Dr. Birdwood ever since he came to Bombay. Besides the eminent services he had rendered to Bombay and the Society, few

232 *Ibid.*
233 *Ibid.*, p. 82.
234 *Ibid.*
235 *Ibid.*, p. 81.

members present would know that one of the earliest of Dr. Birdwood's literary contributions to the press in Bombay was an interesting article on the valuable compilation of papers on the geology of India made by his predecessor, Dr. Carter, which appeared in the *Bombay Quarterly Review* in 1858.[236]

When Taylor returned to Bombay in 1863, after an absence of four years, he found Dr. Birdwood in the office of Secretary of the Society. He himself became a member of the Committee of Management and was in a position to say that it would be difficult to overstate the value of the services rendered to the Society by Dr. Birdwood.

The Society was indebted to Dr. Birdwood for its increase in resources and his judgment in laying out judiciously the funds contributed by liberal-minded Indians.

Dr. Birdwood constantly examined all the important branches of literature in which the library was defective, and supplied all omissions in a regular and systematic manner as the ordinary resources of the Society enabled him.[237]

The unremitting care and assiduity with which Dr. Birdwood constantly watched over the Society was difficult to replace.

Dr. Birdwood, in replying to the President and other members, humbly thanked them for the honour that they had bestowed upon him.

In recalling memories, he said that Dr. Wilson's name was a revered household word to him years before he came to Bombay and it was while he was a student in Edinburgh that he had first read his delightful book, *The Lands of the Bible*. So deep and lasting an impression did it then make on him, that he had carried it about with him amongst his few "household gods."

Dr. Birdwood remembered that he had been proposed by Dr. Wilson in 1855 as a member of the Society. Since then he had met him on an average of probably once a week on some public business or other.

The Honourable Mr. Newton had proposed him as the Honorary Secretary in 1862 and, as the President of the Society, he had come to know Mr. Newton intimately.

Mr. Taylor was one of his oldest and most tried friends in Bombay, and Rao Sahib Mandlik, one of his oldest and most intimate Indian friends.[238]

Dr. Birdwood recounted the contribution of the four members of the Society. In particular he recalled the President's earnest solicitude and zeal in helping Dr. Birdwood in the discharge of his official duties of the Secretary during his illness after his return from Paris in November 1863. He admitted that the brilliant list of rajahs, princes and chiefs as

236 *Ibid.*, p. 82.

237 *Ibid.*

238 *Ibid.*, p. 82.

candidates for admission to the Society was the work exclusively of the President. This was done expressly for Dr. Birdwood's credit . . . 'so that his sun might set in a blaze of glory!'[239]

He commented on the strong *esprit de corps* that existed among the Society's members. They were all proud and determined to preserve the Society's worthy origins and traditions.

Dr. Birdwood referred to Rao Sahib's remark about popularising the Society, for encouraging the admission of Indians.

When he was appointed Honorary Secretary there were only about half a dozen Indians on the Society's role; in 1868 there were nearly one hundred. He added humour by saying, "But, so far as I am concerned, I have only been very selfish in this. Our European members, always coming and going, are not worth more on an average than Rupees 50 each a year for ten years. But every native member is worth the full value of his annual subscription—Rupees 100—for life—and I wish a long life to them all."[240]

He disagreed with the idea that it should be a circulating library.[241] He added that it should always be remembered that this was a library of reference, of standard works and *not* a circulating library, and that novels are only—bait!

He said he would always remember with pride and gratitude the honour which the Society had done him. In the discharge of his duties, he had always sought the members' approval and he was thoroughly delighted that he had found it.[242]

On 10 September 1868, James Taylor the Honorary Secretary read an address to Dr. Birdwood. It contained much of what the Honourable President Mr. Justice Newton had said in August 1868. Dr. Wilson proposed that a subscription be opened among the members for a testimonial to Dr. Birdwood.[243]

CONCLUSION

With Dr. Birdwood's retirement as Honorary Secretary of the Bombay Branch of the Royal Asiatic Society, an era had come to an end. No doubt he had many interests and invigorated several institutions in Bombay, but it seems that the work that he put in to rejuvenate the Society gave him pride, though his ceaseless efforts resulted in ruining his health.

239 *Ibid.,* p. 83.
240 *Ibid.*
241 *Ibid.*
242 *Ibid.,* p. 83.
243 *Ibid.,* p. 86.

Always keeping in mind the educational, literary and scientific objects of the Society, he tackled the task of building a noteworthy library, enlarging it with suitable additions. His work of drawing up an alphabetical catalogue and presenting a tabular form allowing easy access of books to researchers and interested members enabled them to pick out books of their choice.

He was always mindful of the Finances of the Society. He presented a balance sheet that was beneficial to the Society year by year, bearing in mind that judicious economy would benefit the Society.

His sincerity and courteous manner as well as his friendship and camaraderie helped him in winning over Europeans, visitors from faraway places and especially Indians. Among the Indians he awakened a thirst for knowledge and opened doors for them to meet and associate with Europeans on a common platform. In short, the membership of the Society grew by leaps and bounds.

The acceptance of enlightened Indians brought forth benefactions thereby increasing the wealth of the Society. The Indians in turn gained beneficence and respect where it was rightly due.

Dr. Birdwood, while making important contributions himself, revitalised the Journals of the Society encouraging research and scholarship, thus elevating the Society to its pristine glory.

In recounting the tenure of Dr. Birdwood as Secretary of the Bombay Branch of the Royal Asiatic Society, only a few events held at the Society have been described. Yet they give one an idea of the vast and varied subjects handled, the interest created in them by lectures and discussions, the international flavour instilled in the minds of the members and the public by the choice of topics. Above all, promoting the objectives of the Society through literary and scientific research and all this, through valuable contributions in the field of history, geography, sociology, anthropology, astronomy, palaeography, epigraphy, linguistics etc., which speak of but a few of the wide range of subjects in which an interest was inculcated in the people by the Society—a contribution which in no small measure can be attributed to Dr. Birdwood.

CHAPTER IV

The Agri and Horticultural Society of India and Bombay

THE BIRTH OF A SOCIETY

The concept that a number of people uniting and forming a Society to carry forward any undertaking was, generally speaking, only realised fully in the 18th century. In fact before the year 1640 not one Society was formed.[244]

However, in the 18th century there was a surge in the formation of Societies. Diverse objects relating to religion, to science, or the promotion of arts and manufactures were carried forward by a Society formed for that express purpose.

Societies enabled people to pool in their collective ideas. Even the mistakes and slip-ups of its members, when analysed, contributed in their own way to chalk out the correct path for achieving their goals. As Reverend William Carey wrote in 1820, "Men of enlarged minds have been long convinced of the great advantages to be derived from Societies of Scientific men."[245].... "That among these objects for the promotion of which associations can be formed, there are few more important than the agriculture of a country." [246]

In the light of this, Rev. Carey felt that an Agricultural Society in India would undoubtedly produce the most beneficial results with respect to the Peasantry, the Landholders and the Europeans who were engaged in its promotion, and would thereby benefit the country at large.[247]

---

244 *Transactions of the Agricultural and Horticultural Society of India,* vol., I, Appendix, p. 211, W. Carey, 15 April 1820.

245 *Ibid.*

246 *Ibid.,* p.212.

247 *Ibid.,* p. 213.

Rev. Carey believed that it would tend to broaden the ideas of the Peasantry (farmers), to dissipate their prejudices, to call forth their latent energies, to encourage their industry and to promote their respectability and usefulness in Society. Carrying the idea further, he felt that the Landowners would soon feel the benefits of the Agricultural Society leading to increasing value of the estates, and greater comfort and happiness of the tenants, who he believed would gradually stop evading the payment of rents. Rev. Carey tried to prove his point by stating that in England their experience had proved that the produce grown on a particular piece of land had increased four times, consequently raising the value of the land and its rent which had quadrupled.[248]

However, it would be pertinent to observe here that this instance seemed an over-simplification and could not be directly applied to the social fabric of India, where there was much more rigidity of caste and class ingrained in the minds of the people.

It is perhaps this lurking disparity which led Rev. Carey to add, "By associating Native Gentlemen of landed estates with Europeans who have studied this subject, and have made observations upon the practice of Agriculture in different countries, we should gradually impart to them more correct ideas of the value of landed property, of the possibility of improving it, and of the best methods of accomplishing so desirable an end and should at the same time convince them of the importance of studying the true interest of the tenantry (*sic*) and introducing improvements in their estates."[249]

He outlined the scope of the Agricultural and Horticultural Society; and justified his thoughts:

- An Agricultural Society would pay close attention to the improvement of Land.[250]
- It would point out and dwell on the best method of properly cropping Land.[251]
- Another object to be pursued by the Agricultural Society would be the introduction of new and useful plants.[252]
- It would have to endeavour to achieve the improvement of Implements of Husbandry.[253]
- An attempt would have to be made to improve the Stock (Sheep, Goats, Swine, and other useful animals). That is, those animals which come under the denomination of Stock, whether intended for Labour, the Dairy or for Food.
- Yet another object would be to encourage bringing Waste Lands into a State of Cultivation.[254]

---

248 *Ibid.*
249 *Ibid.*, (tenantry (*sic*) should read as tenancy).
250 *Ibid.*, p. 215.
251 *Ibid.*, p. 216.
252 *Ibid.*
253 *Ibid.*, p. 217.
254 *Ibid.*

Reverend Carey substantiated his scheme by stating that India had every variety of climate and geographical features conducive to Agricultural interests.[255]

He suggested that the Agricultural Society should offer rewards to deserving individuals.[256]

Further, he suggested that the Structure of the Society might be conducted by a President, two Vice-Presidents and a Committee that would be chosen annually.[257] It is important to note that he insisted that Native gentlemen should be eligible as members of the Society and should be officers of the Society "in precisely the same manner as Europeans."[258]

These ideas were fair and valuable and worth putting into practice in the interest of India, its land, landowners and farmers.

The Agricultural and Horticultural Society was first formed in Calcutta in 1820[259] and, at a subsequent meeting held on 18 May 1824, it was resolved that a general history of the origin and progress of the Society be compiled.[260]

THE AGRI-HORTICULTURAL SOCIETY OF WESTERN INDIA—BOMBAY

A decade after the Agricultural and Horticultural Society of Bengal was established, it was the turn of Western India to set up a branch of the Agri-Horticultural Society in 1830. It was founded under the patronage of Sir Sidney Beckwith, K.C.B. Its first President was Mr. Newnham; Mr. Vaupell was the first Secretary.[261]

As will be seen later, Dr. George Birdwood's contribution to the working of the Society in Bombay was noteworthy.

In 1835 the Society purchased the Sewri Garden,in Bombay, which was laid out by Colonel Dickinson and Dr. Heddle. They were assisted by a European gardener, Mr McCulloch. The latter had previously been employed by Pasha Mahomet Ali of Egypt. This facilitated a large exchange of plants between Western India and Egypt, contributing to the richness of the Botanical Gardens.[262]

255 *Ibid.*, p. 218.

256 *Ibid.*, p. 220.

257 *Ibid.*

258 *Ibid.*

259 Dossal, Mariam, *"The Hall of Wonder" With The "Garden of Delight"* ,in *Bombay to Mumbai,* Marg Publication, 1997, p. 208.

260 *Transactions of the Agricultural and Horticultural Society of India,* vol. I, Appendix, p. 233.

261 Birdwood, George, *Report of the Government Central Museum and on the Agricultural and Horticultural Society of Western India for 1863,* Appendix B, p. 56.

262 *Ibid.*

However, it was not until 1842 that the Garden was properly laid out. This was when Dr. George Buist and Dr. F. Giraud were appointed joint Secretaries. While Dr. Buist carried out the general arrangements which were followed through right up to the end, Dr. F. Giraud organised the Botanical Department.[263]

But the Sewri Gardens proved too far and did not serve the original purpose of encouraging visitors and inculcating a healthy curiosity in them. It was therefore planned that the gardens be relocated to an accessible site where both Europeans and Natives could benefit and derive pleasure. The Sewri land was decided to be converted into a much-needed burial ground for Europeans.

In lieu of the Sewri Gardens, the Bombay Government provided the Agri-Horticultural Society of Western India land in exchange at Mount Estate, Byculla, on the condition that the Society amalgamated with the Museum Committee for forming the Victoria Museum and Gardens.[264]

The land was situated on the east side of the Parel Road, a few yards north of the Byculla Railway Station.[265]

The estate was finally made over to the Agri-Horticultural Society on 21 May 1861.[266]

Since the properties included in the Mount Estate were not contiguous, the Society was permitted to exchange certain plots with others not in their possession, so as to make it convenient to manage. No doubt there were landlords like Bomanjee Framjee Cama who were reluctant to co-operate, but finally a settlement was struck between the Society and Mr. Cama, by which Mr. Cama's Sindulpara estate situated within the plan of the Botanical Gardens was acquired, with Mr. Cama standing to gain.[267]

BIRDWOOD'S UNSTINTING DEVOTION TOWARDS THE AGRI-HORTICULTURAL SOCIETY

The idea of forming an Agricultural and Horticultural Society in India emanated from Reverend William Carey. Many missionaries like Rev. Carey did think of uplifting the natives, but it cannot be denied that proselytising the natives was also on their minds.

263 *Ibid.*, p. 57. The Society published two parts (1843) and then a volume in (1852) of its Transactions, Govind Narayan, *Mumbai-an Urban Biography from 1863*, Gyan Prakash, p. 359.

264 *Ibid.*, p. 57

265 S.M. Edwardes, *Gazetteer of Bombay City and Island (GBCI)*, vol. III, 1910, p. 336.

266 Government Resolution No. 2512, mentioned in Birdwood's *Report*, p. 57.

267 Birdwood's *Report*, pp.74-75.

Dr. Birdwood, as we shall see, was different. He became Secretary of the Agricultural and Horticultural Society in the mid-1850s after he returned to Bombay from England, and continued as Secretary for many years.[268]

As the Governor of Bombay, Sir Bartle Frere, said, while laying the cornerstone of the Victoria and Albert Museum in November 1862, "Dr. Birdwood whose laborious exertions, so long continued, so unselfishly and energetically rendered, are now, we may hope, destined to be crowned with success."[269]

Indeed, anything that Dr. George Birdwood did for Bombay was 'crowned with success.' He did everything whole-heartedly and putting the need of the people before his own. Dr. Birdwood in his characteristic way set to work at the Victoria Gardens in 1861. In May 1861, the Agri-Horticultural Society was in possession of the Garden within its present boundaries. Almost immediately the transference of plants from Sewri was commenced.[270]

In the last week of July 1861, the laying out and planting of the Garden was begun according to the plans of William Tracey who was assisted by Mr. Terry, the Superintendent of the Jamsetjee Jeejeebhoy School of Arts.[271]

When the Garden was opened by Lady Frere on 19 November 1862, it already had a "handsome promenade." It was expected that the next monsoon would enhance its appearance. Birdwood had then hoped that in three years from the opening, the waters of the Vihar Lake would be available and would add to its beauty.[272]

Indeed, Lady Frere while declaring the Victoria Gardens open had expressed that they would long continue to be "a monument of taste and munificence of the leading merchants of Bombay and a source of pure and rational enjoyments to its inhabitants."[273]

FINANCES OF THE MUSEUM AND GARDENS —CLEAR-CUT DISTINCTION

When the Government Central Museum and the Agri-Horticultural Society were amalgamated and called the 'Victoria and Albert Museum' and the 'Victoria Gardens,' it was agreed that although the Museum and Gardens had become definitely united, the Managing Committees would be unconnected with each other. While the Museum had been funded by

268 Govind Narayan, *Mumbai an Urban Biography from 1863,* Gyan Prakash, p. 359.

269 Birdwood's *Report,* p. 52.

270 *Ibid.,* p. 57.

271 *Ibid.*

272 *Ibid.,* p. 57.

273 *Ibid.*

public subscription and an equal sum of money contributed by the Government, the Agri-Horticultural Society of Western India had undertaken the charge of forming and maintaining their new garden henceforth called the "Victoria Gardens."[274]

In fact, it was the Government of Sir George Clerk that contributed a lakh of Rupees to the Museum, and gave the 'splendid' Mount Estate for the Victoria Gardens.[275]

Birdwood's métier as Secretary of the Agri-Horticultural Society was at once perceived when he presented the Society's Annual Report on 1 January 1864.

Birdwood reported that during the year 1863, fifty-two members were elected, leaving a total of one hundred and thirty-five paying members as against ninety-one paying members on 1 January 1863.[276] An increase in membership would mean a boost to the Society's finances.

Thus the income and expenditure for the year were:[277]

	Rupees	Annas	Pies
Receipts	50,037	9	2
The Expenditure	24,537	15	6
Balance	25,499	9	8

Although the balance included Rupees 17,000 received from Mr. David Sassoon, the venerable head of the Jewish Community, to build a Clock Tower and an amount of Rupees 2,993.12.3 (after accounting for expenditure already incurred), collected by Public subscription on account of the memorial building of the opening of the Garden, the net balance was Rupees 5,505.13.5.[278]

This balance was nearly five times above the balance of previous years.[279] Dr. Birdwood stated that certain outstanding subscription of Rupees 3,375 plus the donation of rupees 5,000 from His Highness Khunderao, Gaicowar, K.S.I., will be required to complete the works going on in the garden. Hence, to meet the normal expenditure of the Society of Rupees 12,000 a year, "the available balance is not more than it is pleasant to have always on hand."[280]

He contended that "the real balance of every well-conducted scientific or philanthropic Society is the public wealth."[281]

274 *Ibid.*, p. 49.
275 *Ibid.*, p. 50.
276 *Ibid.*, p. 67.
277 *Ibid.*
278 *Ibid.*
279 *Ibid.*
280 *Ibid.*
281 *Ibid.*, p. 68.

DONATION

The biggest donation of 1863-1864 was of Vihar water to the Gardens by the Municipal Commissioners. "It is impossible," wrote Birdwood in his Report, "to render in words any acknowledgement of this great benefit ... but for its free gift the newly formed Garden would have been levelled during the heat of last April and May as flat and bare as a table."[282]

A detailed reading of Dr. Birdwood's Report gives a clear picture of how much dedicated effort had been put in by him as Secretary of the Society. Some of the salient achievements of the Society during the year show Dr. Birdwood's visionary and meticulous work for the Society.

During the year 1863, the Society exported a large number of Plants gratis for the Pasha of Bagdad (Iraq); for His Highness Prince Halim, Pasha of Cairo (Egypt); for Colonel Playfair in Zanzibar (Africa) and for the Royal Botanical Garden, Liverpool (England).

In exchange for these, foreign plants were imported gratis from Mrs. Tyreman, Liverpool and Colonel Playfair in Zanzibar.[283]

For the enhancement of the garden in India, Birdwood recorded that vegetable and flower seeds were imported from James Veitch, Junior, of the Royal Exotic Nursery, King's Road, Chelsea (U.K.). These seeds, he had always found in 'first-rate condition' on arrival.[284]

From his Bombay experience, he had recommended and classified flowering plants, dividing them into three categories, Hardy, Delicate and Precarious.

The List of Hardy flowering plants, to name just 8 of the 19 he had picked out, included:

i) Petunia, especially the white, red and purple

ii) *Cape geranium*, red

iii) *Chrysanthemum indicum*, yellow and white

iv) *Zinnia elegans*, yellow, orange, red, white, and pink

v) French Marigold, yellow and red

vi) Balsams, red, white and purple

vii) *Salvia splendens*, scarlet

viii) Pinks

---

282 *Ibid.*, p. 69.
283 *Ibid.*, p. 72.
284 *Ibid.*

He went on to list in the Delicate group, to name 7 out of the 23 that he identified, flowers such as:

i) Portulaca, sps.

ii) Common Marigold

iii) Snap Dragon

iv) Violet

v) Dahlia

vi) Sweet William

vii) Mixed Sweet Peas

He named 6 flowers in the Precarious category including Larkspur, China Aster and Salvia.[285]

With so much emphasis on detail that he implemented, one can only imagine what a feast for the eyes the Victoria Gardens must have been.

LAYING OUT OF THE VICTORIA GARDENS

The garden roads, which were two and a half miles, were all laid out in 1862. During 1861-1862, they were covered with the calcareous sand of Mahim woods, called *Gadha.*[286]

Having completed the borders and avenues of the Garden, Birdwood hoped that his Report would be a sort of guide to the Garden, like the *Kew Garden Guide* of London. He was quick to add that the season from October 1863 to June 1864 was the first attempt for trying the effect of different annual plants in the borders, and was still in the experimental stage.[287]

He hoped that in the next monsoon he would be able to prepare a proper Guide Book.[288]

The whole garden would be completed with zinc labels for all the plants in the Garden, thereby not only rendering the gardens as an object of pleasure but also making it a scientific garden. This, he proposed to achieve by the 1 November 1864.[289]

285 *Ibid.*, pp. 73-74.
286 *Ibid.*, p. 76.
287 *Ibid.*, p. 77.
288 *Ibid.*
289 *Ibid.*, p. 77.

SENT TO KARWAR

His work, no doubt, was appreciated by the Government, and in a Government Resolution issued on 20 March 1863, he was ordered to go to Sudashewghur for its immediate establishment. Birdwood accordingly left Bombay, and selected a charming site at Karwar of about 13 acres between Beitcul and the open sea.[290]

In Bombay, Birdwood thought of every officer employed at the Victoria Gardens and examined every item with a toothcomb. Characteristically, he commended the case of the office clerk Eshvant Krishnarao Palekar and recommended that his salary be raised so as to equal that of the Garden Superintendent, Bhasker Ramchunder.[291] There is no doubt that his favourable equation with all workers, spurred each one to give his or her best for the job on hand.

INCREASED MEMBERSHIP

Birdwood reported that instead of 100 Members that he had expected, only 44 were added to the Society. "This will never do," he wrote, "unless we are always appealing to the public ....Every respectable person residing in Bombay ought to join the Society, and I think it is scarcely fair that any respectable person a permanent resident in Bombay should daily walk in the Garden without becoming a member."[292] He complained also that in spite of his efforts only Rs. 25 were subscribed by the English community. He contrasted this by stating that although the annual subscription was only Rupees 15 it was specially noted that when a Native gentleman Mr. Pestonjee Jehanghier, was sent the bill for his annual subscription for 1863, he sent Rupees 70 instead of Rupees 15, "so highly does he, as a neighbour, value the garden," wrote Birdwood.[293]

That the gardens were a grand success is aptly borne out by the preparation of the Rules and Regulations for the management of the Victoria Gardens. It is interesting to note that Birdwood wrote these out in his own hand on the Printed Copy of the Report.[294]

He outlined the composition of the Establishment stating that the Fixed Labour will be managed by a *Kharbaree* or Native Manager, under whom were the *Muccadam* of *Malees* and

290 *Ibid.,* p. 78.
291 *Ibid.,* pp. 78-79.
292 *Ibid.,* p. 79.
293 *Ibid.*
294 Birdwood, *Report of the Government Central Museum,* in the *ASM (Asiatic Society of Mumbai),* Appendix L, pp.154-166 and Appendix M, pp. 167, contains 3 handwritten pages.

the whole hierarchy of *Malees,* boys and women working regularly with a Gate-Keeper and Night-Guard.

Besides Fixed Labour, Birdwood mentioned the Casual Labour and extra hands to be hired when large gardening operations were to take place.

He delineated the demarcation of duties of each of these persons so that, realistically speaking, there was minimum squabbling.

As was Birdwood's practice, he took care of all details. For instance he urged that "all malis should receive presents of blankets and umbrellas on the Queen's birthday (beginning of the rains), and of turbans, dhotis etc., on the Prince of Wales' birthday (beginning of the cold weather) and presents of sweetmeats and goats and fireworks ... on their own great holidays." But not everything could be satisfactory, for from the 1 July 1864 they would pay fines on stray cattle. However, the killer of venomous snakes would receive eight annas Dr. Birdwood added the last instruction in his own hand.[295]

He specified the work to be done by certain months and dates. Garden operations such as watering plants and shrubs planted in specified areas; using manure for fertilizing, weeding and cleaning, digging, sowing, layering and propagating by cuttings in the rainy season were all overseen by him. Birdwood also advised that no birds except kites and no flying insects except locusts were to be destroyed, and birds with sharp-pointed beaks were to be encouraged in every way.[296]

Dr. Birdwood listed that the date trees, the pummelo trees, the custard apple trees, the mangoes, the plantains and the rose and jasmine beds should be all separately rented out by the year for which they should be all put up for auction,[297] in order to generate funds (which would help to maintain the gardens).

The genuine care and interest that Dr. Birdwood took in the laying of the Gardens was indeed exemplary!

It is this personal touch, which Dr. Birdwood gave to every work that he dedicated himself to, that led the President of the Bombay Branch of the Royal Asiatic Society, Mr. Justice Newton to say on 13 August 1868, when Dr. Birdwood retired as Secretary of the BBRAS, "He had laid other institutions around us under obligations to him and one perhaps—the Agri-Horticultural—may dispute with us the claim to having been his chief object among so many.......I am not unmindful that Bombay is largely indebted to his exertions and his care for the Victoria Gardens."[298]

---

295 *Ibid.,* p. 157. The note about the snakes is added in Birdwood's own handwriting. To be found in the copy of the *Report found in the copy with the Asiatic Society of Mumbai.*

296 *Ibid.,* pp. 163-166.

297 *Ibid.,* p. 166.

298 *Times of India,* cutting in *The Minutes of the Asiatic Society, 1865-1868,* p. 80.

Dr. Birdwood's work as Secretary of the Agri-Horticultural Society leading to the special attention that he gave to the laying out of the Victoria Gardens speaks of his immense devotion and love for plant-life. The Victoria Gardens, like so many other institutions in Bombay, exemplify his Midas touch that helped transform the ordinary Mount Estate and, in Dr. Birdwood's own words, "making a wilderness blossom as the rose."[299]

299 Birdwood, *Report,* p. 69.

CHAPTER V

Birdwood as Sheriff of Bombay and Registrar of The University of Bombay

Dr. George Birdwood adorned many offices in Bombay and, among these, his appointment as Sheriff in 1864 was one of the many forms of recognition of his work in Bombay.

The Sheriff is an old office in Bombay dating back to 1671.[300] Indeed, the practice of appointing Sheriffs in metropolitan cities like Bombay has continued even after independence. It is certain that this office was established, following as a result of India being ruled by the British Crown. In fact, the first Sheriff in the country was appointed in Bombay by *Letters Patent* on 24 September 1726. "It was believed that the office of Sheriff had probably been created by the local government with the assent of the London Company under the *Charter 20 of Charles II of March 1665* which made over Bombay to that Company and empowered the Company to do all things necessary for the complete establishment of justice and enable them or the Governor of Bombay to delegate judges for the purpose."[301]

The Sheriff was and even today is appointed by the Government. In 1864, when Dr. Birdwood was appointed Sheriff there was no well organised Municipality; it was only established in 1865, one year after Dr. Birdwood was appointed Sheriff. Today, the Mayor of the Municipal Corporation of Bombay is elected, whereas the Sheriff, as we have seen, is appointed by the Government. As such, the Mayor[302] is recognized as the first citizen and the Sheriff as the second citizen. In Dr. Birdwood's days, he could well have been regarded as first citizen. In fact, the significance of the Sheriff has been throughout considered a link between the official hierarchy and the common unofficial public. Thus the dignity and importance attached to the office of the Sheriff arises from the customary and time-honoured treatment of

300 *Maharashtra State Gazetteers Greater Bombay District,* Sheriff's Court: Duties of the Sheriff of Bombay.

301 *Ibid.*

302 In November 1931, the designation of President of Bombay Municipal Corporation was changed into that of the Mayor of the Bombay Municipal Corporation, http.//en wikipedia.org/wiki/Mayor of Mumbai#History of the Office

it as a position representing the people. This fact remains today, even in spite of representative institutions having arisen.

Any position of honour is often represented with a badge or symbol. One of the most important items of insignia attached to the office of Sheriff in Bombay was a silver oar first made in 1810 bearing the British Crown and inscriptions that it was given in the 50th year of the reign of George III.[303]

This was changed in 1966 when a new emblem was made in a hexagonal shape and has the State emblem on both sides replacing the crown and inscriptions.[304]

It must be noted that the office of the Sheriff is not judicial, though it falls under the administrative control of the Law and Judiciary Department of the Government; rather by the nature of the duties that the Sheriff performs, it is an executive office.[305]

Thus the main duties and functions of the Sheriff are:

1) To serve and execute the writs, orders and warrants issued by the Supreme Court.
2) To serve witness subpoenas in sessions cases.
3) To sell attached properties by public auctions.

There is a second category of duties of the Sheriff as a public functionary today. Actually, these have become so important that they give justification for the position itself. The direct personal responsibilities of the Sheriff are:

1) To meet very important persons on their arrival in and departure from the city.
2) To entertain dignitaries and prominent people.
3) To convene public meetings.

These functions make the Sheriff a valuable link of much practical utility between the official hierarchy and the public.

The Sheriff's office in Bombay is attached with a great deal of dignity and importance.

There is a considerable amount of work in connection with the serving processes of the courts, the protection of properties attached by the Sheriff in execution proceedings, etc. There are special bailiffs appointed by the Sheriff who are authorised clerks of the solicitors and advocates.[306]

In accordance with one of the main duties of the Sheriff, related to orders issued by Courts of Law, Dr. Birdwood as the then Sheriff in 1864 issued a PROCLAMATION on 1 March 1864, and gave notice on behalf of the High Court of Judicature at Bombay.

303 *Ibid.*
304 *Ibid.*
305 *Ibid.*
306 *Ibid.*

The PROCLAMATION read as follows:

BOMBAY TO WIT: By virtue of a Precept to me directed, I hereby Proclaim and give Notice, that the FIRST SESSIONS of 1864 of OVER and TERMINER, and GENERAL GOAL DELIVERY, will be holden before the High Court of Judicature at Bombay, at the Court House, on FRIDAY, the 18th instant at 11 o'clock in the forenoon, for the trial of all Treasons, Murders, and other Felonies, Perjuries, Trespasses, and other Crimes, Misdemeanours, and Offences had, done, or committed with the Town and Island of Bombay, and the Limits thereof, and the Factories Subordinates thereto; and also to inquire, hear and determine in like manner all Treasons, Murders, Felonies, Forgeries, Perjuries, Crimes, Extortions, Misdemeanours, Offences, Wrongs, and Oppressions, had, done, or committed by any of Her Majesty's British Subjects in any of the Territories which now are subject to, or dependent upon, the Government of Bombay, or within any of the Dominions of the Native Princes of India in alliance with the said Government.[307]

The PROCLAMATION also included orders of the Admiralty in connection with Maritime Crimes, stating:

And also that at the same time and place will be holden a Session of Admiralty; for the trial of all Treasons, Murders, Piracies, Robberies, Felonies, Misdemeanours, Offences, and other Maritime Crimes whatsoever done or committed on High Seas.[308]

The PROCLAMATION further gave notice to the Prosecutors and Witnesses, stating:

And I hereby give Notice to all persons bound to prosecute and give evidence at the above Sessions, or in any way concerned therein, that they are to attend at the time and place abovementioned and not to depart without leave of the Court.[309]

And lastly, the Prosecution issued Notice to all legal functionaries, stating:

And I herby give Notice to all Justices of the Peace, Coroners, Escheators, and also all the Chief Constables and Bailiffs of the Town & Island of Bombay and the Limits thereof; that they be then and there in their own persons, with their Rolls, Records, Indictments, and other Remembrances, to do those things which to their Offices in that behalf appertain to be done.[310]

---

307 *Bombay Government Gazette: January-June 1864, Thursday [d] March 1864,* p. 447.

308 *Ibid.*

309 *Ibid.*

310 *Ibid.*

Ending the PROCLAMATION by stating:

Dated the 1st day of March 1864, and in the twenty-seventh year of the Reign of Her Majesty Queen Victoria.

G.C.M. Birdwood
Sheriff.[311]

We see that Dr. Birdwood signed the same as Sheriff of Bombay.

That the Sheriff had to approach the Government in executing his task becomes clear when Dr. Birdwood addressed a letter dated 27 June 1864 to the Secretary to Government, Judicial Department with a request:

Sir,

I have the honour to request that you will have the goodness to direct the Accountant General to furnish me with a statement of fees collected on account of this Department by the several Mofussil Courts in this Presidency under Act VIII of 1852 and to authorize its payment to me.

I have the honor to be
Sir,
Your most obedient servant
Signed G.C.M. Birdwood
Sheriff

Bombay
Sheriff's Office
27 June 1864[312]

Although the Under Secretary to Government, Judicial Department, H.M. Birdwood, forwarded a copy of Dr. George Birdwood's letter to the Auditor and Accountant General

311 *Bombay Government Gazette, Thursday 3 March, 1864,* p. 447. One finds this same PROCLAMATION on p. 473 of the *Bombay Government Gazette of 10 March 1864.* The PROCLAMATION appears in Gujarati and Marathi.

312 *JD, vol.25 of 1864,* p. 57.

with a request to comply with the Sheriff's desire,[313] it seems that the Sheriff did not receive the required information and had to send another letter to the Secretary to Government, Judicial Department, in September 1864, reiterating the request and stating:

"No answer of Government to this reference (Sheriff's Letter dated 27th June) has yet been received on the subject."[314]

In response, the Sheriff received a letter[315] dated 21 September 1864, from the Judicial Department informing him that the Deputy Auditor and Accountant General has been instructed to take necessary action; a copy of the said letter No. 2823 was forwarded to the Deputy Auditor and Accountant General.[316]

Finally, the Sheriff received another letter dated 2 November 1864, from the Acting Secretary to Government, Judicial Department,[317] stating that:

To,
The Sheriff of Bombay

Sir,

I am directed by the Honourable the Governor in Council to inform you, with reference to Government Endorsement No 2824 of the 21st September last, that the Deputy Auditor and Accountant General states, that the required Statements will be forwarded as soon as information called for on the subject from the several Disbursing officers is received.

B.C. [Bombay Castle]
2nd Nov. 1864

The protracted correspondence between the Sheriff and the Government indicates that the Sheriff had to strive continuously to get the required documents from Government officials.

It is interesting to note that Dr. Birdwood's predecessor M. Cursetjee, the Sheriff of Bombay in 1863, had to inform the Chief Secretary to Government for the information of His Excellency the Governor in Council that the Sealer of the High Court had declined to Seal "the Receipt for the ensuing Criminal Subpoenas (received) from the Clerk of the

313 *Vide, JD, vol. 25 of 1864*, p. 60, No. 3944—2165 of 1864 dated 20 July 1864.
314 *Ibid.*, p. 61.
315 *Ibid.*, p. 61, No. 2823 of 1864.
316 *Ibid.*, *vide* No. 2824 of 1864.
317 *Ibid.*, p. 65, No. 3292 of 1864.

Crown" unless he be paid his fee of one Rupee at the time of Sealing.[318] The Sheriff in his letter went on to state that "the practice hitherto has been for the Sealer to seal such Receipts as also the several Subpoenas issued by the Clerk of the Crown for Witnesses at the Criminal Sessions (which amounted to last Sessions to 115 and for each of which the Sealer receives a fee of one rupee) and to prefer a Bill to the Sheriff after the termination of each Session for the amount of fees payable for Sealing the Receipts and Summons. The Sheriff then includes such Bills in his Contingent Bill which is forwarded to the Civil Paymaster."[319]

The Sheriff then requested His Excellency the Governor to "issue instruction to the Sealer of the High Court to Seal the Receipts and Subpoenas and to prefer his Bills for the same as before and to await payment for the same until the amount has been paid to the Sheriff by Government."[320]

In response to the above letter, the Sheriff of Bombay received a letter from the Judicial Department dated 30 June 1863[321] which stated inter alia "In reply I am desired to inform you, that Government has no authority to give orders to the Sealer of the High Court but H.E. in C would wish to know the name of the Sealer."[322]

The predicament of the Sheriffs of not getting due support from other Government officials can once again be seen in this correspondence.[323]

DR. BIRDWOOD AS THE REGISTRAR OF THE UNIVERSITY OF BOMBAY

It may rightly be said that the Bombay Association comprised of enlightened citizens of Bombay, was instrumental to large extent, in causing to precipitate the famous **Education Despatch of the Court of Directors dated 19 July 1854,** reputably known as **Wood's Education Despatch.** No doubt the education of the Indians was of prime importance to the Court of Directors. However, the two petitions of the Bombay Association, one in 1852, and the second petition sent in 1853, to the British Parliament, accelerated the implementation of

318 *JD, vol. 25 of 1863,* p. 10. Letter dated 15 June 1863.

319 *Ibid.*

320 *Ibid.,* p. 11.

321 *Ibid.,* p. 13, No. 1737 of 1863.

322 *Ibid.,* p. 13.

323 This is even more poignant when we read the <Roots Web:INDIA-L DOMESTIC OCCURRENCES 1863> From "Sylvia Murphy". She reports from the Overland Edition of the Times of India about 'Deaths.' Here we find this information: "HEERAJEE-June 28th of Cholera at Billa Byculla, Mr Heerajee Manockjee, eldest son of Manockjee Cursetjee, Esq, Sheriff of Bombay and second Judge of the Court of Small Causes, aged 23 years, leaving a disconsolate father, two sisters, and two brothers (the latter in England) and a large circle of friends to bemoan his great loss."

the recommendations made by Wood's Despatch. This resulted in the Government of India setting up a Committee to draw up a plan for three Universities in India. The Chairman of the Committee was Sir James Colville.

Thus on 21 December, the Government of India passed the Calcutta University Bill as Act II of 1857. The Act XXII of 1857 related to the establishment of the University of Bombay and Act XXVII of the same year embodied the University of Madras.[324]

The University of Bombay was established, as we have said, by the Act of Incorporation of the Government of India, on 18 July 1857. The preamble to the University of Bombay Act of 1857, states:

"For the better encouragement of Her Majesty's subjects of all classes and denominations within the Presidency of Bombay and other parts of India in the pursuit of a regular and liberal course of education, it has been determined to establish an University of Bombay for the purpose of ascertaining, by means of examination, the persons who have acquired proficiency in different branches of Literature, Science and Art and of rewarding them by Academic Degrees as evidence of their respective attainments, and marks of honour proportioned thereunto."[325]

The same Act of 1857 provided for the offices of the Chancellor (who invariably was the Governor of Bombay), Vice-Chancellor and Fellows of the University; these three categories formed the Senate of the University. The Senate of the University was virtually the Policy Maker.

Another statute in this Act was that the total number of Fellows of the University, exclusive of the Chancellor and Vice-Chancellor, was never less than 26. The Governor-in-Council had the powers, however, to nominate more than 26 Fellows.[326]

The Act also explicitly mentioned the degrees that the Senate was empowered to bestow. These were Bachelor of Arts, Master of Arts, Bachelor of Laws, Licentiates in Medicine, Doctors of Medicine, and Masters of Civil Engineering. A subsequent Act XLVII of 1860 had to be passed to vest the Senate with additional powers to confer degrees over and above those mentioned in the Act of 1857.[327]

At first the University had only four faculties –Arts (which included Science), Law, Medicine and Engineering (which included Agriculture). The only function of the University till 1904 was that of a principal 'affiliating' body, very much on the lines like the University of London. Its authority encompassed the framing of curricula and conducting examinations. The affiliated colleges provided the instruction and prepared the candidates for the University examinations. The University did not directly undertake any teaching.

324 Tikekar, Aroon, *The Cloister's Pale, A Biography of the University of Mumbai*, p. 19.

325 *Ibid.*

326 *Ibid.*

327 *Ibid.*

It may be noted that the Senate was also given power to make and alter bye-laws and regulations, not inconsistent with the Act.[328]

The bye-laws of the University provided that the executive powers of the University be vested in a Syndicate consisting of the Vice-Chancellor and seven others from amongst the Fellows. These were to be annually elected by the Faculties — three by the Faculty of Arts, two by the Faculty of Law and one each by the Faculty of Medicine and Engineering.[329]

Thus the executive arm of the University—the Syndicate—came into existence as a result of the bye-laws. It did not originate with Act XXII of 1857. In the beginning, the Senate, which was the Policy Maker, was treated like a 'parent body', so to speak. The Syndicate did not have the status of a statutory body that exercised jurisdiction and powers to co-ordinate University affairs.[330] Every question decided by the Syndicate had to be approved by the Senate. The Syndicate was empowered to appoint and remove examiners and all other officers of the University except the Registrar. It could hold examinations, grant degrees, honours and rewards, maintain the accounts of the University, and had powers to correspond with the Government and other concerned agencies. It was also empowered to frame bye-laws (as we have seen) and regulations which were subject to the approval of the Senate.[331]

The first batch of successful students from all the faculties were conferred the degrees on 28 April 1862, at the First Convocation presided over by Sir Bartle Frere, the then Governor of Bombay and Chancellor of the University of Bombay.[332]

We may now look closely at the post of Registrar of the University. It was in fact, a part time post until as late as 1930. To a large extent it depended on the way he managed and controlled it. As S.R. Dongerkery aptly put it, "He was and continues to be, a real lynchpin of the University administration."[333]

It must be noted that most of the Vice-Chancellors were esteemed personalities who were otherwise busy in civic and professional capacities. Being honorary officers, they came to the University for a few hours in the day to peruse papers that called for their attention and advice. On the other hand, Syndics, Deans and Fellows were tenure posts, who actively took part in University affairs. However, it was the Registrar who had to assume the entire responsibility of advising the University authorities on every matter connected with the working of the University.[334]

328 Dongerkery, S.R., *A History of the University of Bombay, 1857-1957;* University of Bombay, 1957, p. 12.
329 Tikekar, *op.cit.,* p. 20.
330 *Ibid.*
331 *Ibid.,* p. 20.
332 *Ibid.,* p. 22.
333 Cited in Tikekar, *op.cit.,* p. 123.
334 *Ibid.,* p. 123.

It is noteworthy that the University of Bombay was singularly lucky in having men of repute and outstanding ability as Registrars. Their efficiency, integrity and sincerity of purpose helped build sound traditions and set laudable academic standards. The first Registrar, Dr. R.S. Sinclair, held the office for eight years. Dr. G.C.M. Birdwood, renowned scholar whose many-sided contribution to enhance the development of Bombay, held the post for a little over a year. James Taylor, who was responsible for organizing the laying of the foundation stone of the University, was Registrar for nearly five years and nine months. Peter Peterson lived on the second floor of the Rajabai Tower and held the post for 13 years; Rev. D.C. Boyd for nearly three years; D. MacDonald for nearly 11years; followed by Khan Bahadur Furdunji M. Dastur with a record of meritorious service for 28 years. Dastur's protégé, S.R. Dongerkery, who wrote a learned history of the University followed his able guide with a 26-year term, and set the stage for T.V. Chidambaran who held the office for 21 and a quarter years.[335]

During the course of the years the University of Bombay has been functioning under successive Acts of the Government, particularly those of the State Government of Maharashtra after India became Independent. In 1994, however, the State Government promulgated an Act entitled "**The Maharashtra Universities Act, 1994**" which became applicable to all the Non-Agricultural Universities of the State. The name of the University of Bombay was changed to ***University of Mumbai*** in the year 1996.

Under the 1994 Act : "The Chancellor, Vice-Chancellor, Pro-Vice-Chancellor, if any, the members of the Senate, Management Council or Academic Council for the time being holding office as such in each university are hereby constituted and declared to be a body corporate ... and (who) shall have perpetual succession and a common seal and may by that name sue or be sued."[336]

Also, "Each university shall be competent to acquire and hold property, both movable and immovable ... which it may transfer or dispose ... or contract ... provided that no such lease, sale or transfer of such property is made ... without the prior consent of the State Government."[337]

The objects of the University are laid down in the Act. They are "to disseminate, create and preserve knowledge and understanding by teaching, research, extension and service and by effective demonstration and influence of corporate life on society in general."[338]

The University is expected "to promote discipline and the spirit of intellectual inquiry and to dedicate itself as a fearless academic community."[339]

335 *Ibid.*, p. 123.

336 *Maharashtra Universities Act, 1994,* p. 6. (1994:Mah. XXXV)

337 *Ibid.*

338 *Ibid.*

339 *Ibid., 4. Objects of University, No. 2.*

It is "to encourage individuality and diversity within a climate of tolerance and understanding."[340]

The object is to promote freedom, secularism, equality and social justice as enshrined in the Constitution of India.....to carry out social responsibility

And

To promote equitable distribution of facilities of higher education.

In short it is to be a catalyst in the socio-economic transformation and must add to the values needed for national development.[341]

The objects stated an expectation for better interaction and co-ordination among different universities and for generating a sense of self-respect and dignity amongst the weaker sections of society.

All in all, it is "to strive to promote competitive merit and excellence as the sole guiding criterion in all academic and other matters relating to the students."[342]

It may be pertinent to say that the scope of the University had widened enormously.

OFFICERS OF THE UNIVERSITY

The offices of the University include inter alia the Vice-Chancellor, Pro-Vice-Chancellor, Deans of Faculties and Registrar.

It is stated in the Act of 1994[343] that "The Governor of Maharashtra, for the time being, shall be the Chancellor of every university and the Chancellor, by virtue of his office, shall be the Head of the university."

One of the important duties of the Chancellor is that "when present (he) shall preside over the Convocation of the university and may issue direction to the Vice-Chancellor of the university for specific purposes, whenever necessary, and the Vice-Chancellor shall submit the minutes of such meeting to the Chancellor for his perusal."[344]

340 *Ibid., No. 3.*

341 *Ibid., No.4-7-Objects of the University in Maharashtra Universities Act, 1994,* p. 6.

342 *Ibid.,* p. 7. Nos. 13, 14, 15.

343 *Ibid.,* p. 16 [9.(1)]

344 *Ibid.,* p. 16. [9.(2)].

The other officers of the University besides:

1) The Vice-Chancellor
2) The Pro-Vice-Chancellor are:
3) The Deans of Faculties;
4) The Registrar;
5) The Controller of Examinations;
6) The Director of sub-campuses of the university;
7) The Director, Board of College and University Development;
8) The Librarian of the university library;
9) The Finance and Accounts Officer;
10) The Director of Students' Welfare;
11) Such other officers in the service of the university as may be prescribed[345]

In the Maharashtra Universities Act, 1994, the Functions and Duties of the Senate, the Management Council and the Academic Council are clearly defined.[346] It reads:

1) The Senate shall transact the following business at its annual meeting, namely:-
   - Review current academic programmes and collaborative programmes;
   - Suggest new academic programmes consistent with the societal requirements in higher education;
   - Suggest measures for improvement and development of the University;
   - Suggest institution of new degrees, diplomas, certificates, and other academic distinctions; and
   - Confer, on the recommendations of the Management Council, honorary degrees or other academic dictions.
2) The Senate shall receive, discuss and approve the annual financial estimate (budget), the annual reports, accounts and audit reports of the University.
3) The Senate shall review broad policies and programmes of the University and suggest measures for its improvement and development.

The erstwhile Syndicate is now called the Management Council. It is and "shall be the principal executive authority to formulate statutes and forward the same to the Senate for approval and make Ordinances and administer the affairs of the University and shall carry out all such duties which are not specifically assigned to any other authority."[347]

"The Academic Council shall be responsible for laying down the academic policies in regard to maintenance and improvement of standards of teaching, research;" extending collaboration programmes in academic matters and evaluation of the work-load of teachers.[348]

345 *Ibid.*, p. 17.[10.(1-11)].
346 *Ibid.*, p. 34. [26. (1-3)].
347 *Ibid.*, p. 34. [27. (1)].
348 *Ibid.*, p. 38.[29. (1)].

By tackling Cowasjee Jehanghier discreetly, Governor Frere paved the way for the University to receive more donations.

Cowasjee Jehanghier's gift to the University in 1863 was followed by another on 27 August 1864, when Premchund Roychand, a *Srawak* Jain businessman came forward with a sum of Rs. 2,00,000 (two lakhs), towards "the creation of a University Library, which may be an ornament to the city."[361]

The Chief Secretary to the Government of Bombay, the Hon'ble H.L. Anderson, acted immediately and on 31 August 1864, forwarded the offer to the Registrar of the University, R.S. Sinclair.[362] In his letter, he made an important point and wrote:

"In tendering, at Mr. Premchund Roychand's request, this benefaction, splendid in its amount and unfettered by any condition which could detract from its immediate or permanent utility for the acceptance of the Vice-Chancellor and Senate, I am directed to add that, should the University accept this gift, the Government will be prepared for arranging a site for the University buildings so as to give the utmost effect to this and other benefactions at as early a period as possible."[363]

On 10 September 1864, the Vice-Chancellor moved the resolution at a meeting of the Senate to "unanimously accept with the best thanks, Mr. Premchund Roychand's noble gift." The motion was seconded by Dr. Buehler and was carried with great approval and praise.

But Premchund Roychand's generosity was ever forthcoming, and he gave a further donation of another two lakhs on 6 October 1864, when he wrote to H.L. Anderson conveying his thoughts. This time he wrote: "Sir—I have the honour to request that Government will do me the favour to offer to the University of Bombay in the name of my good mother two (2,00,000) lakhs of rupees for the erection of a Tower to contain a large clock and set of joy-bells. If there be no architectural objections, I should like the tower to be in connection with the University Library."[364]

On 10 December 1864, the Senate unanimously resolved to accept the noble gift and agreed that the Tower be named 'The Rajabai Tower' in commemoration of Mr. Premchund Roychand's mother.

Dr. Birdwood and Premchund Roychand were close friends. Although Dr. Birdwood became the Registrar of the University in 1866, he had always been associated with it in other

---

361 Tikekar, *op.cit.*, pp. 35-36. Letter of Premchund Roychand to H.L. Anderson, Chief Secretary, Bombay Government.

362 *Ibid.*, p. 36.

363 Tikekar, *op.cit.*, p. 36.

364 Wacha, D.E., *Premchund Roychund: His Early Life and Carreer,* The Times Press, Bombay, 1913, pp. 223-225.

capacities. For instance, he was a Fellow of the University in 1863.[365] He was also an examiner for the year 1866-67 for the First Examination in Arts, in Chemistry, Heat and Electricity, along with Mr. J.B. Lyon.[366]

It is quite likely that this friendship influenced Mr. Premchund Roychand to donate freely to the University.

However, it was only on 29 December 1868 that the Foundation stone of the University was laid.[367]

This delay troubled Sir Cowasjee and he politely reminded Sir Seymour Fitzgerald, the new Governor, who succeeded Sir Bartle Frere in 1867 of this fact. This was followed by another reminder to the Acting Registrar of the University Mr. Hughlings.

The delay was caused neither by the University authorities nor by Government. The architectural design of the University had been allocated to Gilbert Scott, the well-known British architect. Since Gilbert Scott had never visited India, important details about architectural design encumbering him to give prime importance to tropical climatic conditions caused delay and a vast amount of correspondence back and forth.[368]

But what is of great relevance here is that it was during Dr. Birdwood's term as Registrar that he informed the Syndicate[369] that the dates of the fixed deposit receipts for the University Hall Fund would fall due on the 4 October next, (that is the coming month of 1866) and the dates of the fixed deposit receipts for the University Library Fund would fall due on the 6 October next. It was then Resolved that the funds be invested 5 per cent in Government paper, keeping Rs. 4,711 in the Bank of Bombay in a current account from the University Hall Fund and Rs 2,802 - 8 annas from the University Library Fund for the payment of a claim of Mr. Gilbert Scott for designs, and for other expenses incurred by the University under these heads.[370]

It is to the credit of the University and the Registrar that he was 'on the dot' and exactly on time with the affairs of the University as Gilbert Scott had submitted the drawings of the University Hall in 1866.[371]

---

365 *Bombay University Calender, 1864,* p. 91, Letter dated 24 September 1863, of Cowasjee Jehanghier, Esquire, Justice of Peace, to G.M. Birdwood, Fellow of the University.

366 *Bombay University Minute Book IV,* pp. 52-55.

367 Tikekar, *op.cit.,* p. 326.

368 Tikekar, *op.cit.,* p. 41.

369 An Ordinary Meeting of the Syndicate held in the Town Hall on Saturday the 29 September 1866 at 4.30 p.m. pp. 96-101. The above reference is on pp. 99-100 of the *Bombay University Minute Book IV.*

370 *Bombay University Minute Book IV,* pp. 99-100.

371 Tikekar, *op.cit.,* p. 326.

Although the Maharashtra State Universities Act was passed in 1994, we find that many of the stipulations in the Act were, in fact, being followed by Dr Birdwood as Registrar even in 1866-67 and then in 1868.

As chief administrative officer he conducted meetings of all the then present Faculties.

- The first meeting, at which his signature appears, was held on 7 July 1866 at 4:30 p.m. It was a Meeting of the Faculty of Arts.[372] At this meeting J.P. Hughlings, who was to officiate later as Registrar for a brief period between April 1867 and January 1868, when Dr. George Birdwood again became Registrar and continued till September 1868, was unanimously confirmed in the office of Syndic in place of H. M. Birdwood (Justice of the Bombay High Court,[373] and Dean of the Faculty of Arts[374]) for the remainder of the current year. Likewise, F.J. Candy was elected Syndic in the place of Rev. C.D. Duport, for the remainder of the year.[375]
- At the Meeting of the Faculty of Civil Engineering held on 13 July 1866, Dr. Birdwood recorded that it was resolved that in the Master of Civil Engineering Examination, each candidate would be required to submit the working drawings and specifications of such Engineering works as may have been designed and executed by himself (the examinee) during the two previous years.[376]

The Meeting of the Faculty of Medicine was held on 17 July 1866. The Requirement of First and Second Examinations for the Degree of L. M. (Licentiate of Medicine) were passed, namely that Physiology and General Anatomy be added to Descriptive Anatomy in the first examination and form a substantive part of the Degree, while the subject could cease for the second examination of L.M.[377]

The Meeting of the Faculty of Law was held on 21 July 1866. Birdwood meticulously recorded that the two Barristers J.C. Hayllar and R.M.A. Branson were appointed to conduct the ensuing Law Examinations.[378]

- An Ordinary Meeting of the Syndicate was held on 28 July 1866 at which time the Registrar submitted drafts and Notifications for Honours in Arts and M.A. Examinations, and for Matriculation[379] and the Jugonnath Sunkersett Sanskrit Scholarships Examinations.[380]

---

372 *Bombay University Minute Book IV*, pp. 64-65.
373 Tikekar, *op.cit.*, p.132.
374 *Ibid.*, p. 42.
375 *Bombay University Minute Book IV*, pp. 64-65.
376 *Ibid.*, p. 68.
377 *Ibid.*, pp. 69-70.
378 *Ibid.*, pp. 71-72.
379 The Matriculation examination was held by the University, the age-limit for candidates appearing at the Matriculation examination was fixed at 16 years; S.R. Dongerkery, *History of the Bombay University*, p. 15.
380 *Bombay University Minute Book IV*, p. 74.

At this meeting, a letter from the Bank of Bombay for one Government Promissory Note of Rs. 4,500 standing in the name of the University of Bombay pertaining to the Jam Shri Vibhaji Scholarship was read by Birdwood. This Scholarship was alluded to at the Convocation of 1867.[381]

Again it was resolved that the Senate be requested to authorize the Syndicate to receive donations of Books to the University.[382]

It was also Resolved that the Honourable A.J. Hunter be invited to become a member of the Board of Accounts in place of Dr. Birdwood who had been appointed Registrar and that in case of his declining, the Honourable G. Foggo be invited to become a member of the Board.[383]

It was resolved that the Senate be requested to pass a Grace for the

admission of four students of the Poona Civil Engineering College and the First Examination for the Degree of Licentiate of Civil Engineering in November next.[384]

Also, the Regulations for the Degree of Master of Civil Engineering as modified by the Faculty of Civil Engineering were considered.[385]

It is interesting to note details that the Registrar had to consider. For instance, certain proposals for furniture to be used at the University Convocations with the estimate were put forward by the Registrar.[386]

On 29 September 1866 at the Ordinary Meeting of the Syndicate, the Registrar stated that the large Room of the Town Hall did not afford sufficient accommodation for the number of students who had applied to appear for the Matriculation Examination. It was therefore resolved that the Registrar apply for the use of the Asiatic and Geographical Society's rooms.[387]

In view of the heavy work on the Registrar's Establishment on account of the ensuing Examinations, an additional clerk was employed for three and a half months from October to the half of January.[388]

The Registrar was called upon to publish Notification of certain University prizes in the Government Gazette — like for instance the Homejee Cursetjee Prize for 1866.[389]

381 *Ibid.*, p. 174.
382 *Ibid.*, p. 75.
383 *Ibid.*, p. 75.
384 *Ibid.*, p. 76.
385 *Ibid.*, p. 77.
386 *Ibid.*, p. 89.
387 *Ibid.*, p. 96.
388 *Ibid.*, p. 96-97.
389 *Ibid.*, p. 98.

Dr. Birdwood along with W.G. Hunter was nominated as one of the judges to decide upon the merits of the Manockjee Limjee Gold Medal Essay for 1866.[390]

As Registrar, Dr. Birdwood had to take some firm decisions against erring students. On 29 September 1866, at the Meeting of the Syndicate of the University, he read out letter No, 1304 dated 22 September 1866, from the Director of Public Instruction, wherein names of certain candidates from a Private English School at Rutnagherry[391] were mentioned. These candidates had sent in their applications for permission to attend the ensuing Matriculation Examination through their Head Master. Taking note of the contents of the letter from the Director of Public Instruction, Dr. Birdwood as Registrar wrote to the Head Master of the School stating that the applications of the candidates were rejected on account of their insubordinate and improper conduct at the Rutnagherry High School.

The Syndicate was pleased to Resolve that the action taken by the Registrar in this matter be approved.[392]

Among various duties Dr. Birdwood, as Registrar, had to submit a statement of account to the Syndicate. At the Syndicate Meeting of 24 November 1866, he submitted statements showing how the University Hall Fund of Rs. 1,06,548,, 13annas,,10pies and the University Library Fund of Rs. 2,24,043,,6annas,,3pies had been invested in Government 5 per cent paper. The Syndicate referred this statement to the Board of Accounts for their audit.[393]

It is seen from a Meeting of the Syndicate held on 22 December 1866, that it was the responsibility of the Registrar to make all necessary arrangements for the smooth conduct of the Convocation ceremony to be held on 8 January 1867. It is interesting to note that the University provided the prospective recipients of the degrees with the gowns and scarfs belonging to the University, for the day. It is also seen that the Convocation ceremony was open to the public who had to acquire tickets of admission from the Registrar.[394]

At the same Meeting, Dr. Birdwood laid before the Syndicate, a Resolution of the Government dated 11 December 1866, authorising him to proceed to Paris to superintend the exhibits contributed by Bombay to the exhibition to be held there in 1867.[395]

The Syndicate was then pleased to Resolve that "Dr. Birdwood should be allowed to proceed to Paris on the full pay of his appointment as Secretary and Curator of the Government Museum; and be absent for a period of six months; his passage both going and returning being defrayed by Government. With respect to the University Registrarship, he

390 *Ibid.*, p. 99.
391 Now spelt Ratnagiri.
392 *Ibid.*, p. 100.
393 *Ibid.*, p. 105.
394 *Ibid.*, pp. 155-156.
395 *Ibid.*, p. 156.

should be requested to place himself in communication with the Senate, and inform that the Government will acquiesce in any arrangements he may be able to effect with that body, both with regard to length of absence and salary."[396]

"The Syndicate taking into consideration the suggestion here made, and the importance on public, scientific and economical grounds of Dr. Birdwood's visit to Paris, recommend to the Senate that Bye-Law 26 (p. 53 of last Calendar) be held in abeyance in his case, and that leave of absence for six months be granted to him, if the consent of the Governor of Bombay in Council be given to the suspension of the Bye-Law in his favor (sic) [favour]."[397]

However, at the time of confirmation of the Minutes of this meeting at the Subsequent Meeting of the Syndicate held on Wednesday the 2 January 1867, when the Vice-Chancellor Sir Alexander Grant, called attention of the Syndicate to certain points of informality in the earlier Resolution on the matter, a consideration of the entire subject of the Resolution took place. The former Resolution was then cancelled and it was resolved: "To inform Dr. Birdwood in reference to Resolution of Government No. 2481 of 11 December 1866 that the Syndicate regret to find it inexpedient to recommend the suspension of the University Rules with regard to the period of leave to be allowed to the University Registrar."[398]

Three months leave was then granted to the Registrar from the date of his departure from Bombay and he was directed to inform Government to that effect, and that he would be entitled to the whole salary of the office for the period.[399]

It may be inferred that Dr. George Birdwood, with his achievements in the field of Science and public life enjoyed immense respect and confidence from the members of the Syndicate, that they had resolved the suspension of a Bye-Law in his favour; it was only after the Vice-Chancellor pointed out the "informality" in the Syndicate's Resolution IV at their Meeting of 22 December 1866, that the said Resolution was rescinded and a suitable Resolution, abiding the provisions of the Bye-Laws was passed to permit Dr. Birdwood's participation in the Exhibition at Paris.

Subsequently, in 1867 Dr. Birdwood was sent by Sir Bartle Frere, at the express desire of the leading merchants of Bombay, as Special Commissioner for the

Government, to the Universal Exhibition held in Paris in that year.[400]

It is well known that Dr. George Birdwood worked with the Hon'ble Jugonnath Sunkersett especially to promote and set up a Museum in Bombay and in laying the Victoria Gardens.

396 *Ibid.*, pp. 156-157.
397 *Ibid.*, p. 157.
398 *Ibid.*, pp. 158-159.
399 *Ibid.*, p. 159.
400 *Wikisource, Men of Time,* eleventh edition/ Birdwood, George Christopher Molesworth, by Thompson Cooper.

As Registrar of the University of Bombay, Dr. George Birdwood was in charge of the University Examinations and issuing notification for the same. These include Matriculation examination, various degree and post-graduate examinations, as well as the Jugonnath Sunkersett Sanskrit examination.

At the Meeting of the Syndicate of 2 January 1867, Dr. Birdwood read out a letter from Venayakrow Jugonnathjee Sunkersett, son of the Hon'ble Jugonnath Sunkersett, with whom Dr. Birdwood had very close and cordial relations. The Syndicate was pleased to resolve that "the Registrar in acknowledging the Receipt of the Rupees 1,620, inform Mr. Venayakrow Jugonnathjee Sunkersett of the hope of the Syndicate that the whole endowment may soon be paid."[401]

In the Convocation held on 8 January 1867, Dr. Birdwood had the privilege of presenting to the Chancellor, Sir Bartle Frere, a Report of the proceedings of the University since the previous Convocation held on 6 April 1866. In his report Dr. Birdwood lucidly conveyed information about, Results of various Examinations, an account of the several Meetings of the University Authorities such as the Senate, the Syndicate, Faculty of Arts, Faculty of Law, Faculty of Medicine and Faculty of Civil Engineering, as well as of various Boards of Examiners and Board of Accounts. He then dwelt upon the approval of the Governor in Council to the Alterations and Additions to Regulations and Bye-Laws, and assured that the modified Regulations have been acted upon.[402]

During Dr. Birdwood's tenure as the Registrar of the University, the Government offered on 8 October 1866 an additional site in continuation northwards of the existing site and towards the north-east corner fronting the entrance to Church Street.

At the Annual Meeting of the Senate, held on 22 December 1866, it was unanimously resolved "that the additional site offered by Government be respectfully accepted with the best thanks of the Senate."[403]

Dr. George Birdwood continued to remain the Registrar of the University till April 1867 when John Powell Hughlings took over as Acting Registrar in place of Dr. Birdwood. Dr. Birdwood resumed as Registrar of the University again in January 1868 and remained in that post till September 1868.[404]

Thus he was once again responsible for organising and managing the seventh University Convocation of 14 January 1867-68.

---

401 *Ibid.,* p. 159.

402 *Ibid.,* pp. 172-174.

403 *Ibid.,* p. 174. (It is this site on which the Rajabai Tower, the Library building, and the building housing the present offices of the Vice-Chancellor, Pro-Vice-Chancellor and the Registrar have been constructed.).

404 Tikekar, *op.cit.,* p. 337.

The Convocation ceremony was held in the Town Hall, which was appropriately decorated for the purpose. The occasion was graced by the Chancellor, His Excellency the Right Honourable Sir William Robert Seymour Vesey Fitzgerald, the Vice-Chancellor Sir Alexander Grant, the Deans including the Reverend John Wilson, Richard Tuohill Reid, Inspector-General Francis Shortt Arnott; Syndics including H.M. Birdwood; Members of the Council, Judges of the High Court, Members of the Legislative Council, Fellows of the University including Dr. Bhau Dajee and several other distinguished persons and Dr. George Birdwood himself as the Registrar.

Subsequent to the presentation of the candidates to the Chancellor for conferring the Degrees of Bachelor of Arts, Bachelor of Laws, Master of Arts, Licentiate of Medicine, Dr. Birdwood laid before the Chancellor, a Report of the Proceedings of the University since the previous Convocation held on 8 January 1867. In his Report, Dr. Birdwood referred to the various examinations held by the University and the University Prizes, Gold Medals and Fellowships. He proceeded to outline the Alterations of the Bye-Laws and Regulations in Arts, Medicine and Law which had been made by the Senate and approved by the Governor of Bombay in Council. Significant among the Alterations in the Arts Regulation included the abolition of Examination for Honours in Arts and introduction of a clause to the effect that Candidates when placed in First Class either at the B.A. or M.A. Examination will be considered to have taken honours in the B.A. or any branch of M.A. Examination, respectively. Further, by making extensive changes in Regulation for Medicine, the whole course of medical studies was altered and improved.[405]

In his address to the Senate, the Chancellor stated, inter alia, "To all of us, I think, who have listened to the very complete and clear report just read by the Registrar, the account that he has given us of the progress and of the prospects of this University must be highly satisfactory; and to most of you, gentlemen, who have attended previous Convocations, it must be a source of gratification to find that the progress established in former years has not only not been lost, but that the University continues in the same onward and steady march of success that has called for congratulations hitherto."[406]

The Chancellor also said that in the Report that the Registrar read, it was evident that University education was not confined only to those who were brought into communion with professors and teachers connected with the University, but that it had taken wide root throughout the Presidency and it was felt by every class of people. In other words, there was not a district of this Presidency from North to South, from East to West that was not represented in it.[407]

405 *Bombay University Minute Book IV*, p. 359.

406 *Ibid.*, p. 360.

407 *Ibid.*, p. 361.

The Chancellor then alluded to Mr. Cowasjee Jehanghier, one of the most enlightened citizens of the city, who was among the first to promote the highest interests of his people, the highest interests of society here, and to promote the best interests of this University in particular, was now the very latest benefactor of the University of Bombay.[408]

The Chancellor added, "And I do not think that there is anything which is more pleasing, in looking back to the history of this University, than to find that alike in times of prosperity as in times when prosperity is past, there are enlightened men amongst the native community of this country who, feeling and knowing the duty they owe to Society, are desiring to discharge that duty by nobly supporting this valuable institution."

"I see near me a friend and colleague of my own, who himself must feel the greatest pleasure in a portion of that report which refers to a travelling fellowship established by him—I mean Mr. Munguldass Nathoobhoy. It must be a satisfaction to him to find that the first person who has obtained the travelling fellowship which his munificence has established, has distinguished himself by attaining the honour of the membership of the College of Physicians and the membership of the College of Surgeons of London, has in open competition obtained the admission to the Medical Service of this Government, and is now pursuing those studies which will lead him hereafter to a distinguished career."[409] The Chancellor was referring to Mr. Atmaram Sadashiv Jayakar.[410]

It is to the credit of Dr. George Birdwood, that as Registrar of the University of Bombay he was able to bring about the fruition of several projects of the University.

With the respect he commanded amongst Indians, which endeared him to them, he was able to garner their support. Donations to the University from prominent persons like Cowasjee Jehanghier and Premchund Roychand prompted the Government to seriously consider the question of providing the University with a plot of land for erecting its buildings.

The foundation stone of the University buildings however, was laid on 29 December 1868 by Sir William Robert Seymour Vesey Fitz-Gerald, the Chancellor.[411] This was soon after Dr. Birdwood's term as Registrar ended; but it would not be wrong in saying that he initiated the process of actually facilitating the construction of the magnificent buildings of the University, mainly the Convocation Hall and the Library with the Rajabai Tower.

It is undoubtedly Dr. Birdwood's organisational skills that led the Chancellor at the Convocation of 1867-68 to say:

---

408 *Ibid.,* p. 362.

409 *Ibid.,* p. 362.

410 *Ibid.,* p. 359—University Prizes.

411 Dongerkery, *op.cit.,* Chapter II—Development from 1857-1902, pp. 18-35.

"...I am amply and fully satisfied with the statement which the Vice-Chancellor[412] has made as to the position and the merits of the University of Bombay. But there is one thing that he brings to notice which is peculiar to this University, and which I hope this University will be firm in maintaining; and that is, that whereas in the other Universities the examinations are not conducted solely at the head quarters of the University, but at various towns and other places throughout the country, and are conducted by means only of written papers without any oral examination, that in the case of the Bombay University, over and above an examination upon paper upon fixed subjects, there is also a probing and searching oral examination which must test the merits of the candidates, all of whom have to appear for their examination in Bombay."[413]

It must be remembered that Dr. Birdwood, as Registrar, was in charge of the examinations and the above observation is, in no small measure, an accolade which he could justly claim. But Dr. Birdwood, in his very correct and humble manner, considered it as his duty and diligently wrote lucid and detailed reports about every matter of the University.

During Dr. Birdwood's tenure as Registrar, several important University Prizes were awarded:

The Munguldas Nathoobhoy Travelling Fellowship was awarded on 5 March 1867.

The Senate, on the recommendation of the Syndicate, introduced some changes in the Manockjee Limjee Gold Medal Endowment Regulations, so that an opportunity was given to **all the Graduates** of the University of **five** years' standing instead of only to the **Bachelor of Arts** of **two** years standing and the former could now compete for the medal.

Bhugwandass Purshotumdass Sanskrit Scholarship of Rs. 400 was awarded in 1867 to Kashinath Balkrishna Marathe, B.A. of the Poona College.

In 1867-68, **The Homejee Cursetjee Prize** was successfully awarded to Mr. Barjorji Edalji Modi of Elphinstone College.

The **Jugonnath Sunkersett Sanskrit Scholarship** had as many as 34 candidates as against 21 of the previous year from various parts of the Presidency.

The **Jam Shri Vibhaji Scholarship** was awarded in January 1867 to Mr. Kalianrai Lakshumishanker Vohora (sic) of Surat High School.[414]

In other words, six endowments in the form of Scholarships and Prizes were entrusted to the University during Dr. Birdwood's term as Registrar.[415]

412 Alexander Grant was the Vice-Chancellor.

413 *Bombay University Minute Book IV*, p. 361.

414 *Bombay University Minute Book IV*, pp. 369-70.

415 *Ibid.*, p. 177.

It is noteworthy that handsome gifts in the shape of a University Seal and Mace[416] were received.[417]

The Registrar, Dr. Birdwood, at the Convocation of 1867 had said in his report when the then Chancellor Sir Bartle Frere was present:

"With the history of all these things the memory of your Excellency's administration will remain associated. And, as the noble-minded Lord Elphinstone was regarded as the founder of this University, so we shall take the liberty to regard your Excellency as our Second Founder. Lord Elphinstone's Arms[418] were incorporated with those which we bear, and we will now ask Your Excellency to permit your bust, (to be provided at the expense of the existing Fellows and Graduates) to be placed in our future University Hall, surmounted by a shield bearing your Excellency's Arms' in perpetual token of our grateful appreciation of your rule."[419]

While bidding good-bye to Sir Bartle Frere, with whom he had a special equation, Dr. Birdwood wished him well and concluded with words of surety, "We feel sure," he said, "you will continue to watch over the welfare of the University of Bombay, as being the part not the least interesting to you of this Empire of India."

These were words that echoed his own feelings, for a premonitory happening would soon take place, and Dr. George Birdwood would be forced to leave India in 1868 for reasons of ill-health.

---

416 *University Mace, Bombay University Calender 1864,* p. 91 C "Munguldas Nathoobhoy, Esquire, Justice of Peace, in a letter to the Registrar, dated 18 November 1864, offered Rs. 1,200, for the purpose of providing the University with a Mace."
At a meeting of the Senate held on 10 December 1864, it was unanimously resolved that "Mr. Munguldas Nathoobhoy's handsome offer of Rs.1,200 for a Mace for the University be accepted with thanks."

417 *Bombay University Minute book IV,* p. 177.

418 *Bombay University Calendar, 1864,* p. 91 reads: "University Arms and Common Seal: Cowasjee Jehanghier Readymoney, Esquire, Justice of Peace, in a letter to G.M. Birdwood Esq. M.D. Fellow of the University, dated 24 September 1863, forwarded a donation of Rupees 1,200 to meet the expenses of a Grant of Arms to the University and the engraving of the University seal . This donation was accepted at a Convocation of the Senate held on the same day with a vote of thanks to the donor for his timely and liberal benefaction."

419 *Bombay University Minute Book IV,* p. 177.

CHAPTER VI

Absent in Person, Present in Spirit: Sir George Birdwood and India After 1868

Sir George Birdwood left an indelible mark on Bombay when he had to leave India as a necessity because of his ill-health.

In fact his work on the *Economic Vegetable Products of the Bombay Presidency* had reached its twelfth edition in 1868.[420]

Ironically, in his preface to the second edition, he had expressed some doubts. Having added an Index to the first edition which was sold off within a few months, he humbly wrote, "I have added very little else to the volume, so that it is at least three years behind the times."[421]

He admitted that he had been closely engaged otherwise during the last three years and that it was in fact impossible to complete a work of the present kind satisfactorily in Bombay or even in London. Being dissatisfied with the second edition, he actually wanted to destroy it. But an experienced and trusted friend advised him candidly that he "would simply be doing an act of folly to destroy it,"[422] and hence he let it appear.

However, he hoped that a third edition would appear to his satisfaction; although he had a preference for the first edition since it truly represented the years of labour that he had spent in bringing it out. In concluding his preface to the second edition, he reiterated his displeasure on 30 October 1865.[423]

That the book reached its twelfth edition confirms the belief that his work was valued and prized and that he was a truly respected person.

---

420 *Wikipedia, George Christopher Molesworth Birdwood,* p. 1of 1.

421 Preface to the second edition, *Catalogue of the Vegetable Productions of the Presidency of Bombay; Including a list of the Drugs sold in the Bazar of Western India.* Second edition with Index, Bombay: Printed at the Education Society's Press, Byculla, 1865.

422 *Ibid.*

423 *Ibid.*

1757 on the "plain of Placis" or Plassey. Birdwood writes that this volume is of the highest interest. At that time it was in perfect condition of preservation and he felt that it was worth publishing separately.[434]

Another interesting find of Birdwood needs to be mentioned in his own words: "I discovered the original grant of arms to the "New" Company dated 13 October 1698. They are identical with the arms borne by the late Honourable East India Company, thus affording another proof that the "Old" Company was altogether swallowed up by the "New."[435]

The delicate flavour of tea has for years titillated the palate of the British. But its introduction into England is traced by Birdwood.

The entry of tea is recorded in the first volume of the Joint Stocks (of the East India Company) which incidentally runs into five volumes from 1671 to 1709.[436]

The fourth entry in Volume I deals with "Goods remaining on hand ...." Here, there is a mention of "Thea" [Tea] [valued at 20s. per lb.]. There is a footnote attached to the word "Thea."

Dr. Birdwood's footnotes besides revealing interesting facts show his erudition.

In his footnote on Tea he writes, "Tea had been introduced into England some years previously. The first mention of it by any English writer, so far as I can find, is in Pepy's Diary, 25 September 1660—'I did send for a cup of tea (a China drink), of which I had never drank before.' In the same year, by Act 12 of Charles II, chh.23 and 24, a duty of 18d.is imposed on every gallon of chocolate, sherbet, and *tea* made for sale; coffee being charged only 4d." Birdwood quotes with reference to India, Waller's lines------

"The best of Queens, and best of herbs, we owe
To that bold nation which the way did show."

"These words about India are well-known," Birdwood writes.[437]

---

434 *Ibid.,* p. 57.

435 *Ibid.,* p. 21., footnote. Plate II on p. 20 displays the Arms of the 'New' East India Company.The East India Company was established in 1600 as a joint-stock association of English merchants trading to the 'Indies.' Over a period of 250 years the Company underwent several substantial changes in its basic character and functions. A period of rivalry with a 'New' Company after 1698 resulted in the formation in 1709 of the United Company. This 'new' East India Company was transformed during the second half of the eighteenth century from a mainly commercial body with scattered Asian trading interests into a major territorial power in India with its headquarters at Calcutta. The political implications of this development eventually caused the British Government to institute a standing Board of Commissioners for the Affairs of India(or 'Board of Control') to exercise supervision over the Company's Indian policies. [*The National Archives|Access to Archives,* p. 1 of 86].

436 Birdwood, *Report on the Old Records Of The India Office: With Supplementary Note And Appendices,* p. 25.

437 *Ibid.,* Footnote, p. 26.

The East India Company purchased and presented 2lbs. of tea to King Charles II in 1664, and 23 ½ in 1666. The first order for its importation by the Company was in

1668—"Send home by these ships 100lbs. weight of the best *tey (sic)* you can get". The first consignment of it, amounting to 143 ½ lbs. was received from Bantam[438] in 1669. The generally received story is that Lords Arlington and Ossory were the first to introduce tea into this country (England) in 1666 from Holland.

The earliest mention of tea, in the *Old Records of the India Office* is in a letter from Mr. R. Wickham, the Company's Agent at Firando, in Japan[439] who, writing on 27 June 1615, to Mr. Eaton at Miaco, asks for "a pot of the best sort of chaw."

A present of tea was prized in England during the 17th century, as is seen from the "Court Books" of the Company.

Writing to Madras on 13 February 1684, the Directors of the Company say, "In regard Thea (sic) is grown to be a commoditie (sic) here, and we have occasion to make presents therein to our great friends at Court, we would have you send us yearly five or six canisters of the very best and freshest Thea (sic); that which will colour the water in which it is infused most of a greenish complexion is genuinely best accepted."[440]

Looking at the *Unclassed Papers Relating to the Miscellaneous Affairs of the Company,* we get an idea of the goals of the Company as Administrators.

The Commissioners namely Henry Vansittart, Luke Scrafton and Francis Forde, appointed by the Company were given powers to superintend, direct, control, manage, and transact all the business and affairs of the Company in and through all parts of India.

This document dated !5 September 1769, also gave Instructions to the same Commissioners to *restore peace* to India upon a solid and permanent basis ... providing effectually for the honour and security of the faithful ally "Mahomed Ally Cawn of Arcot" (the Nawab Mahomed Ali, styled "Prince of Carnatic")[441]

If war was necessary they were to direct operations of the three Presidencies upon a uniform plan of action. However, the preservation of security of Bengal was always to be the most important object and consideration to the Company;[442] While Bassein and Salsette were to be obtained under a solid right of title.

438 Bantam was an important port of trade,in Java (East Indies) where the English had a factory. In 1677 the Javanese at the instigation of the Dutch, sacked the East India Company's factory at Bantam and assassinated the Agent. In 1682-83 Bantam was taken by the Dutch, and the English, Portuguese, French and Danes driven out. Birdwood, *Report on the Old Records of the India Office,* p. 186 and pp.225-227.

439 *Ibid.,* Footnote, p. 26. Also see p. 52 C- *Japan.*

440 *Ibid.,* Footnote, p. 26.

441 *Ibid.,* pp. 33-35.

442 *Ibid.,* p. 35.

Going back in time, "*The Joint Voyages*" are of historical interest; they record that Peyton commanded the fleet which in January 1614/15 took Sir Thomas Roe [on board the *Lion*] to India, as Ambassador from James I to the "Court of the Great Mogol" [Jehangir, 1605-27] at Agra.[443]

In the ***Factory Diaries and Consultations***[444] one comes across the BOMBAY RECORDS[445]

These consist of:

A. Seventeen volumes of Diaries and Consultations, from 1669 to 1702-3.

B. Forty-five volumes of letters from Bombay, from 1672 to 1708-10.

C. Forty-two volumes of letters to Bombay, from 1673-74 to 1703-4.

Besides, [The Tannah "PROCEEDINGS" extend from 1777 to 1799.]

Bombay was transferred to the East India Company in 1669; and their first Governor was Sir George Oxenden, (1668-69). The previous four Governors of Bombay, appointed by the Crown, were Sir Abraham Shipman; his Secretary, Mr. Humfrey Cooke, who first took possession of the Island in 1665; Sir Gervase Lucas, who succeeded in 1666; and Captain Henry Garey, who officiated in 1667-8.[446]

This is but a brief account of the enormous amount of work that Dr. Birdwood, Special Assistant, Statistics and Commerce Department of the India Office undertook from 1 November 1878. He gave a detailed history of:

i) The Portuguese in Asia

ii) The Dutch in the East

iii) The English in India[447]

Cataloguing the English in India, he writes, "The first English attempts to reach India were by the north-west passage. In 1496 Henry VII granted Letters Patent to John Cabot [Giovanni Gavotta] and his three sons to fit out two vessels for the discovery of this passage to India. They failed, but discovered the islands of Newfoundland and St. John, and explored the coast of America from Labrador to Virginia.[448]

He goes on to record chronologically till the time of Queen Elizabeth who also sent Sir John Mildenhall by way of Constantinople to the Great Mogol to apply for privileges for the English Company, for whom she was preparing a charter; and on 31 December 1600

443 *Ibid.*, p. 49.

444 *Ibid.*, pp.82-86.

445 *Ibid.*, pp.85-86.

446 *Ibid.*, pp.85-86.

447 *Ibid.*, Refer to the Contents.

448 *Ibid.*, pp. 193-199.

the English East India Company was incorporated by Royal Charter under the title of "*The Governor and Company of Merchants of London trading into the East Indies.*"[449]

This then is only a whit of the very large compilation of records of the East India Company undertaken by Dr. Birdwood.

Besides these records, while at the India Office he devoted a great deal of time and energy to the encouragement of Indian Art. He wrote valuable monographs on various items of art.

His celebrated work is of course *The Industrial Arts of India.* Dr. Birdwood praised the Industrial and Decorative arts of India. He believed that these were mostly represented in the form of articles of utility. These forms of art were passed on from father to son. He did not believe that 'Fine Art' existed in India----that is Art for Art's sake.

HISTORICAL RETROSPECT OF INDIAN ART

He studiously traced the character of Hindu and Indian art by the influences that it had absorbed due to the antiquity of Indian trade. Indeed he traced this back to the Bible.[450]

In the *Handbook to the British Section of the Paris Exhibition* of 1878, he states that the very name of India was unknown among the nations of the Mediterranean Sea, although its costly perfumes had been in daily use in the service of the Jews' Tabernacle at Shiloh and Jerusalem, and earlier had been used for embalming the dead in Egypt.[451]

Dr. Birdwood believed that in order to appreciate the relative force of influences that had affected Indian art, it was necessary to review the history of the states and nations of Southern and Western Asia and the Mediterranean with which India was connected.

He believed that our real knowledge of Indian history begins with Alexander the Great's invasion of India in B.C. 327. Before that the only sources to depend upon were the Vedas (B.C. 1400), the Code of Manu (B.C. 900-300), Ramayana (B.C. 400-350), and Mahabharata (B.C. 525-500). He felt that although the Puranas composed during the revival of Brahmanism, and Mahommedan conquest, give dynastic history of India from the time of Chandragupta (Sandrocottus of the Greeks) they lean towards mythology and doctrine.[452]

The first Greek, he writes, who speaks of India by name is Hecataeus of Miletus, B.C. 549-486. However, Dr. Birdwood feels that Strabo gives the best account of India,[453] until the

449 *Ibid.*, p. 199.
450 *Handook to the British Section of the Paris Exhibition. Paris Universal Exhibition of 1878*, p. 20.
451 *Ibid.*, Introduction.
452 *Ibid.*, Introduction.
453 *Ibid.*, p. 15.

travels of Marco Polo (b.1254, d. 1324) and Ibn Batuta of Tangiers in 1341, then Stevens and Fitch and Bernier and Tavernier and others in the 16th and 17th centuries.

Be that as it may, Dr. Birdwood feels that art, science and literature reached the highest perfection during Ashoka's reign (B.C. 250) when intimate relations existed between India, Syria, and Egypt.[454]

While tracing the foreign influences on Indian Art, he dwells on the '**Knop and Flower Pattern**'[455]

Dr. Birdwood believes that the Knop and Flower, or cone and flower pattern is represented, with local variations, on early Indian monuments in the same form and general style as on the marbles of Assyria and in the Bharhut sculptures.[456].... Dr. Birdwood writes, "At least the lotus is repeatedly represented in the identical half conventional form in which we find it, *en silhouette,* in the Hieroglyphic paintings of Egypt. Here again India is the copyist."[457]

It is not always easy to accept this latter theory of Dr. Birdwood. No doubt Buddhist Gandhara sculpture was influenced by Hellenistic Greek trends. But the lotus as a motif could easily have been an indigenous one. Bharhut sculpture is attributed to the Sunga period, that is, the mid 2nd century B.C. This sculpture decorated the great stupa or relic mound of Bharhut in Madhya Pradesh.

The Bharhut style marked the beginning of a tradition of Buddhist narrative relief and decoration that continued for several centuries.

The flat planes, rather stiffly posed figures and precise elegant detailing and ornamentation suggest the continuance in stone of an earlier tradition in wood.

The composition is simple, even naive, used in an attempt to distinguish planes.[458]

In fact Dr. Birdwood seems to falter on his theory of 'Art for Art's sake' when he says, "Indeed, in Hindu art imagination is let loose as in a dream. In Amravati and Bharhut sculptures the transformations go on under your eye and reveal the whole mystery. The cone is generally the lotus bud and the elephant is never represented in carved stone without its trunk."[459]

---

454 *Ibid.*

455 *Ibid.*, p. 124.

456 *Ibid.*, p. 127.

457 *Ibid.*

458 *Bharhut Jatland Wiki.*

459 *Handbook to the British Section of the Paris Exhibition,* Paris Universal Exhibition of 1878, p. 129. Elephants with their trunks raised in a trumpeting effect and standing on their rear legs were considered to be excellent symbols of protection and power and bonding. (*Elephant Symbol & Meaning, Elephant in FengShui, in Chinese culture).*

Indeed, the Indian lotus (*Nelumbo nucifera Gaertn*)[460] with its impressive white, pink or sometimes yellow flower, also called Hindu lotus, is an aquatic plant from the Nelumbonacea family.

The flowers, seeds, young leaves, stems and rhizomes (roots) are edible.

Lotus flowers have for generations been a Buddhist and Hindu symbol of purity and non-attachment and are often used as offering to Lord Buddha and Hindu Gods. In India, the lotus flower is considered to be of divine origin and is viewed as sacred by both Hindus and Buddhists.[461]

In Hindu mythology the lotus flower or *Padma,* which Vishnu holds in his lower right hand, represents Purity, Spiritual liberation, Divine Perfection and Spiritual consciousness enfolding within the individual.

Dr. Birdwood himself says, "Anything full of glory becomes the symbol of life."[462]

Yet, Dr. Birdwood also remarks, "All that is monstrous in the decorative form of Indian and Assyrian art, all that is obscene in Indian symbolism, is derived from common Turanian sources, anterior to direct commercial intercourse between India and Assyria."[463]

On the contrary, he also says, "It is quite possible, however, that some of the very forms in India which can be proved to be copied from Assyrian temples and palaces may have originally been carried to Egypt and Assyria on Indian cotton or woollen fabrics and on jewelry."[464]

DECORATIVE ART OF INDIA

When he speaks about decorative art, he is quite nostalgic.

"It is quite impossible," he says, "to enumerate all the smaller village wares of India, although they are the most interesting of all, illustrating as they do the infinite variety in unity of the decorative art of India."[465]

460 The name Nelumbo is derived from Tamil and nucifera from the Latin, meaning 'nut-bearing.' It is also known under several different Sanskrit names, mainly *padma, kamala,* or *pushkar. The Sacred Lotus, Nelumbo nucifera Nymphaeceae;* p. 1 of 3.

461 The idea of enlightenment is symbolized by the life cycle of the sacred lotus plant because it begins its life humbly in the mud of ponds but soon grows and sends stems and flowers well above the surface of the water (up to 50 cm), thereby showing the path of spiritual enfoldment. It also has unusual flowering habits; its flowers 'wake up' (open) at dawn and 'go to sleep' (close) at about 2 p.m. Some lotuses are even known to open up at night and close during the day, transcending normal time cycles. *http://www.holisticaroma.co.uk/shp/The Sacred Lotus.htm* p. 1 of 3.

462 *Handbook,* p. 130.

463 *Ibid.,* p. 125.

464 *Ibid.,* p. 127.

465 *Ibid.,* p. 87.

Speaking about the lacquer work of Sawantwadi in Western India he mentions individually the native toys such as models of hand-mills, cooking utensils etc., and Hindu playing cards. "These last are circular, and being painted with mythological subjects in bright colours are most pleasing objects, and interesting also as illustrating the state of art of painting in India, in districts where it has remained uninfluenced by European teaching and example."[466] He also agrees that ivory combs are most artistic as are Bison horn figures of Sawantwadi.[467]

Dr. Birdwood also appreciates Indian Musical Instruments, which he says, "are remarkable for the beauty and variety of their forms."[468] He admits that viewing ancient sculptures and paintings it is evident that they have remained unchanged during the last two thousand years.

He adds, "The harp *chang* is identical in shape with the Assyrian harp on the Nineveh sculptures, and the *vina* is of equal antiquity. The Hindus claim to have invented the fiddle-bow,"[469] he concludes.

Dr. Birdwood also comments that fine weaving probably passed from India to Assyria and Egypt and through the Phoenicians into Southern Europe and gold interwoven with cotton is still practised all over India.[470]

In contrast he says, "It is surprising that a people who possess, as their ivory and stone carvings and clay figures incontestably prove, so great a facility in the appreciation and delineation of natural forms should have failed to develop the art of sculpture. Nowhere does their figure sculpture show the inspiration of true art."[471]

Dr. Birdwood found fault with the Indian use of sculptured forms only in architecture, so much so that he perceived a tendency to subordinate sculpture to architecture. He felt that sculpture lacked the individual touch and conformed to convention. "Their very gods are distinguished only by their attributes and symbolical monstrosities of body and never by any expression of individual and personal character."[472]

As such, figure sculpture even in the noblest temples relegated itself to the idol often found to be "some obscene or monstrous symbol."[473]

He felt figure sculpture failed in the sense of true art, a fact that would be realized if they attempted to produce it on a natural heroic scale. It was only because their ivory, clay and stone figures of men and animals were on so minute a scale that they excited admiration.

466 *Ibid.,* The Toys and arts of Sawantwadi in Western India are fast disappearing, especially the charming doll 'Thakki' and must be revived again. The playing cards are called 'ganjifa.'

467 *Ibid.,* p. 83.

468 *Ibid.,* p. 88.

469 *Ibid.*

470 *Ibid.,* p. 90.

471 *Ibid.,*p. 84.

472 *Ibid.,*p. 85.

473 *Ibid.*

"Their larger figure sculpture is indeed never pleasing, except when treated conventionally. It is a strange feeling."[474]

That notwithstanding, his name was identified with the representation of India at all principal International Exhibitions from 1857 to 1901.[475]

A CRTICAL REVIEW OF THE EXHIBITIONS

It has been said that the main objectives of the exhibitions in which India was presented as a British Colonial possession was to educate the British public on the merits of the empire and to reinforce the idea of a Great Britain inextricably linked with Imperial gains.[476] The Royal Commission in charge of Colonial exhibitions hoped the pride in empire could be instilled among the common people who came to visit these exhibitions. Pride in the empire would also forge national identity.

Dr. Birdwood did not entirely fall in with the philosophy of the Royal Commission. Being an Indophile at heart, his approach was not necessarily related to reaping Imperial gains. He had been largely responsible in India for setting up the Government Central Museum in Bombay. At this time he genuinely wanted the people of India to be aware of their produce, their arts and crafts and their value *vis-a-vis* the world market. He had, with interested persons, hoped to inculcate an enlightened attitude. The Museum he had hoped would be a *College of Inquiry.* True, that he also felt the need for the British to realize India's potential. His way of thinking was not one-sided.

Modern historians have felt that the objective of the exhibitions was to present a dual picture of technological backwardness on the one hand and the exotic artifacts that titillated the imagination and desire to possess on the other.[477] This visual display of difference, would therefore justify Britain's Imperial designs and its right to dominate as the superior culture.

The organisers of the exhibitions were necessarily those who were in their own way intensely interested and involved with Indian Art. Some were charmed by it, others expressed disapproval, but their sympathy and tolerance of Indian art was impossible to untangle from the situation of their being British and therefore a part of British Imperialism. They wanted to make it clear that India had a living artistic tradition, although the natives were unaware of

474 *Ibid.,* p. 85.

475 *Journal of Indian Art,* vol. viii., *The Life and Work of Sir George Birdwood.*

476 Chattopadhyay, Swati, *A Critical History of Architecture in a Post-Colonial World: A View from Indian History,* Department of Architecture, University of California at Berkeley, Posthumus Destinies, p. 3 of 8. POSTED BY DEBBANERJI, Published July 15, 2009.

477 *Ibid., art.cit.,* p. 3 of 8.

it. Therefore, they felt that it was their responsibility to make this fact known to Indians and thereby rescue them from oblivion.[478]

"In consequence also of the improvement of national taste in this country and the spread of higher education and culture among the natives of India, we may hope for a rapid increase in the demand for Indian hand-loom made and artistically dyed and printed piece goods;"[479] Dr. Birdwood wrote in regard to textiles; in other words, the art of weaving was known to the Indians but a taste for artistic presentation had yet to be sharpened and diffused.

In their conscientious pursuit to rebuild India's artistic past, men like George Birdwood and John Lockwood Kipling developed their own standards for judging and categorising Indian arts and crafts. They collected art specimens and organized them on 'scientific' principles. This seems to have become the nineteenth century British preoccupation "with division and classification exaggerated in the colonial context by the desire to fathom the diversity of Indian culture. More importantly the classification of arts and crafts were tied directly to economy, it was supposed to provide a medical, social and economic understanding of native society."[480]

Chattopadhyay feels that "In their classification process Birdwood and Lockwood Kipling blatantly ignored the Indian view of 'types' of artifacts, and adopted historical evolution as the criteria for classification and regional, even state boundaries, as appropriate lines of division. Such an exercise produced categories that had little relevance to cultural processes, but they found profitable use in International exhibitions."[481]

This assessment as regards Birdwood's work especially, cannot be entirely accepted. Firstly, Chattopadhyay makes her comments largely based on the presentation of India in the 1886 Colonial and Indian Exhibition in London. In fairness to Birdwood one must also study the *Handbook to the British Section of the Paris Exhibition* of 1878.

The *Handbook* was almost wholly written by Birdwood, except for the Preface written by C. Purdon Clarke.

True that even here, he paid much importance to the historical perspective; tracing foreign influences on Indian art. This was Birdwood's point of view and many a time, he expressed it clearly with proof. Nevertheless, it could not be completely accepted by all.

At the British Section in 1878, the various objects exhibited in the Grand Vestibule of the Palace of Champs de Mars, numbered over twelve thousand specimens. These were

478 *Ibid., art.cit.,* p. 3 of 8.

479 Birdwood, *Handbook to the British Section of the Paris Exhibition,* 1878, p. 95.

480 Chattopadhyay, Swati, *art.cit.,* p. 3 of 8. (John Lockwood Kipling: A renowned teacher of sculpture, his creative genius is seen in several sculptures located in the splendid buildings built during his time in south Mumbai.)

481 *Ibid.*

arranged into the following collection, one might add both for convenience and to provide a clear line of demarcation for easy explanation.

The Indian presents to the President, His Royal Highness the Prince of Wales, and other private collections lent to the Indian Committee.

Articles of Indian manufacture exhibited by the principal importing firms in London and Paris, exhibited in the Indian Pavilion.

Supplementary collection of native art manufacture exhibited by the Indian Committee (objects priced for sale at the close of the exhibition.)

Raw Products, and food substances, woods and forest specimens, dye, etc.[482]

The Raw Products and Food consisted of [i] Dyed Tusser Silk [ii] Tea (by various Companies and Estates) [iii] Pickles and Preserves [iv] Bottled Beer (Murree Beer Company) [v] Sugar and Spirits (Minchin Brothers, Aska, Madras) [vi] Book Binding and Printing [vii] Embroidery and [viii] Triplicane[483] Embroidery.

In the first part of the *Handbook*, "The Settlement of the Old World and Historical Dates" were enumerated, and the "Routes of Indian Commerce" such as Caravan Routes, Routes via the Persian Gulf and Red Sea were delineated by Birdwood.

He then drew up the Section "The Master Handicrafts of India".

Under this section he speaks of "Gold and Silver Plate".[484]

Amongst these, the presents given to the Prince of Wales were displayed first. Dr. Birdwood points out a silver-gilt service for *pan* and *atar* (betel leaf and perfumes) from Mysore, which he classifies as a good example of pure Hindu work; while the elaborately chased goblets (*surahi*) and rose-water sprinklers, some in ruddy gold and others in parcel-gilt, are "almost perfect examples of the exquisite goldsmith's work of Cashmere and Lucknow; the work of Cashmere being distinguished by the introduction of the shawl pattern cone in the chasing."[485]

There is no denying that the art of South India has its own character, as does the art of places in North India. Each region specialises in its own form of Art, and in this sense a geographical identification of art styles is justifiable.

But Dr. Birdwood does not restrict himself to geographical boundaries. He also speaks of

482 Birdwood, *Handbook to the British Indian Section of the Paris Exhibition,* following Preface; Section V.

483 Triplicane: situated about a half km from the Bay of Bengal coast and Fort St. George is one of the oldest central business districts of Madras (Chennai) South India. Triplicane owes its name to its Puranic existence as *Tiruvallikeni* or *Tiru-Allekeni* (sacred lily pond in Tamil denoting the pond in front of the famous *Parthasarathy* Temple located there. It is also referred as *Vrundha-raNyam* (Beautiful garden) in Puranic scriptures.http://en. Wikipedia.org/wiki/Triplicane, p. 1 of 4.

484 Birdwood, *Handbook to the British Indian Section of the Paris Exhibition,* 1878, pp. 59-60.

485 *Ibid.,* p. 60. Chasing—engraving metal.

the types of art. Take for instance Damascened Work.[486] He explains that Damascening is the art of encrusting one metal in another, 'not in *crustae,* which are soldered on or wedged into the metal surface to which they are applied, but in the form of wire, which by undercutting (weakening) and hammering is thoroughly incorporated with the metal which it is intended to ornament.'[487]

Practically, Dr. Birdwood says damascening is limited to encrusting gold wire, and sometimes silver on the surface of iron, steel or bronze. This oriental form of ornamentation takes its name from Damascus, where it was carried to perfection by goldsmiths.

In India, damascening in gold was carried on in Kashmir and Gujarat, and Sialkot in the Punjab, and in the Nizam's dominions in Hyderabad. It was called *kuft* when worked in gold and *bidri* (from Bidar) when damascening in silver. Birdwood observes that this art was originally imported from Persia by the Mahommedans.

"Gold and Silver Plate" is followed by a description of Metal Work, in Brass, Copper and Tin.[488] After this is "Damascened Work" (discussed earlier) and this is followed by "Enamels".[489]

Enamelling, Dr. Birdwood writes, "is the master art craft of the world and the enamels of Jeypore rank before all others and are of matchless perfection."[490]

Here again his penchant for tracing foreign influence comes to the fore. He believes that enamelling was probably a Turanian art, introduced into China by the Yuechi and he feels that it was carried as early, if not earlier into India.[491]

The culminating point of the Prince's presents lies in the ARMS, presented to him.

"For variety, extent and gorgeousness and ethnological and artistic value, such a collection of Indian arms has never been brought together before, not even in India itself, and it fairly defies description."[492]

486 *Ibid.,* p. 63.

487 *Ibid.,* p. 63.

488 *Ibid.,* pp. 61-62.

489 *Ibid.,* p. 64.

490 *Ibid.*

491 *Ibid.,* p. 65. Turanian is a term used in references to diverse groups of people, such as Iranian, people from Transoxiana (Turkestan), the Huns or Mongols (related to the Turks). The nomadic Yuechi tribe are regarded as a branch of the Kushanas. The Kushanas invaded India after the downfall of the Mauryas. The Yuechi lived in the west of the Hwang-ho River in China. These Yuechi tribes were expelled from their original homeland of China. The main branch moved west and met the Sakas whose orginal homeland was the Kashmir region. Kujala Kadphises of the Kushana branch united the four tribal branches of the Yuechi under his supremacy. Kujala Kadphises set out to capture Kabul and annexed the Western border of India including Kashmir. In his coins he described himself as 'Dharmasthita'and 'Satyadhamasthita'—indicating his allegiance to Buddhism. He was succeeded by his son Wema Kadphises in 64 A.D. and reigned upto 78 A.D. *Origin of the Kushanas;* http://www.indianetzone.com/21/the origin_early_history_kushanas.htm p. 1 of 2.

492 *Ibid.,* p. 66.

The collection presented the armourer's art in every province of India, from the rude spears of the Nicobar islanders, to the costly damascene, sculptured and jewelled swords and shields and daggers and matchlocks of Cashmere (Kashmir), Lahore, Sialkot, Gujarat, Cutch, Hyderabad, Singapore and Ceylon. "Good arms," Dr. Birdwood adds, "are also made at Monghyr in Bengal and at Kuduru and Vizianagram in Madras."[493]

Commenting upon the sword of Shivaji in the Prince's collection, Birdwood hastens to add that it is not his famous sword '*Bhowani*' at Satara.

The sword in the Prince's collection is not this deified weapon, but the one that has always been kept, since Shivaji's death in 1680, at Kolhapur.

"The political value of the gift is simply incalculable. It was a family and national heirloom, which nothing but a sentiment of the profoundest loyalty could have moved descendants of Sivaji (sic) to give up, and which has been sacredly guarded for the last 200 years at Kolhapur as the palladium[494] of their house and race, by the junior branch of the Bhonsla family."[495]

The surrender of this weapon, Birdwood ventures to interpret as "vain regrets for the past and, sensible of the present blessings of a civilised rule, desire to centre their hopes of the future in the good faith and wisdom, and power of the British Government."[496]

This remark smacks of Imperialistic leanings and is somewhat surprising coming from Dr. Birdwood.

Even so, his pejorative remarks about European influence debasing Indian design are well-known. Whether it was debasement of a design in gold plate, armoury or any form of art, Dr. Birdwood thoroughly despised such infringement. "The mechanical character of European manufactures requires a consistent general finish which is quite out of place in the bold and free hand compositions of the best native art work ... with the spread of middle class English ideas among the princes and chiefs of India, Indian arms and jewellry will soon be lost arts."[497]

A description of "Arms" is followed by "Jewellry"—which presents a greater variety of style than arms.[498]

Besides aboriginal and peasant jewellery, there was a collection of grass ornaments worn by the wild *Thakurs* and *Katkars* of Matheran.[499] The variety is tremendous.

493 *Ibid.,* p. 67.
494 Palladium: a rare silvery-white metallic element.
495 *Ibid.,* p. 68.
496 *Ibid.,* p. 68.
497 *Ibid.,* pp.68-69.
498 *Ibid.,* p. 69.
499 *Ibid.,* p. 69-71.

"In nothing do the people of India display their naturally gorgeous and costly taste so much as in their jewellry and jewelled arms, which are not only fabricated of the richest and rarest materials, but wrought likewise with all the elaborateness, delicacy, and splendour of design within the reach of art."[500]

In this section, diamonds including a perfect example in the Prince's collection are discussed.

Jewellry is followed by a section on ART FURNITURE AND HOUSEHOLD DECORATIONS. This is followed by subheadings as for instance 'Bombay Blackwood.'[501]

Writing about 'Pottery', Dr. Birdwood has to say, "Purest in art, in directness and simplicity of form and decoration, of all the homely arts is the pottery of India, the Hindu pottery of Madura and the Indian pottery of the Punjab and Scinde (sic)."[502]

At the same time he expresses his disappointment when he says,

"Every endeavour was made to represent this pottery at the Paris exhibition, with a view of bringing it into European demand; but the Bombay Government has sent instead an overwhelming collection of the Bombay School of Art."[503]

Dr. Birdwood is clearly appalled when he remarks, "It is quite a misapplication of Doulton's methods to apply them to friable Indian earthenware. The shapes also of the Bombay School of Art pottery are detestable, taken neither from Scinde or Western India but from Chinese sugar jars, Japanese flower vases and English jam and pickle pots."[504]

There are notes about Lac Wares, Miscellaneous Wares, Trappings and Caparisons, Musical Instruments, Woven Stuffs, Felt, Fine Needlework and Carpets, followed by Pottery, which has just been discussed.

These classifications are quite complete and informative, and interesting to the reader. Of course, one cannot help saying that Birdwood expresses the triumph and tragedy of Indian Art. Also, there are debatable questions raised by Birdwood. Take for instance his discussion of the representation of the custard apple in the Ajanta Cave paintings. He calls it an extraordinary example of "anachronisms in pictures."[505]

His compatriot James Fergusson, in whom he had implicit faith, dated Ajanta Cave paintings not later than the 7th or 8th century A.D.

Dr. Birdwood believes that the Portuguese introduced the custard apple into India, therefore, it could not have been introduced into India until the beginning of the 16th century.

500 *Ibid.,* p. 73.
501 *Ibid.,* pp. 77-83.
502 *Ibid.,* p. 120.
503 *Ibid.*
504 *Ibid.,* p. 122.
505 *Ibid.,* Introduction.

He feels that a probable solution of the enigma is that it is a misrepresentation of the jack fruit [*Artocarpus integrifolia*], which is profusely portrayed at Bharhut.

Alexander Cunningham's thorough work on the Bharhut sculptures is well-known. The Plates and illustrations are remarkably clear and discernible. Cunningham, talking about trees writes: "In a few instances the fruits only have been sculptured such as the Mango, the Jack fruit and the Custard Apple."[506]

Here the jack fruit—the *Khatahal* or *Artocarpus integrifolia*—is carved in proliferation.

"The Jack Tree with its huge fruit is too well known to need description. In some scenes I think that I can distinguish the Jack Tree with its fruit, but there is no doubt about the identification of the fruit itself in many bas-reliefs and the coping."[507]

Speaking about the Custard Apple, Cunningham writes:

"The *Sita-phal* or *Annona squamosa*—the Custard Apple—my identification of this fruit amongst the Mathura sculptures has been contested on the ground that the tree was first introduced into India by the Portuguese."[508]

Cunningham adds that he does not dispute the fact that the Portuguese brought the custard apple into India, but he believes that it was only an exercise of bringing coals to Newcastle. He supports this statement by saying, "I have now travelled over a great part of India, and I have found such extensive and such widely distant tracts covered with the *wild* custard apple that I cannot help suspecting the tree to be indigenous. I can now appeal to one of the Bharhut sculptures for a very exact representation of the fruit and leaves of the custard apple."[509] He also cites a second sculpture with a Monkey represented on a branch of a custard apple tree eating one of the fruits; and on a third custard apple tree a striped squirrel is also represented.[510]

At Bharhut the *Lotus* flower is also used extensively "in the ornamentation of the basses of medallions of Pillars and Rails" and also the coping. The plant itself with its buds and blossoms is found on a large scale in one of the Jataka medallions.[511]

In so far as Dr. Birdwood's theory of the custard apple, being wrongly placed when it seems to have belonged to another time, can be confidently said to be a mistaken view. The jackfruit, as represented in the Bharhut sculptures, is huge and grows on the bark of the tree,

506 Cuuningham, Alexander C.S.I. C.I.E. Major General Royal Engineers (Bengal. Retired), Director General Archaeological Survey of India, *The Stupa of Bharhut,* p. 45; Published by the Order of State for India In Council, London, 1879.

507 *Ibid.,* No. 13, p. 47.

508 *Ibid.,* No. 14, p. 47.

509 See Plate XLVII fig. 2. In Cunningham's book *The Stupa of Bharhut., Ibid.*

510 Cunningham, *op. cit.,* p. 47.Also see Plate XXXIII fig. 6.

511 See Plate XL fig. 1 for the coping flower, and See Plate XXVII fig. 10 for the plant.

and is easily identifiable. The custard apple is represented in small clusters among the branches and is much smaller than the Jack fruit. Thus it is quite possible that as Cunningham points out the custard apple, and one might add, the lotus flower were indigenous flora.

Turning to a comparison between '*The Handbook to the British Section of the Paris Exhibition*—1878 and the '*Official Catalogue of the Colonial and Indian Exhibition* in London ---1886, an interesting aspect is revealed.

While one perceives a more intimate approach of George Birdwood in the *Handbook*, the *Catalogue* does not seem to have the same style. It must surely have had Birdwood's inputs; but there are others who took a prominent role.

Birdwood no doubt was on the Committee to the Royal Commission and on the Reception Committee for the exhibition. However, it was the Secretary of the Royal Commission, Sir Philip Cunliff-Owen, K.C., M.G., C.B., C.I.E., who made arrangements that year for the utilisation of Art Work (as far as possible) in the construction and decoration of the Courts at the exhibition. He submitted these plans for the approval of H.R.H. the President.

Again, a plan was submitted for draping the vestibule with Indian cottons, and for the separation of the Courts by carved wooden and stone Mens.[512] Permission was granted by H.R.H. the Prince of Wales for the construction of a Palace Durbar Hall in carved wood with a peculiar feature of most Oriental Palaces—a *Karkhaneh(Karkhana)* or workshop where jewellers, weavers, carvers and others carried out their trade and produce to impress the visitors with their beautiful handiwork.

In fact C. Purdon Clarke C.I.E. visited India with the permission of H.R.H. the Prince of Wales and brought back wood-workers who immediately commenced work on the Durbar Hall.[513]

This exhibition in South Kensington, London, was intended to be different from the previous exhibitions that had served to illustrate some of the multitudinous Arts and products of the Indian Empire. On this occasion, the technical processes of their manufactures, the application and use of objects which otherwise would have remained beautiful curios to be displayed in Museum cases, were to be brought out; hence these were used in the decoration of the Courts; and the *Karkhana* was put up to display how artisans would ply their trade in India.

The artisans who worked in the screens and gateways were instructed by the Royal Commission to use as many patterns as possible on condition that they were purely Indian

---

512 Mens: an architectural term for a window directly within a triangle that forms the pediment (triangular upper part of the front of a classical building, above the columns) for the building.

513 *Catalogue to the 1886: Colonial and Indian Exhibition in London.*

and traditional.[514] One can only imagine that this overcrowding and exuberance of carving could not have been very pleasing.

What was then presented at the Exhibition of 1886 was an Indian Palace with the purpose to represent the distinctive qualities of a Royal Residence in feudal India. Typically, it had a grand fortified entrance gateway, a forecourt with shops for the use of the Rajah and his entourage, and beyond this the Durbar Hall or Hall of Audience.

Both the Palace and the forecourt were designed by C. Purdon Clarke. The Gateway to the Palace called the Gwalior Gateway was designed by James Keith, the Curator of Antiquities at the Gwalior Fort, who incidentally also supervised its execution.[515]

The Durbar Hall was made of carved pine wood to portray the "Punjab Style." A triple-arched opening led to the greatly decorated rectangular room, its walls divided by piers into several recessed bays, each with its own style of ornamentation.[516]

The illustrated Journal, *The Graphic,* found fault with many details. Indeed the Gwalior Gateway, which was intended to be the Gateway to the Indian Palace was criticised by *The Graphic* for lack of authenticity because it was of a combination from various sources, therefore, strictly speaking, not an accurate Gwalior Gateway.[517]

However, "in the choice of artifacts and architectural vocabulary, the exhibition organizers faithfully reproduced the authoritative pronouncements of men like Birdwood and Lockwood Kipling and Fergusson."[518]

One also tends to agree with Chattopadhyay when she comments on the impressive carriers of Dr. Birdwood and Kipling. Both men indulged in collecting, cataloguing, exhibiting and explicating Indian art, but they differed in their sympathetic awareness of Indian arts and crafts. Both concerned themselves with tracing the foreign influences in Indian art and crafts. Kipling was very critical of labour practices in India and had a more conservative approach about 'reviving' the craft industry for economic gain. He took pride in technological changes in the nineteenth century India as long as they did not affect architecture and crafts. Birdwood on the other hand had a happy, idyllic and theocratic idea of village life. In his commentary on the state of Indian art he conjured a picture of India as an imaginary land of princely patrons and simple people absorbed in tradition, a world where everybody had a secure and fixed position. He believed that 'The Code of Manu' was implicitly behind the unchanging tradition of India. Change and imitation of foreign art forms led to grotesqueness and mongrelisation.[519]

514 Chattopadhyay, *art.cit.,* p. 5 of 8.

515 *Ibid.*

516 *Ibid.*

517 *Ibid.*

518 *Ibid.,* John Lockwood Kipling came out to India in 1865 as one of the three British members of staff of the J.J. School of Art. - Allen, Charles, *Kipling Sahib - India and the Making of Rudyard Kipling,* Little Brown, u.k. 2007, p. 32

519 Chattopadhyay, *art.cit.,* p. 3 of 8.

Turning back to the Exhibition in London of 1886, one perceives Imperialism surfacing blatantly in the write-up of the *Catalogue.* There is for instance the 'Historical Retrospect of the Indian Empire.' This traces the history chronologically from the East India Company established in 1600. It ends with the lines, "In 1886 the British power is paramount over an area of more than a million and a half square miles, containing upwards of two hundred and fifty millions of inhabitants."[520]

This was clearly meant to impress the British.

The products of each of its colonies was displayed under approximately 37 headings---naming each colony.

Reading this catalogue, one is convinced that the British were trying to exhibit their supremacy over the colonies.

The grounds of the Exhibition were lit up by about 9,700 electric glow lamps of 5 and 10 candle power, with a few 20 candle lamps on the Band Stand on the verandah of the Conservatory. The objective was to produce a general effect of being a charming arrangement of light and colour. This was enhanced by illuminated Fountains.

One can only imagine that the whole would have resulted in a kitschy effect. Indeed, 'kitsch' would be the appropriate word to describe this showy display.

This of course is not in keeping with Dr. Birdwood's cautious views. He kept up his connection with India, while at the India House. This he did by making constant contributions to the Indian press. From his boyhood he was a diligent contributor of special information to magazines and newspapers. In India he is said to have helped to convert the *Standard* into the *Times of India* and edited the *Bombay Saturday Review;* after his return to London he wrote for the *Pall-Mall, Athenaeum, Academy* and *The Times.*

His research on the subject of *Incense*[521] is a good example of his mastery of detail, which has made his historical and botanical account of this subject, a classic.[522]

His connection with Indian princes helped him to encourage many Maharajas to contribute products made in their State. Indeed in the Paris Exhibition of 1878, Dr. Birdwood was no doubt responsible for convincing various Maharajas as for instance (1) The Maharaja of Kashmir; (2) Patiala; (3) Oodeypore (Udaipur); (4)The Raja of Jind and (5) The Rajah of Nabha to display their commercial collections.[523]

520 *Catalogue of the 1886: Colonial and Indian Exhibition in London, 'History of the Indian Empire.'*

521 *Trans. Liun.Soc. xxvii 1871, Ency. Brit. 9th ed; Incense, 1881* revised.

522 Wikipedia, *George Christopher Molesworth Birdwood.*

523 List of Exhibitors, *Handbook.*

Again it was surely Dr. Birdwood's influence that gave confidence to (1) H.H. Nizam of Hyderabad; (2) H.H. Maharajah Gaekwar of Baroda; (3) H.M. Maharajah of Mysore; (4) Scindia of Gwalior; (5) Holkar of Indore; (6) Oudipore; (7) H.H. Maharajah of Travancore; (8) H.H. Nawab of Bahawulpore; (9) H.H. Maharaj of Jeypore; (10) Jodhpor; (11) Patiala; (12) Benares; (13) H.H. The Thakur Sahib of Bhownugger; and (14) The Maharajah of Vizianagram to take an interest in the Exhibition of London in 1886.[524]

Actually Birdwood's friendship with Princes and leading educated native Indians and his intimate knowledge of the country was of immense value in handling problems of the Indian Empire. He was honoured by the British Empire; in 1887 he was created a K.C.I.E., given his LL.D. by Cambridge and also made an officer of the Legion d'Honneur and a laureate of the French Academy.[525]

He truly deserved these honours and remained an "Indian" in spirit.

The Dedication in Dr. Birdwood's Collection of Essays, which he calls 'SVA' emphasises his philosophy which prompted his writings and is a Preview of the Chapter that follows; it reads:

AUM

TO

THE BRAHMANA

THE GOLDEN CENSER OF THE PRAYERS OF INDIA

TO

THE KSHATRIYA

THE CONSECRATED SWORD OF HER DEFENCE

TO

THE VAISHYA

THE CUP OF HER PLENTEOUS RICHES

AND EVER OVERFLOWING CHARITIES

AND TO

THE SUDRA

THE KEEN, WIDE-GATHERING SICKLE

OF HER BOUNTIFUL HARVESTS----

524 List of Maharajas in the Colonial and Indian Exhibition of 1886, *Official Catalogue. This list is quoted as it appears in the original reference.*

525 Wikipedia, *George Christopher Molesworth Birdwood.*

TO THESE
THE FOUR VARNA, "COLOURS," OR "CASTES"
THE ARK OF THE SOUL OF INDIA
OF THE HINDUS
I DEDICATE THIS BOOK
IN TESTIMONY OF THE AFFECTION THAT
GLOWS WITHIN MY HEART FOR MY MOTHERLAND
HRI BHARATA
AND ITS SACROSANCT PEOPLE
AND EVER MORE AND MORE FAITHFULLY
AND FERVENTLYAS MY LONG PROLONGED
PROBATIONARY DAY ON EARTH
RINGS TO EVENSONG

VIII DECEMBER, MCMXIV **GEORGE BIRDWOOD**

CHAPTER VII

Birdwood's Perception of Communities and Customs

Dr. George Birdwood was a man with a multiplicity of interests. He was a prolific writer who touched upon a plethora of subjects.

A little after the first decade of the twentieth century — 1912 or thereabouts, Dr. Birdwood felt the need to reproduce a collection of his 'casual writings.' Although his desire was not fulfilled immediately, it did take shape in 1914.

The essays that Dr. Birdwood chose for reproduction were precious to him as a record of his "progressively wider and clearer 'open vision' of the future enchanted India."[526]

He called his collection of twelve essays *Sva*. *Sva* to Birdwood implies that these essays are "a part and parcel" of himself—facts of human history that "in the course of a long and all- absorbing studious life have most deeply pervaded and impressed"[527] him.

The Sanskrit *Sva* means "his," "her," or "itself." The word *Svastika* is Sanskrit and is composed of *svasti* meaning "well-faring" and *tika* meaning "mark," "sign," "token," etc.[528]

At the start of any auspicious ceremony, Hindus draw the *Svastika* sign to invoke goodness. In short the Svastika is with you in whatsoever you do and withersoever you turn in India and enters into the whole scheme of sacramental life of the Hindus.[529]

By reading the essays one is able to gather Dr. Birdwood's perception of communities and customs. Birdwood pans across a whole gamut of subjects. His historical leanings prompt him to trace events in their pristine condition; his appreciation of art steers him to perceive the beauty of objects and humanity; his sociological bent of mind leads him to analyse societal issues, and his training in medicine helps him view cases and issues scientifically. All in all, it is a unique point of view to be considered and digested.

526 Birdwood, George, *Sva,* edited by F.H. Brown, London: Philip Lee Warner. Humphrey Milford, Oxford University Press, Bombay, Melbourne, Toronto, MDCCCCXV, *Author's Preface,* p. xiv.

527 *Ibid.*

528 *Ibid.*, p. xxviii

529 *Ibid.*, p. xxviii

Dr. George Birdwood was a person with a high degree of sensibility—an ability to understand emotion and art.

He had a sentient judgement about the sharp ethnic characteristics of various communities. Take for instance his essay on "The Mahratta Plough." To this effect he wrote about the *Chit pavan* or *Konkanst* Brahmins of Maharashtra, that they were a "handsome race of men with fair complexions, light grey eyes and strikingly intellectual faces"...... presenting "in their manly and joyous national temperament, a complete moral antithesis to the witty and plaintive Bengali Babus, a radically Turanian race."[530]

About the *Chit pavan* women, he had to say "they are the most refined type of feminine loveliness; and in the sweetness of grace, and dignity of their high-bred beauty, at once modern in its delicacy, and antique in its fearless freedom, they might well be taken for the Greek originals of the Tanagra "figurines" awaked to a later life among the tropical gardens and orchards and cocoanut groves of Southern Konkan."[531]

His word pictures capture the everyday life of these women. "One never wearies of watching them, as they are to be seen in the dewy morning in their gardens, perambulating, in archaic worship, the altar of Holy Basil [*tulsi, Ocymum sanctum*] placed before every Hindu house."[532]

The characterization of these women reveals that his observations were not merely superficial, for he remarks that, "the outward and visible charms of these fair *Chit pavanis* faithfully mirror the innate virtues of their pure and gentle natures; for they are perfect daughters, and perfect wives and mothers... remaining modestly at home, as the proper sphere of their duties, unknown beyond their families, and seeking in the happiness of their children their greatest pleasure."[533] Dr. Birdwood knowingly adds that these women pride themselves in the reverence of their husbands, decorating their hair with flowers signifying their married status, "the crown of a true woman's glory in the highest."[534]

There is no doubt that he respected the Mahrattas (Marathas), "the true sons" of Maharashtra; "the hardy, brave, shrewd, hospitable and intensely devout *mavalis* (sic)[535] of the south of India."[536]

530 Birdwood, *Sva, The Mahratta Plough,* p. 38. Turanian--- meaning Iranian and Aryan by inference.

531 *Ibid.,*pp.38-39. Tanagra figurines were Greek figurines produced in the later fourth century B.C. primarily in the Boeotian town of Tanagra.

532 *Ibid.,* p. 39.

533 *Ibid.*

534 *Ibid.*

535 *Ibid.,* p. 28, *mavalis* should read as *mavalas.*

536 *Ibid.*

While he draws upon a comparison of the afternoon picture that the *chit pavan* women present as they make their way towards the river to fetch water, to the chromatic effects of a glowing Turner or a Claude,[537] he contrasts the comely *Deshast* Brahminis, though not so fair as their *Konkanast* sisters, to a study worthy of a Lombard master's canvas with classical tendencies. Yet they are all known at a glance by their great beauty and richer clothing, for as they sweep past in their flowing gold-bordered *saris* of crimson, "nothing can be nobler than its glow against the olive flesh-tints of the stately *Deshast* Brahminis," he expresses admiringly.[538]

Talking about the Mahratta women of the *rayat* class, he remarks that they lose the good looks of their girlhood as they reach maturity but are a fine, healthy race, tall and straight, modest, frank and chatty and in their colourful attire are welcome objects to the artistic eye.[539]

He surreptitiously hints and treads cautiously while speaking about dancing girls, (although he does not mention them per se) "loitering in the shadows of the big temple" and he emerges strongly when he states the fact that they are, "not illicit, degraded, and depraved, but a recognized institution, established, endowed, and sacramental."[540]

Later he comments about the town of Jejuri on the right bank of the River Nira in Maharashtra. Jejuri is famous for *Khandoba,* an incarnation of Lord *Shiva,* in the figure of an armed horseman. Next to the *Khandoba* temple is the temple of *Vithoba* or *Vitthal,* the most popular object of worship throughout Maharashtra. Attached to this temple of Jejuri is a large establishment of dancing girls or *devadasis.*[541]

Birdwood hastens to comment on the rich culture of Maharashtra; for not far from the Jejuri temple, is the village of Valhe, the reputed birthplace of Valmiki, the legendary author of the classic *Ramayana.* The geography and history of Maharashtra, he writes, were most familiarly impressed upon him from his earliest infancy in India 1832-1839; and just as Robin Hood and Rob Roy lived on in the memories of Englishmen and Scots, so the names of Hindu gods and such titular names as the Peshwa, Holkar, Scindia, the Gaekwar's (of

537 *Ibid.,* p. 39.

538 *Ibid.* Lombard painters were active in the 18th century in Valtellina, the small Alpine valley on the border between Lombardy and Switzerland. Lombard painters were influenced by Roman models around 1700. Pietro Ligari (1686-1752) created large altarpieces characterized by a balanced composition. He produced the most beautiful canvases during this Milanese period of classical tendencies around 1717-1720 including 'Immaculate Conception.'

539 *Ibid.,* p. 81.

540 *Ibid.,* pp. 81-82.

541 *Ibid.,* p. 42. This institution lives even today. Though some might perceive it as an aberration, the dancing girls are still in demand and are invited for special occasions such as weddings and other happy events. They are a matriarchal society in which the men folk are relegated to a subsidiary role, playing the 'second fiddle' as it were, as 'escorts' and drivers of transport vehicles like tempos; for the dancing girls are now divided into troupes and travel from place to place in a tempo.

Baroda) ambassador Gangadhar Shastri and his assassin Timbakji Danglia (sic)[542] were vividly ingrained in his memory.[543]

While he is retrospective about the Mahratta countryside, he makes keen observation about the character of the Mahratta people; their intense patriotism in regarding Maharashtra not merely as their mother country but also as their heavenly inheritance, which is probably why they regarded Mohammedans not merely as religious persecutors and foreign intruders but as profane and sacrilegious regarding the Hindu religion and therefore to be expiated at any cost.[544] Indeed, a feeling that some Maharashtrians hold even today!

Going back to the days of Shivaji, the great Maratha ruler, Birdwood enlarges upon Mahratta character by quoting the instance of the murder of Afzal Khan by Shivaji. He calls it a "foul and treacherous murder" for the "unsuspecting Bijapur general walked from Koyna valley with a single attendant." Yet he condones Shivaji's assassination of Afzal Khan when he writes: "The deed was damnable; but Sivaji (sic), in all truth and sincerity, deemed it high and worthy, and the last sacrifice of his devout patriotism to the welfare of his sacrosanct country; and it will be a bad sign for the Mahratta people if they ever come to think less of Sivaji (sic) for it. The Bijapur army lay between him and the independence of his country, and the only way of its overthrow in his power was by destruction of its commander. Hardening his heart to the necessity, he enticed his noble victim into an ambush, and in a paroxysm of sacramental ecstasy determinately slew him."[545]

Dr. Birdwood had made a thorough study of the people of Maharashtra; their ways of life, the implements that the farmer used in his day-to-day living. Indeed nothing would seem inscrutable about the observations he made about the social aspects of a Deccan village. He considered the villagers living as a large contented family. His descriptions of a villager's routine, which to some, would be relegated to a position of ubiquity, are to him an epitome of simple, perfect living.

The day would begin with "the house father" who having worshipped the family gods, would gently arouse the bullocks and oxen, stalled either in a yard behind the house or in the porch in front. "It is a devoutly soothing sound," Birdwood remarks, "for it tells you at once that you are among a people setting about their daily duties actually hand in hand with God."[546]

He goes on to talk about the man leaving the house heartened by the soft strains of his wife's song as she grinds flour on the hand-mill to gather the supply of flour for the day. He

542 Danglia should read Dengle.
543 *Ibid.*, p. 43.
544 *Ibid.*, p. 50.
545 *Ibid.*, pp. 51-52.
546 *Ibid.*, p. 76.

continues to describe her day's routine. Her set sequence of doing things however, bursts into happy activity with the onset of festivals. He speaks of this as a way of life that has been followed for the past 3,000 years. He then asks a rhetorical question:

"And is not this co-operative agricultural life of the people of India high farming in its noblest sense?"[547]

Elaborating on this belief he states, "The enactments embodied in the Code of Manu and cognate law books of the Hindus, have achieved this consummation for India from the foundations of Athens and Rome. Through all the dark backward, and abysm of time, we trace there the bright outlines of a self-contained, self-dependent, symmetrical and perfectly harmonious industrial economy, deeply rooted in the popular conviction of its divine character, and protected, through every political and commercial vicissitude, by the absolute power and marvellous wisdom and tact of Brahminical priesthood."[548]

Without appearing to be cynical, one cannot resist from saying that the views of the people of India have changed radically. No matter how hackneyed it may sound, it is a truism that, 'The old order changeth, giving place to the new.'

In fact, Birdwood almost pre-empted this when he ended his essay on "The Mahratta Plough" as:

"Thus the lesson of the Indian plough, if rightly read, goes deep; ...and the deepest gulf before England is that we are ourselves digging, by forcing the insular institutions of this country on the foreign soil of India, - India of the Hindus."[549]

Here Birdwood is very forthright in his thoughts about English colonialism In India.

BIRDWOOD'S WRITING ABOUT THE RAJPUTS OF INDIA

Birdwood's view of the Maharashtrians is intimate and first hand. When he writes about the Rajputs[550] he bases his writings on the work of Miss Gabrielle Festing's *From the Land of Princes* and on James Tod's *Annals and Antiquities of Rajasthan (1829-32)*[551]

Birdwood points out that Tod's *Annals and Antiquities* is a "veritable 'Open Sesame' to the heart and mind and soul of the great and sacrosanct military caste of India; and the

547 *Ibid.*, p. 83.

548 *Ibid.*, pp. 83-84.

549 *Ibid.*, p. 88

550 Birdwood, *Sva, The Rajputs in the History of Hindustan*, pp. 93-148.

551 While Tod was fascinated by the vibrant colours of Rajasthan *(Ibid.*, p. 98). Festing's collection of stories is from 'definite and unimpeachable family traditions and documents.' (*Ibid.*, p. 100).

only Hindu caste with any quickening and controlling traditions of political power and responsibility."[552]

Miss Festing's book helps in exerting a salutary influence about the Rajputs and in arousing a feeling of romantic sympathy with the noble *Kshatriya* Caste of the Rajputs.[553]

Birdwood believes in the idea that there is a basic and fundamental, indeed "a radical brotherhood with the 'Twice born' castes of Hindus, generally Brahman, Rajput (Kshatriya) and Vaishya; who in blood and brawn and bone, and in their ineradicable virility, are one and the same Aryan people with ourselves."[554]

Birdwood expounds a theory of Aryan Migration whereby the Aryans who descended on India from the regions of the Caspian and Aral Seas made their way southward and eastwards down into Hindustan first and then down to the Deccan. As they moved, "they set up every one his throne by the way" subjugating the peoples already in the peninsula.[555] Simultaneously they formed settlements and their needs for a garrison for their defence were contained. As a consequence, several warriors were left without an occupation and these gradually turned to trading and over the centuries became the *Vaishya* caste of Brahminical India.[556]

He speaks of the origin of the *Rig Veda,* 'the only true Veda' which he feels was an outcome of a 'lyrical heartburst of devout joy.' The hereditary guardians of the Vedas segregated themselves as the *Brahman* caste differentiating themselves from the *Kshatriyas* and *Vaishyas.*[557]

He expands his view by stating that, "The usurping Brahmans in their sacerdotal intolerance of the natural superiority of the Rajputs, sought to brand them with artificial inferiority, not only by writing them down second in order of their four theocratic castes, but by striving, and on the whole with remarkable success to impose upon them all manner of ceremonial disabilities."[558]

This, he writes, is indicated in the *Aitariya Brahmanam,* an Appendix to the *Rig Veda,* giving guidance to the Brahmans and giving the earliest explanations on the sacrificial prayers and rituals of the *Veda.*[559]

This then is Birdwood's theory of the origin of the four castes and the Brahman predominance over the *Kshatriya* Rajputs - who were themselves "Sons of Kings."[560] They

552 *Ibid.,* p. 100.
553 *Ibid.*
554 *Ibid.,* p. 100.
555 *Ibid.,* pp.100-101.
556 *Ibid.,* p. 101.
557 *Ibid.,* p. 102.
558 *Ibid.,* pp. 102-103.
559 *Ibid.,* p. 103.
560 *Ibid.,*p. 94.

are said to have been raised by the royal and saintly Agastya, the famous author of several "Hymns" of the *Rig Veda.*[561]

The Rajputs pride themselves as the warrior caste devoted to self-sacrifice. They claim to be descended from the *Kshatriyas* the primitive Aryas of India. The Rajputs never lost their pride of belonging to the Aryan race.

Birdwood's own opinion is that the purest Aryas of India are to be found among the Jains who became the *Vaishyas*, who, influenced by Buddhism, form their own religion of "the twenty-four Victorious Jains."[562]

BIRDWOOD'S VIEW ABOUT THE ARABS

In Part II of the Essay on the Rajputs, Birdwood speaks about 'The Ismailites in India.'[563]

The Arabs were a Caucasian or Noachian race, a "highly intellectual people who had the keenest alacrity and zest.......in the arts of war and peace."[564] They at once gauged the opulence of India and realized that Afghanistan had to be occupied before they set their eyes on India.

Thus it was only when the military and religious superiority over the Afghans was assured that Caliph Walid I in A.D. 711, sent a naval expedition to Sindh under the command of Muhammad ibn Kasim. He acted in co-operation with Hijaj, the Governor of Bassora and managed to subjugate Sindh.[565]

It is at this stage that we see the Rajput feelings for their country and their pride as warriors who could not accept defeat. It is said that the Rajput *Deshpati [desh:* land, *pati:* lord] made a determined defence, but he was hopelessly "outclassed "by the newly gotten "Greek Science of the Arabs."

THE RITE OF JOHUR

This defeat led to the woeful Rajput rite of *johur.* The Rajput *Deshpati* fell fighting amongst the Arab cavalry, but his widow continued the defence of the city till the depletion of provisions of the garrison. "Then she, and all the women with their children, gathered

561 *Ibid.,* p. 103.
562 *Ibid.,* p. 105.
563 *Ibid.,* p. 109.
564 *Ibid.*
565 *Ibid.,* p. 110.

themselves together, and built up a great funeral pyre in the garden of the Palace and mounting it, were sacrificed in the flames of their own kindling."[566] This then was the beginning of the establishment of the ritual of *johur.*

Much later the Arabs were defeated at Mewar by Prince Bappa. The Arabs in India never recovered from this reverse. The Rajputs in Sindh rose successfully against them in A.D. 750; Prince Khoman of Chitor finally expelled them from India in A.D. 812.[567] The Rajputs considered India as their sacrosanct soil.

THE AFGHANS

It is the Rajputs that countered all attacks on India. After the Arabs they tackled the Afghans. In A.D. 979 Jaipal, the Rajput Prince of Lahore, came face to face with Subuktegin at Lagman, on the road from Peshwar to Kabul[568] and inflicted a defeat.

The son of Subuktegin was the bigot "Mahmud of Ghazni" who, continuing the quarrel his father had started, defeated Jaipal in 1001. This defeat triggered off another *johur.*

However, the Rajputs persisted in their endeavour to ward off the foreigners from their invaluable motherland—India. The Rajputs continued to put up a fight with the invaders. In all their encounters, their romantic and chivalrous nature coupled with their pride was always visible.

The first Afghan dynasty was succeeded by the second, with Muhammad Ghori 1153-1206 succeeding to the throne.[569]

For six hundred years thereafter, "India of the Hindus never recovered from that 'doubly redoubled' deadliest stroke of doom."[570]

In 1206, Muhammad Ghori was assassinated. On his death one of his "favourite" slaves seized the government of Hindustan. They called themselves the 'Slave Kings' (1206—1288), with their throne at Delhi.[571]

The only connection with the Rajputs was the capture of the hill fort of Ranthambore in Jaipur State and a rising of the princes against Balin the ninth Slave King (1266-88) in which many Rajputs lost their lives.[572]

566 *Ibid.,* p. 111.
567 *Ibid.,* p. 112.
568 *Ibid.,* pp. 113-114.
569 *Ibid.,* p. 117.
570 *Ibid.,* p. 120.
571 *Ibid.,* p. 121. This was actually the third Afghan Dynasty.
572 *Ibid.*

Risings of the Rajputs were put down constantly. The seventh dynasty of the Afghans consisted of Three Kings of the House of Lodi, (1450—1526); they were the last abhorred Afghan dynasties of India.

The Afghan Governor of Lahore, himself a Lodi, revolted against Ibrahim Lodi, the last of his dynasty and sought the aid of Zahiruddin Muhammadan, surnamed Babar—the 'Lion-Hearted.' Thus began the rule of the Mo(n)gol or Mughal Emperors of Delhi (1526-1806).

When the Rajputs realized that Babar had come to stay in India they made a last desperate effort to restore *Kshatriya* supremacy.[573] They were led by Rana Sangha. In February 1527 they suffered a blow at the battle of Sikri.

In 1532, Chitor was stormed for a second time by Sultan Bahadur of Gujarat. The noble Rajput queen, before committing *johur* sent her bracelet to Humayun, the son of Babar. This act was to bind Humayun in brotherhood, to protect her son.[574] Humayun marched against Bahadur, and drove him back to Gujarat. But Humayun, though brave and generous, was not free of the Afghans during his reign of 25 years, 1530-1556.

It was left to his son, Akbar the Great, 1556-1605, to stamp out the Afghans with the help of his general Beiram. The second Battle of Panipat, November 5, 1556[575] was fought against Hemu, the *Kshatriya* general of the Afghans. Subsequently, 1567-73 were spent in subjugating the resurgent Rajputs. This was cleverly tackled by Akbar by intermarriages and by the employment of the *Kshatriya* Hindus in high office.[576]

Not all Rajputs accepted this degradation. The Rana of Chitor defied Akbar and Akbar laid siege on Chitor when the Rani solemnised the rite of *johur* . This was the 'third sack of Chitor 1567-8.'[577]

Udai Singh, the Rana of Chitor, left the defence of the city to Jai Mal, chief of Bednor and sought refuge in the neighbouring forests, where he later built the city of Udaipur. At the same time he took a vow that so long as Chitor remained a ruin, neither he nor his successors would twist their beards in the Rajput fashion, or eat or drink from anything but leaves, or sleep on anything but straw; it is said that the Ranas of Udaipur continued this practice, altering it somewhat by sleeping on sumptuous beds *laid on straw,* and eating from golden and silver plates *laid on green leaves* and of course never twisting their beards![578]

In short, it was their pride that forced them to take certain vows, which they followed for years to come.

573 *Ibid.,* p. 124.
574 This was perhaps the beginning of *Raksha Bandhan.*
575 Birdwood has incorrectly referred to this as "the third Battle of Panipat," *Ibid.,* p. 125.
576 *Ibid.,* pp. 125-126.
577 *Ibid.,* p. 125.
578 *Ibid.,* p. 126.

In 1592, Akbar made himself master of Hindustan keeping a strong hold on Afghanistan, as the key to the plains of the Indus and Ganges.[579]

In 1601 Akbar's health failed him and he struggled for 5 years knowing that there was none to carry on his work.[580]

Akbar was a genius. He abolished the infamous poll-tax on Hindus, forbade the practice of *sati* and encouraged remarriage of widows.

He repressed the attempts of Rajputs to act independently in matters of high policy and State necessity; but so long as they were submissive of their political relations with the Paramount Power he respected their social prejudices and sympathised in their misfortunes; and valued and trusted them as friends. He did not interfere in their military ideas or in the internal economy of their sovereign states. He resisted forcing an alien system of education on a people, "who, through at least 2,000 years of history, had elaborated the most perfect type of Aryan speech, and created a splendid literature and unique architectural and industrial arts of their own, and a highly spiritualised idiosyncratic religious culture."[581]

Reading about Birdwood's perception about communities in India, one may observe that Birdwood has an intimate affinity to Maharashtra and Maharashtrians; he is able to make observations about the Rajput character by studying the history and comment on their perseverance and pride through the ages. Both communities combated against the Muslims and both had some commonalities, for instance, the fact that they were pitted against foreigners, and religious intolerance of many of the Muslim rulers was at the bottom of their clashes.

By steadily avoiding mixed marriages, the Rajputs were able to sustain the pristine purity of their pan-Aryan strain.[582]The outstanding characteristic of this feature is seen in their virility, their temperance, endurance, patience, courage, fortitude, equity and above all their magnanimity.[583] They took an unflinching view of life, of its inexorable necessities and stern responsibilities.[584]

Birdwood perceived that the crux of regenerating the national life of Aryan India was through three conduits, these being the "still living industrial arts of India, the still living chivalry of Rajputana and the still living religion of the Hindus—of the Mahratta and Tamils in special."

His perception may not apply quite so relevantly in today's scenario; nevertheless these are pointers that might help revive our degenerated standards.

579 *Ibid.,* p. 126.
580 *Ibid.*
581 *Ibid.,* p. 127.
582 *Ibid.,* p. 141.
583 *Ibid.,* p. 141.
584 *Ibid.,* pp. 145-146..

BIRDWOOD'S STUDY OF ISLAM IN INDIA

Dr. Birdwood has written an essay on *The Muharram in Bombay.*[585] Here he has chronicled the history of Islam. One can deduce the volatility of a people, which led to deceit, intrigue and bloodshed amongst the factions. The cruel streak in humans is brought to the surface and one is saddened by the killings between blood relations—'the internecine feuds.'[586]

The Muslims may be divided into two great sects of Sunnis and Shias. The Sunnis or "Traditionalists," literally "those of the Path" are so called because "they acknowledge the authority of the received traditions of the sayings and doings of Mahomet, 'the Prophet of the God.'"[587] The Shias or Muhammadan Dissenters, declare that Ali 'the Lion God,' his two sons Hasan and Hussain and the descendants of the latter, are the only two *Imams* or Sovereign Pontiffs.[588]Hasan and Hussain were the sons of Fatima and Ali, the daughter and son-in-law of Muhammad the Prophet.[589]

The Muharram or Moharrum festival was the biggest annual festival of the Muslims. It is celebrated in commemoration of the martyrdom of Hasan and Hussain.[590]

Dr. Birdwood writes about the Muharram in Bombay; he talks about the Shia celebration of Muharram; "Attached to every great Shia house is an Imambarrah—a hall or enclosure –built expressly for the celebration of the anniversary of the death of Hussain. The enclosure is decorated on all sides with arcades and generally has a domed roof. On the side of the Imambarrah, facing Mecca, is set the *tabut* or *tazia* which is a model of the tombs of Kerbala."[591]The *tabut* is a framework of bamboo in the shape of a mausoleum and is made with a network of paper pasted on it.[592]

In the houses of the wealthier Shias these *tabuts* are fashioned of silver and gold or of ivory and ebony, embellished all over with inlaid network. The poorer Shias make do with a *tabut* of lath[593] and plaster, adorned with mica, silver, gold and green tinsel.[594]

A week before the new moon of the Muharram, the Muslims enclose a space called the *tabut kana,* where the *tabut* is prepared. At the very moment the new moon is seen, a spade is stuck into the ground. A pit is then dug there, and lighted, the fire is kept burning for

585 Birdwood, *Sva, The Muharram in Bombay,* pp. 159-181.
586 *Ibid.,* pp. 159-173.
587 *Ibid.,* pp. 159-160.
588 *Ibid.,* p. 160.
589 Gupchup, Vijaya, *Bombay, Social Change 1813-1857,* p. 276.
590 Gupchup, *op.cit.,* p. 276. Also Birdwood, *Sva,* p. 173.
591 Birdwood, *op.cit.,* p. 173.
592 Gupchup, *op. cit.,* p. 277.
593 Lath—thin flat strips of wood.
594 Birdwood., *Sva., art.cit.,* p. 173.

ten days of Muharram. Birdwood is not sure about the origin of the fire; but states that the Hindus as well as Muslims regard the fires with great awe and make their vows over them.[595]

On the 10th day of the Muharram every house wherein a *tabut* is kept, sends a separate cavalcade or its company on foot to join the general funeral procession.[596]

Birdwood writes, "In Bombay, after gathering its contingent from all Shiah (sic) households, as it winds its way through the tortuous streets of the native town, the living stream at length emerges upon the Esplanade on the side bordering Back Bay."[597]

The Esplanade, for that day, is signified as "the plain of Kerbala."[598] The procession leads to the sea with the wail of "*Ya Ali! Ai Hasan Ai Husain, Ai Hasan, Ai Husain, Husain Shah!*" [drowned, drowned, drowned, in blood, all three, fallen, and prostrate, and dead!][599]

The general scene was one of noise, bustle and confusion. There was also the danger of Hindus converted to Islam fighting against the people of their own caste. For many Hindus had faith in the *tabuts, ullums* (or artificial tombs intended to represent Hasan and Husain) and the *buraq* or horse (which was intended to be a facsimile of the one which the Almighty sent from Heaven by the angel *Jibreel* (Gabriel) to His Highness Muhammad Mustafa (the chosen).[600]

There could also be a clash between Shias and Sunnis; for while the former regarded Muharram as a period of mourning, the Sunnis considered it as an occasion for frolic.[601]

The route to the sea was thus lined by native policemen. In fact, the disturbing aspects of Muhorrum when Bombay experienced bedlam, were quelled by the policemen who were representatives of British law and managed to keep check on "the infuriated zealots." In Bombay the Muharram procession was confined in 1846, (this was before Dr. Birdwood wrote about the scene in his essay "*Muharram in Bombay*")[602]to an irregular procession wending its way to the sea.[603]

595 Birdwood., *Sva, art.cit.,* p. 174.

596 *Ibid.,* p. 177.

597 *Ibid.,* p. 178.

598 The plain of Kerbala or Kurbala is significant because Husain was the younger brother of Hasan who succeeded to the throne of Medina. Hasan was poisoned by Ayzeed who had been given the Government of Syria. Later Husain was killed on the tenth day of the month of Muharrum, after a desperate twenty day battle at Kurbala.[Gupchup, *op.cit.,* p. 276.]

599 Birdwood., *Sva., art.cit.,* p. 179.

600 Gupchup, *op.cit.,* pp. 277-280.

601 Gupchup., *op.cit.,* p. 276.

602 Birdwood., *op.cit.,* p. 179.

603 *Report of the Superintendent of Police submitted with the report of the Senior Magistrate of Police, No. 493 of 1854, dated Sept. 22, 1854, JD vol. 64 of 1854,*p. 207.

Dr. Birdwood writes that "the 11th and 12th days of Muharram should be spent in meditation by the graves wherein *tabuts* have been laid in Bombay beside the sad seashore."[604]

It is interesting to note that the procession of Muharram on the 10th day is all that is known to the Europeans in India. It is they who, on repeatedly hearing the wail of *Ai Hasan Ai Husain,* popularly designated the words with a semi-voluntary corruption as "Hobson-Jobson"! which indeed was the title given by Sir Henry Yule to his great and fascinating glossary of similar Anglo-Indian colloquial words and phrases. In fact Sir Henry Yule repeatedly quoted Sir George Birdwood's writings.[605]

This is proof that Dr. Birdwood was recognized as an authority on India, its people and their customs even by men like Sir Henry Yule. There is no denying that Birdwood had a vast knowledge of facts and an eye for detail. From his descriptions one is able to gather that his writings were based on personal experience and not mere hearsay.

BIRDWOOD'S VIEWS ABOUT DISEASES LIKE LEPROSY IN INDIA

Birdwood's tendency for preference to Science and Medicine prompts him to write about the Leper in India.[606]He writes that it may be premised that because of the constant ceremonial ablutions of the Hindus, it was absolutely unknown in India before the arrival of Vasco Da Gama's ships in Calicut in 1498. But within a few months of his sailors landing there, the *Zamorin* became contaminated with it through his *zenana* (harem); and within seventeen years of its appearance on the Malabar Coast, it spread all over India even as far north as the Himalayas.[607]

Birdwood was familiar with the special practice of his friend, the well-known physician Dr. Bhau Daji, who treated many cases of leprosy. However, Birdwood states that never, as far as he could remember, was there any suspicion of "their having originated in leprous contagion."[608]

Let us see how Hindus viewed leprosy. For this Dr. Birdwood goes back in time to the *Manu Smriti* or the Code of Manu. He writes that in the Code of Manu *white* (leprosy) was believed to be the punishment for stealing *clothes,* that is *white* cottons cloths.[609] Dr. Birdwood goes on to say that, the *Bavishya Purana,* is a work of a very late date compared to

604 Birdwood, *Sva,*pp. 180-181.

605 *Hobson-Jobson: A Glossary of Colloquial Anglo-Indian Words and Phrases* (New edition. London: John Murray 1903).

606 Birdwood, *Sva, Leper in India,* pp. 183-199.

607 *Ibid.,* p. 185.

608 *Ibid.,* p. 186.

609 *Ibid.,* p. 188.

the Code of Manu, but is most instructive on the point. It was never printed in the original Sanskrit, therefore, Dr. Birdwood does not give the Sanskrit name for the disease. It states eight varieties of the disease;[610] the worst is the eighth variety, white leprosy. According to the Puranic ordinances, a leper is excluded not only from domestic sacrifices but also from inheritance of property.[611]

Remarking about its contagion from his medical knowledge, he says it is extremely sluggish. Even when the disease has established itself, it takes years to flare up; in its earlier stages it may lie latent throughout a lifetime.[612]

Birdwood comments that in India it prevails chiefly among the Hindus and affects the males more than the females. He states that all the cases that came under his observation in Dr. Bhau Daji's practice were from the estuaries of rivers. He makes an interesting observation when he says that cases of cancer also come from similar geographical surroundings; he further adds that they are invariably associated with a diet largely made up of pickles of all kinds and candied preserves.[613]

Elephantiasis is a form of the disease[614] which is mentioned in the *Bavishya Purana.* Dr. Birdwood comments that the Hindus believed that it can only be removed by immolation, or suffocation in some sacred stream or tank, or by burying the victim in a newly dug grave.[615]

But under the British rule, this practice was treated as either suicide or murder and, therefore, it could not have happened on a large scale.[616]

In 1911, Mr. Gail's Census Report recorded a fall in leprosy since 1891 from 126,000 to 109,000 and he attributed this to the improvement of material conditions among the lower castes; and also on the efforts to house lepers in asylums.[617]

Birdwood indicates that it is the responsibility of the Government of India, to learn from the experience of other European countries in the 16th and 17th centuries and take the necessary simple and efficacious steps. Practical measures such as Isolation of lepers and amelioration of sanitary conditions, cleanliness in food habits will go a long way, he advises.[618]

Birdwood feels that an attempt to drive leprosy from India can only be entirely successful if it is aimed to simultaneously drive syphilis out of India. Dr. Bhau Daji always suspected an obscure connection between them.[619]

610 *Ibid.,* p. 189.
611 *Ibid.,* p. 190.
612 *Ibid.,* p. 183.
613 *Ibid.,* p. 193.
614 *Ibid.,* p. 189. No. 4 in the variety of leprosy in the *Bavishya Purana* translation.
615 *Ibid.,* p. 193.
616 *Ibid.,* p. 193.
617 *Ibid.,* p. 194; Footnote.
618 *Ibid.,* p. 195.
619 *Ibid.,* p. 197.

Birdwood's own conjecture was that leprosy and syphilis were types of a protean disease that tends to generate itself where bodily cleanliness is habitually neglected.[620]

Birdwood states emphatically that he feels strongly that if "we are to succeed in the benevolent movement for the alleviation of the leper in India, we must, and all the more unhesitatingly, in view of the humiliating history of syphilis in that country, combine the religious obligations of penitence and reparation with the burden and the glory of a great imperial and international work of duty and mercy."[621]

Birdwood's vast knowledge, his eye for detail and his candid remarks must be acknowledged. It is amazing that even when he wrote his essays, he was able to foresee many truths that hold true even to this day.

BIRDWOOD AND SOCIAL REFORMS

Even after Birdwood returned to England, he remained actively involved with Indian affairs.

On 19th November 1907, he wrote an Introduction to the Jubilee Volume of *Stree Bodhe* from West Ealing, near London.

The *Stree Bodhe or* "Woman's Wisdom," was founded in 1857 by a group of young Hindu and Parsi social reformers who spared no pains working for the emancipation of women in the Western Presidency. It was therefore decided that the jubilee of the *Stree Bodhe* could be celebrated in a manner that would portray the progress of social reform during the past half century.[622]

The Jubilee Celebrations were carried out from Saturday 1 February 1907 according to the arrangements made by an executive Committee under the Presidentship of The Hon. Mr. Justice N.G. Chandavarkar and other eminent citizens of Bombay.[623] The celebrations lasted for five days.

The President, Justice Chandavarkar referred to the late Mr. Kaikhusro N. Kabraji, 1865-1904 (Editor of *Stree-Bodhe* and *Rast Goftar)* as "having worked not only for his community, but as one who had the catholicity to work zealously for the advancement of Social Progress among Hindus and Mohammedans also."[624]

620 *Ibid.*, p. 198.

621 *Ibid.*, p. 199.

622 G.C.M. Birdwood, *The Stree Bodhe and the Social Progress in India:A Jubilee Memorial, Together with the Account of Jubilee Celebrations and Lectures*, p. 177.

623 *Ibid.*, p. 178.

624 *Ibid.*, pp. 178-179.

Mrs. Sarojini Naidu delivered an eloquent speech in English on the fourth day of the festival given over to the Ladies exclusively.[625]She called the Jubilee Celebration a renaissance.

That the *Stree Bodhe* had stirred many enlightened Indians is evidenced by the fact that they received a very gratifying response of their invitation for funds to work towards several objectives that they had in view.

Among the donors were eminent people like H.H. the Maharaja Gaekwar of Baroda, H.H. the Nawab of Junagadh and H.H. the Begum Saheb, and many others; but it is interesting to note that even Mrs. N.G. Chandavarkar and her daughter, Mrs. D. Sirur contributed to the funds in their own right. They were ladies from the *Chitrapur Saraswat* Community, who respected traditional customs and yet were forward-looking probably because of their distinguished and respected husbands who gave so much to society.[626] The total subscriptions at that time amounted to Rs. 5,400.

It is fitting that the Introduction to the *Stree Bodhe* should have been written by Dr. George Birdwood who did so much for Bombay and India. In his Introduction, he is able to capture the momentum given to the movement at its inception in 1857.

Birdwood writes about the zealous band of young reformers of whom the three most memorable, in his opinion, were Karsondas Mulji (1832-1871), Sir Munguldas Nathoobhoy (1832-1890) and Nanabhai Haridas (1832-1889). Birdwood writes that these young Hindus were warmly supported by a number of active sympathisers among the Parsis, of whom Birdwood specially mentions Dosabhai Framjee Cama. Interestingly he writes, "It is a strange coincidence that not only the three Hindus afore named but two or three others of this group of courageous reformers were all born in 1832, the year of the British Reform Bill."[627] Which Birdwood feels might have influenced their minds.

---

625 *Ibid.*, p. 194.

626 *Ibid.*, pp. 179-180.Mr. Justice Narayan Ganesh Chandavarkar B.A., LL.B. was a practising lawyer, a politician and public man. He was also a past President of the Indian National Congress. He was appointed Judge in 1901 and held that office till 1913. He took a prominent part in the affairs of the Bombay University and was later appointed Vice-Chancellor. Dattatreya Sirur was a mill-owner whose mills in Bangalore, the Minerva and Mysore and Modern Mills in Bombay flourished during his lifetime. He contributed to the setting up of the *Prarthana Samaj* in 1867 with the aim of refining the Hindu religion.He also set up an orphanage for boys in Parle, Bombay, called the *D.N. Sirur Balakrishna Orphanage.*It has functioned since 1932 and is an orphanage for boys aged 8-18; currently it has 70 children. It is not an adoption agency.

627 *Ibid.*, pp.1-2. Sir Munguldas Nathoobhoy was a wealthy, enlightened and public-spirited member of the *Bania (Kapol)* caste of the Hindu sect of *Vallabhacharyan Vaishnavas.* He received the Companionship of the Star of India in 1872 and was knighted in 1875. He was one of the most liberal supporters of the agitation against the *Vallabhacharyas.* Nanabhai Haridas was also a *Vallabhacharyan Vaishnava,* the most able co-adjudicator of Karsondas Mulji and the first Indian to be appointed to the Bench of the High Court of Bombay (*Ibid.*, pp. 1-2.).

Karsondas Mulji belonged to the *Kapol Bania* Caste of the Hindu sect of *Vallabhacharyan Vaishnavas.* He felt very strongly about some of the distressing social customs; thus in 1853 he wrote an essay in favour of widow remarriage. This offended many including his aunt, who had brought up the orphaned Karsondas; she actually turned him out of her house where he lived. This only ignited his feelings about other unpalatable customs, and led him to use the hospitable columns of the *Rast Goftar,* "Truth Speaker."

There were certain stipulated conditions of proprietorship in the *Rast Goftar:*

1) Loyalty to the British Raj.
2) Advocacy of female education.
3) Opposition to Infant marriages.
4) Advocacy of re-marriage of widows.
5) Opposition to the Tyranny of Caste.

Opposition to the traditional "Immoralities of the Maharajas" of the *Bhatia* and *Bania* castes of the Hindu sect of *Vallabhacharyan Vaishnavas.*[628]

Kaikhushro Naoroji Kabraji (1842-1904) became the joint editor with Karsondas Mulji of the *Rast Goftar.* He became sole editor in 1863 and continued to edit the paper till 1904, when he died after a period of 41 years. He was associated with Birdwood's close friends, in the management of the paper *Rast Goftar* with Sorabji Shapurji Bengali, C.I.E. and Dadabhai Naoroji, all distinguished Elphinstonians (students of the well-known Elphinstone College in Bombay) of the highest integrity and fearless in the cause of social reform.[629]

While writing the Introduction to the Jubilee volume of *Stree Bodhe* and while dwelling on education and enlightenment of women, Birdwood feels that two quotations from the Old Testament containing the portraiture of a good woman are very apt—one from "The Confessions of Augustine" and the other from *"The Proverbs* (said of Solomon—written *circa* B.C. 1000) Ch. XXXI, v. 11.31; and the other from "The *Confessions of St. Augustine,* IX, 24.5.

Remarking about Saint Augustine on the Death of his Mother, Monnica at Ostia [circa A.D. 390], Birdwood says, "The love of his mother, Monnica, to St. Augustine was in a word, the highest revelation of the Love of God. The thought would have occurred to an Asiatic (he was a Numidian)—and no Christianized European ever first came upon it, or ever re-read the passage without undergoing something of a momentary transfiguration. But in Bombay Monnica and her son are to be found in every Hindu and Parsi household. Nowhere indeed is the Divinity of Motherhood and the Divinity of Childhood understood as in India."[630]

Speaking about the Indian woman at the Jubilee Celebrations Sarojini Naidu had said: "Yet as an Indian woman myself....I venture to reiterate the urgent necessity for a wide and

628 *Ibid.,* pp. 2-3.

629 Birdwood,*Stree Bodhe,* p.2.

630 *Ibid.,* pp. 6-7.

Birdwood's view was that the handicrafts of India could not be classified on the same basis as the art and industry of Europe. The latter were based as it were, on the broad distinction that industrial productions are no longer hand wrought but manufactured by machines. "In India however, everything is hand wrought, and everything down to the cheapest toy or earthen vessel is therefore more or less a work of art.[638] The village communities have been the stronghold of the traditional arts of India," he wrote. The typical Hindu village consisted exclusively of farmers; but agriculture and manufactures could not exist without each other; historically the village was obliged to receive artisans as members of its hereditary governing body—and as a matter of convenience to the farmers, they were on a sort of service contract. Later they sought their livelihood in towns that began to spring up. It is in this way that the great polytechnical cities of India were formed.[639] Thus the hereditary handicraftsmen were dislodged from the village communities in hundreds and thousands to flock to the mills of Bombay for tempting wages. They then manufactured piece goods in competition with those from ' Manchester.' Birdwood felt that machinery "should be the servant and never the master of men."[640] Birdwood feared the social and moral evils of the introduction of machinery into India. When he wrote his book he could confidently say that "in every Indian village all the traditional handicrafts are still to be found at work."[641]

Thus Birdwood felt that Industrial Arts arising out of manufacturing raw products into artistic forms within which decorative art took shape, is what existed in India. He did not believe that fine art existed in India.

One can then venture to interpret that Sir George Birdwood respected the art forms produced by the Indian artisans in common life, as well as decorative art of the artists of India. But it seems that he distinguished between the artists of Europe and India and proposed that Indian art form could be revived to be appreciated by the beholder of European art.

Prophetically, Indian art was gradually viewed more favourably in England, as we shall see.

APPROBATION OF INDIAN ART IN BRITAIN

In 1843 when John Ruskin's first volume on *Modern Painters* appeared, a sizeable section of the British population was attracted to the Arts and Crafts movement. It was an interest that continued till just before World War I. Ruskin was both appreciative of and repelled by Indian art.[642]

638 *Ibid.*, p. 131.
639 *Ibid.*, p. 137.
640 *Ibid.*, p. 136.
641 *Ibid.*, p. 135.
642 Lipsey, Roger, *Coomaraswamy: 3. His Life and Work,* Princeton University Press, p. 55. John Ruskin (8

Ruskin was mainly familiar with Indian decorative arts—the textiles, jewellery, inlaid boxes, metal work and the like—that Birdwood enthusiastically and meticulously delineated later in '*The Industrial Arts of India.*' Ruskin seems to have had only a general opinion of Indian sacred art, and its exotic iconography shocked him.[643]

Ruskin had exact standards for beauty. He believed that Nature—natural form—was the source for beauty. He thought that Indian art failed in this respect; he vilified Indian art because it seemed neglectful of nature.[644] This view exemplified the fact that in England in 1859, during Ruskin's time, even its leading art critic knew little about Indian art.[645]

The delightful representation of trees, flowers and landscape in Rajput paintings, as also compassionate studies of various animals in temple architecture which struck contemporary art critics as sculptures revelling in nature, were unknown to Ruskin.[646]

On the other hand he fiercely criticized the Indian artists in his book of 1859 *The Two Paths.*[647] His thoughts no doubt were coloured by the aftermath of the Indian Uprising of 1857. Great Britain was shocked by this turn of events; in the light of this 'the art of a subject people could not be accepted on equal terms.'[648]

The polarity of views regarding Indian art amongst Englishmen is evident when one reads Birdwood, whose respect for the Indian artist and craftsmen is borne out in his writings. His ardour expressed in his description of a village scene where the potter at the wheel, the weaver at his loom, the brass and coppersmiths hammering their pots and pans and the jeweller in the verandah of a rich man's house highlight the way of life of a people, in which their literature, art and civilization have continued for 3,000 years.[649]

Summing up thus far we might say that very little of a positive nature about Indian art was expressed in England throughout the remainder of the nineteenth century.

Birdwood admired the crafts but did not recognize the existence of fine art and like Ruskin, was horrified by the depiction of Puranic deities as "eight-armed monsters."[650]

February 1819—20 January 1900) was an English art critic and social thinker. He is also remembered as a poet and artist. His essays on art and architecture were extremely influential in the Victorian and Edwardian eras.

643 Lipsey, *op.cit.,* p.56.

644 *Ibid.,* p. 57.

645 *Ibid.*

646 *Ibid.*

647 Ruskin, *The Two Paths,* 185, in the Collected Works, XVII, 262; cf. esp., pp. 265-266, cited in Lipsey, *op.cit.,* p. 57.

648 Lipsey, *op.cit.,* p. 57.

649 Birdwood, *The Industrial Arts of India,* pp. 135-136.

650 Lipsey,*op.cit.,* p. 60.

There were men like Morris, Burne-Jones, Millais, Edwin Arnold, Walter Crane, and others who were associated with the Arts and Craft movement and petitioned the British Government in 1878, through a much-talked-of letter, seeking the preservation of Indian craft industries.[651] However, their appeal had nothing to do with sacred art, to which they were not yet close nor with "understanding the nature of Indian," as Ananda Kentish Coomaraswamy (AKC) was to put it.[652]

So while there were some in England who were indifferent to Indian Art, Coomaraswamy and his friends strived to awaken an interest. Thus in England it was a group of artists and Arts and Crafts persons with Roger Fry, that first experienced a *metanoia,* a change of mind with regard to Indian Art.[653]

In India it was Ernest Binfield Havell, artist, and Principal of the Calcutta School of Art and keeper of the Government Gallery, who was responsible in inculcating an interest in Indian Art. From 1884—1892, he was superintendent of the Madras School of Art conducting an official investigation of indigenous arts and crafts; from 1896—1906 he directed the Calcutta School.[654] He revamped the teaching methods and established a balanced curriculum now giving importance to "the principles and methods of Indian painting and sculpture" which had hitherto been neglected. He sold "a miscellaneous collection of European paintings owned by the Calcutta Art Gallery so that he could buy good examples of Indian painting and sculpture for Indian students. His move was opposed, but the programme succeeded attracting brilliant students like Abanindranath Tagore and other younger pupils."[655]

In 1908, Coomaraswamy published *Mediaeval Sinhalese Art,* while Havell published *Indian Sculpture and Painting: Illustrated by Typical Masterpieces with an Explanation of Their Motives and Ideals.* This was hailed as an important and convincing new study. Roger Fry in his key article of 1910, *Oriental Art* praised Havell's book and *excused its morally right indignation* while Coomaraswamy held that it was "the first serious attempt to understand and appreciate Indian art."[656]

The publication of Havell's and Coomaraswamy's books in England in 1908 led to the emergence of two schools of thought on Indian art: the old school, best represented by Sir George Birdwood and the new school of critics sympathetic to Indian art. Roger Fry tried to

651 Cited in part by Ashbee in his introduction to Ananda Kentish Coomaraswamy, *The Indian Craftsman.* AKC introduced another passage from Morris on *Commercial War* in Appendix III of that book. Cited in Lipsey, *op.cit.,* ft.nt. 14, p. 60.

652 Lipsey, *op.cit.,* p. 60.

653 Lipsey, *op.cit.,* p. 61.

654 Lipsey, *op.cit.,* p. 61.

655 *Ibid.,* p. 62.

656 AKC, (Ananda Kentish Coomaraswamy) *The Hindustan Review (1910),* p. 271, cited in Lipsey, *op.cit.,* p. 63.

mitigate the sensitive issues between these two schools through his mildly informative article in *The Quarterly Review.* It was a personal approach to Oriental Art, with some intentional and unintentional remarks revealing that he himself was not yet fully able to justify that approach. His article was at once seen as a sign of change by the admirers of Indian art.[657]

Almost at the same time as the publication of Fry's opinions, the two schools of thought on Indian art came face to face with one another at a meeting of the Indian Section of the Royal Society of Arts. The great rift at that private gathering was exposed on the editorial page of the *London Times.* The complete minutes of the session were published in the *Journal of the Royal Society of Arts* for February 4, 1910. Chairing that session was Sir George Birdwood, while its principal speaker was E.B. Havell. Havell discussed the problems of art schools and government patronage in India.

While taking an overview of the educational scenario in India, E.B. Havell said in his paper on *Art Administration in India* that we must remember that at one time Lord Macaulay's[658] view that Indian culture was worthless prevailed over the British educational administration, this with the intention of "bringing to the benighted East that which academic Europe believed to be the higher artistic culture of Greece and Italy." It was only in about 1880, through Sir George Birdwood's writings, that different views of artistic policy in India began to prevail at the India Office.

We have to therefore give the entire credit of changing deep-set British views about Indian art, to a more liberal and acceptable outlook to Dr. Birdwood's writings.[659] Havell also made several comments on which the Chairman sometimes agreed and at other times disagreed. However, Sir George in his reply concentrated on the existence of fine art in India.[660]

He said: "As to this recently raised question of the existence in India — India of the Hindus,- of a typical, idiosyncratic and idiomatic "fine art" ... I have up to the present, and through an experience of seventy-eight years, found no (such) examples in India; and judging from my experience, I should say that India had never prized art for art itself's sake alone. I never saw a Hindu painting, sculpture, bronze ... etc., that was not first, throughout and last ... either a sacrosanct article of utility ... or a ritualised, and generally monstrous representation of the high gods, and epic heroes,...the materials, shapes, and colours of these

657 Cf. Vincent A. Smith, *History of Fine Art in India and Ceylon,* (London 1911), Introduction, where the author gives an account of the years leading up to 1910; cited in Lipsey, *op.cit.,* p. 69.

658 Thomas Babinton Macaulay (25 October 1800—25 December 1859) arrived in India (Madras) on 10 June 1834, as a member of the Supreme Council, when William Bentinck was Governor General. Although Macaulay was in India for only about four years, he was destined to impact the lives of millions of Indians. He studied a variety of subjects but was very critical and had a negative approach to Indian art, theology and sciences during his period.

659 *Journal of the Royal Society of Arts, 4 February 1910,* p. 274.

660 Lipsey, *op.cit.,* p. 69.

objects being all determined by the most arbitrary principles, and the most peremptory and stringent canons, that could have possibly been devised for the creation and perpetuation of such conventional forms ...."

"....My attention is drawn to the photograph, on my left, of an image of the Buddha as an example of Indian "fine art" .... Few of us have the faith of the new school of "Symbolists" in a symbolism that outrages artistic sensibilities and proprieties by virtually regarding art as but a framework for its myths ....and strange semeiological devices; and one might as reasonably rave over Algebraical (sic) symbols as examples of "fine art" .... The senseless similitude, in its immemorial fixed pose, is nothing more than an uninspired brazen image vacuously squinting down its nose to its thumbs, knees, and toes. A boiled suet pudding would serve equally well as a symbol of passionless purity and serenity of soul."[661]

Actually, Birdwood was looking at an Indonesian stone sculpture, a *dhyani* Buddha (Buddha seated in mediation) from Borobudur.[662]

Birdwood was drawing a parallel of the Buddha with a suet pudding, made with flour, bread crumbs, seasonings or fruits and thickened to the proper consistency by purified animal fat or suet.

This unexpected remark by Birdwood precipitated varied responses.

Walter Crane was the first to respond to Birdwood's remarks. He lauded Sir George's contribution to the welfare of the arts of India and for the idea of reorganisation of Art Schools. His own experience of the sculptured temples of south India necessitated him to rank them with the "splendid vital sculpture of the French thirteenth century." Walter Crane, while talking about sculptures of Southern temples, had also remarked that, "There were some typical figures taken from ordinary life and they were treated with great beauty, tenderness and an immense amount of imagination and character, while owing to the extraordinary richness and fantasy of the purely decorative casing, the whole effect of the temples was very impressive. It was therefore wrongly supposed that the higher imagination was not present in Indian (Hindu) art."[663]

Perhaps Birdwood did not see the inner beauty, which Walter Crane saw, and compared it to the French Art of the thirteenth century.

Coomaraswamy then spoke for perhaps fifteen minutes, criticised Birdwood regarding the display at the South Kensington Museum of which Sir George was the Curator. He said that the South Kensington Museum was " an emporium of industrial art, valuable as far as it went," but probably not able to bring about any special feeling of respect for, or any enlarged

661 *Journal of the Royal Society of Arts, 4 February 1910,* pp. 286-287. Algebraical should be Algebraic.

662 Cf. Sherman E. Lee, *A History of Far Eastern Art,*(New York, 1964), figure 152, for a representative example; cited in Lipsey, *op.cit.*, p. 70, footnote 43.

663 *Journal of the Royal Society of Arts, 4 February 1910,* pp. 288-289.

comprehension of, the expression of Indian thought and feeling in art. This criticism was followed by his thoughts on the inadequacies of art schools in India and the shortcomings of critics when they turned to Indian art. He praised Havell's work as "the beginning of a new order of things." As to Birdwood's theory that fine art did not exist in India, "this appeared to be only a question of terminology; the distinction of fine and decorative art was artificial... he could only say that if Sir George Birdwood chose to call the art of the Royal Academy or the Paris Salon, 'fine' and such a figure as the *Avaloketesvara* of Mr. Havell's book (Plate XI) 'decorative' then he preferred decorative to fine art, and regarded the decorative as a profounder revelation, a more living utterance than the fine."[664]

Havell brought the evening to a close with an observation that France and Germany (France, which had been the teacher of several generations of British artists) were far ahead of England in the size and quality of their museum collections of Indian art; furthermore educated Indians were beginning to understand and appreciate their own art. It would be "impolitic" of Great Britain to lag behind.[665]

It is interesting that at the same meeting of the Indian Section of the Royal Society of Arts views were expressed which prompt an acceptance of fine art in India. Take for instance Mr. Havell's reply to Sir George Birdwood. While thanking him, Mr. Havell said, "Art was primarily subjective, and when we talked of the limitations of Indian fine art, we were only unconsciously describing the limitations of our own ideas, our own mind, and our own knowledge."

A story that he related aptly brings out this point. This is the story of the English landscape painter Joseph Mallord William Turner (April 1775 — December 1851). JMW Turner was showing one of his wonderful pictures of a sunset, to a person who objected — "I can't see colours like that in a sunset," "Don't you wish you could?" replied Turner tersely.[666]

Mr. Robert Chisholm, former Principal of the Madras Government School, from whom Mr. Havell took over in 1884, and who had spoken at the meeting of 'Art Administration in India' after Mr. Havell, later wrote, "Fine art in a picture, as I understand it, is not only an appeal to higher emotions, suggesting higher ideals than mere language can convey, but an appeal presented in such a way as to combine executively the greatest number of truths, both literal and conventional, so that the discernment by the beholder of the hidden thought, may be awakened, undisturbed by qualities widely different from the ordinary conventional methods of presenting such truths, such as unusual or bad drawing, crude colouring, or obtrusive nothings which command attention."[667]

664 *Ibid.*, pp.289-290; also cited in Lipsey, *op.cit.*, p. 71.
665 Lipsey, *op.cit.*, p. 71; *Journal of the Royal Society of Arts, 4 February 1910,* p. 291.
666 *Journal of the Royal Society of Arts, 4 February 1910,* p. 291.
667 *Journal of the Royal Society of Arts, 4 February 1910,* p. 297.

He himself tended to agree with Birdwood regarding fine art. He thought it (Indian art) beautiful in its way and idealistic, but it was not what would be called fine art, as it was known to Europe.

He did not feel that the pictures exhibited by Mr. Havell in the School of Art, judged by these standards fell in the category of fine art. He firmly believed that Ruskin did a great deal for fine art in his day, especially Whistler's and Turner's Art, exhibited in the Tate Gallery. Chisholm did not entirely subscribe to Mr. Havell's view that in India he could advance art better by adopting native methods of teaching drawing. Yet he added that Havell's twenty years of experience and earnest study in India should not be lightly set aside. Thus he did give Havell the benefit of the doubt regarding his personal views on Indian art.[668]

Again Mr. Luther Hooper also wrote in connection with Havell's paper and said: "I take it that art, which is the expression by the craftsmen in his earnest and happy work of his true sense of proportion and colour, must of necessity be fine, whether the object in which it is wrought be a common cup and platter, a peasant's gown, a stately building, or the *statue of a goddess.*"[669]

Predictably, the minutes of this meeting, which were published in the *Journal of the Royal Society of Arts,* brought forth a response from artists and critics, some of whom had attended this meeting. They wrote a letter to the London *Times,* which contained the quintessence of Birdwood's remarks where he compared the Buddha in meditation to a pudding, and countered these remarks by their own view of Indian art:

"We find in the best art of India a lofty and adequate expression of the religious emotion of the people and of their deepest thoughts on the subject of the divine. We recognize in the Buddha type of sacred figure, one of the great artistic inspirations of the world. We hold that the existence of a distinct, a potent, and a living tradition of art is a possession of priceless value to the Indian people."[670]

The next day, an editorial appeared in the *Times* entitled *Art in India.*[671] The editorial by and large was in agreement with the "distinguished artists and critics" who had written the

668 *Ibid.,*p. 289.

669 *Ibid., p. 295.*Luther Hooper was born on 4 April 1849-died in 1932. He developed a skill in ornamental writing and illuminating; he was introduced to Mr. Henry Shaw, well-known as an antiquary and authority on old manuscripts. In 1890, Hooper began to study the history, principles and technique of weaving; and assisted in development of a handloom silk weaving firm in Ipswich. He mastered the techniques of weaving and became interested in the Art and Craft movement (about 1890). He wrote seven books on weaving. His most famous book is 'Draw Loom'. His book on silk is translated into Chinese.

670 *The Times* (London) (28 February 1910), clipping in the notebooks of AKC, family collection. Cited in Lipsey, *op.cit.,* p. 71.

671 *Ibid.,* 1 March 1910. Cited in Lipsey, *loc.cit.*

letter. It further propounded the theory that art in the West, at its worst, was entirely realistic and inexpressive, while art in the East, at its worst, was entirely symbolic and inexpressive.

Each had something to learn: to exhort expressiveness, over and above the conventional subject matter to which each was accustomed to, within its boundaries. In other words 'Expressive power' was recommended as a norm for the East and West. This would help to "understand the art of the other in spite of all differences of convention." The editorial was an attempt to ease ruffled feathers, and put things in order, but superficial.[672]

The most important result of the meeting of the Royal Society of Arts was that it encouraged William Rothenstein, Coomaraswamy, Havell, Roger Fry, the illustrious scholar W.R. Lethaby, and a few others, to found the 'India Society.' When Rothenstein penned his autobiography, *Men and Memoirs,* in the 1930s, the India Society was changed to the 'Royal Indian Society,' which took pride in the publications it sponsored and particularly for its periodical *Indian Art and Letters.*[673]

A year after its formation Coomaraswamy spelt out the Society's goals to an audience in London and talked of "the India Society, in which English and Indian and other Continental ladies and gentlemen combined for the study of the aesthetic aspects of Indian culture. We find before us not only an enormous amount of work to be undertaken but many willing workers to undertake it ... *The Discovery of Asia, then, has become to Europe no longer a piratical expedition, but a spiritual adventure.*"[674]

Ironically, Ananda Kentish Coomaraswamy (1877-1947) evolved from a person who earlier subscribed to the views of the "old guard" which believed that no "fine art" existed in India, into an astute scholar of Indian art, giving credit to the existence of "fine art" in Indian art. Let us see how this happened.

At the beginning of his study of Indian art, Coomaraswamy gathered the remarks of English writers who expressed the view that 'Gandharan sculpture' never reached the heights of Rome. Thus we find Vincent Smith in his *Early History of India* writing that while Gandharan sculpture was the best that India could offer it only "echoes ... the second-rate Roman art of the third and fourth centuries;" and again that Indian art "has scarcely at any time, essayed an

672 Lipsey, *op.ci.,* p. 71.

673 In 1910 the Birdwood controversy culminated in the foundation of the 'India Society,' later the 'Royal India Society,' to combat 'the views of the Birdwoods of this world.' Coomaraswamy played a major part in this endeavor. In 1944 The Society was granted permission to become The Royal India Society under the patronage of the Dowager Queen Mary of Teck. After partition, its name was again changed to the Royal India and Pakistan Society, and then again to the Royal India, Pakistan, and Ceylon Society. In 1966 it merged with the East India Association.

674 AKC, *Education in Ceylon,* p. 140, included in *Art and Swadeshi* (Madras 1911). Italics in the original.

By making this statement was Birdwood not admitting the fact that India no doubt had the capacity to make 'fine art' forms? He was inadvertently confuting his stand that only Industrial and decorative art existed in India. In point of fact, the proclivity of fine art was a living phenomenon. It had been taken for granted and was discovered and accepted by Art historians after other Art forms had been identified.

All in all there was a change in viewing Indian art. Even at the India Office, the Secretary of State affirmed in the despatches that the intention of the Schools of Art in India was not to force upon Indians European ideas of art, but to promote the development of Indian art and craft upon their traditional lines.[686]

Mark Sedgwick in his book *Against the Modern World Traditionalism and the Secret Intellectual History of the Twentieth Century,* believes that the comments Birdwood made about the Buddha at the meeting of the Indian Section of the Royal Society of Arts where Mr. E.B. Havell read his paper on *Art Administration in India,* were made "somewhat unwisely."[687]

With the utmost respect to Sir George Birdwood it must be said that although he did so much for the Indians and their art, he doggedly held the view that fine art did not exist in India; and perhaps he made the extremely severe, harsh and hostile comments to drive home his belief about the non-existence of fine art in India—comments which in a sense were almost self-destructive and certainly enigmatic!

686 *Journal of the Royal Society of Arts, 4 February 1910,* p. 274.

687 Sedgwick Mark, *Against the Modern Traditionalism and Secret Intellectual History of the Twentieth Century,* p. 52; Oxford University Press 20D4 (2004).

CHAPTER IX

Birdwood the Man with Éclat

One now comes to the fascinating subject of 'Letters.' Letters can be informative, fantastic, strange, colourful and exotic. The world famous letter of Abraham Lincoln to his son's teacher[688] may be inspirational to some, and pedantic to others.

The Romantic letters of Ludwig von Beethoven, Napoleon Bonaparte to Josephine, or Lord Byron's famous love letter,[689] Victor Hugo to Adele, John Keats to sweetest Fanny, may evoke a feeling of old charm.

Letters may reveal the person's typical quality; as the little-known letters of Bernard Shaw and his lady love, Mrs. Patrick Campbell, a widow and actress.[690] When she wanted to publish his passionate correspondence he retorted in his characteristic sharp manner, "I will not dear Stella, at my time of life, play the horse to your Lady Godiva."

Nearer home, there are the *Letters from a Father to His Daughter* by Jawaharlal Nehru.

They are an endeavour on the part of a forcibly absentee father, to explain his absences and at the same time play a role in Indira's life and upbringing.

Coming to the Letters to Birdwood, their multifarious nature at once bring out the many sides and aspects of his personality. He was no doubt a perspicacious personage. Recognizing his quality of quickly gaining an insight into things, he was consulted by scholars, statesmen and politicians, aficionados of art, and the common man. He was a friend to all!

In order to appreciate the many sides of George Birdwood's personality, one could divide these letters, chronologically, into groups dealing with various subjects.

688 Last lines of the last stanza:"Teach him always/to have sublime faith in himself,/because then he will have/ sublime faith in mankind." Abraham Lincoln's World famous letter to his son's Teacher.

689 'If all that I have said and done,and am still but too ready to say and do, have not sufficiently proved what my real feelings are and must be ever towards you, my love, I have no other proof to offer'—Lord Byron to his lady-love.

690 In 1898 Shaw (1856-1950) married the wealthy Charlotte Payne-Townshend. He remained with her until her death, although he was occasionally linked with other women. Mrs. Patrick Campbell played the starring role of Eliza in PYGMALION.

PRIDE IN INDIA

A letter that catches the eye is a confidential letter from the Council of Education, Kensington Museum, which was probably written in the late 1870's. It is signed with initials, all of which are not entirely legible, but the first P and the last O can be deciphered. It was therefore from Philip Cunliff-Owen (8 June 1828 to 23 March 1894) who was an organizer of exhibitions and who became Director of the South Kensington Museum in London, retiring in 1893, when the Museum was split into the Victoria and Albert Museum and the Science Museum.[691]

In this letter to Birdwood, Sir Philip Cunliff-Owen congratulates Birdwood heartily for what he is doing.

It is obvious from the letter that they were both intently interested in India. For Sir Philip writes with wanton abandon,

"At length we shall be able to do great things and no trade, no proviso of our Great Indian Empire shall now be represented. For we can take troubles to show the World what India can produce."[692]

This indeed is an esoteric letter, intended only for Birdwood's eyes.

Birdwood in the 1870's was the Curator of the South Kensington Museum. While he was criticized by some, like Ananda Coomaraswamy, of making the Museum a show-case for the Industrial Art of India, to which Birdwood was partial,[693] there were others like W. Hart who not only recognized his work in India but what he had done for the Kensington Museum.

On 6 October, about 1878,[694] Hart wrote:

"I often smile at the recollection of your zeal in whipping up the native gentry of Bombay in Horticultural and Scientific matters."

About the Museum he wrote:

"I did not know that you had given up the Museum, which, from all I have been told you must have reconstructed and brought to perfect order out of the utter chaos. I trust that your present occupation makes up, by its superior importance and lucrativeness, for this hard work with which it is accompanied and if so I congratulate you on having obtained it."[695]

Although he had officially left the Museum, his interest in it was alive and he visited it, once in a while; visits which were obviously prized. For a letter written in the early 1880's says:

691 http://en.wikipedia.org/wiki/Philip_Cunliff_Owen pp.1-2.

692 MssEur F 216/1; Letters to Birdwood, India Office Select Materials.

693 *Journal of the Royal Society of Arts, 4 February 1910,* pp. 288-89.

694 Dr. Birdwood left the Museum and joined the India Office.

695 MssEur F 216/1 Address: Westwood Landsdowne Bath, Date: 6 October [? 1878]; Signed: W. Hart.

"Early in June I called on you at the Kensington Museum and after wandering hopelessly about was informed your visits there were like angels—from there I went to the India Office with little better success, though on the premises you were not to be found......depend upon it, the next time I come to Town I shan't let you off so easily."[696]

Obviously, Birdwood was on the go, and was rather tantalising for the writer of this letter.

LITERARY ABILITY

Birdwood's literary talents were highly valued.

Edmund Backhouse Eastwick, who wrote *Handbook of the Bombay Presidency: With an Account of Bombay City*, in his letter of 11 September 1880 to Birdwood, expresses his obligation for the excellent review of his book, which appeared in *The Times* that morning. He then adds:

"Have you received from Messrs. Bradbury Agnew & Co the sheets of the 'Bombay Handbook' up to p. 268? Please insert anything you would like or instruct me what I should put in."[697]

Another scholar who shared his views with Birdwood was Colonel Henry Yule.[698] On 11 December 1888[699] while explaining why he disagreed with Birdwood on a matter regarding the removal of 'architectural valuables' (for the third time) from the India Museum and pointing out that they would suffer by each removal, he stated that in his opinion, they might suffer fatally. In the same letter he also talks about another matter.

"Did you know of Pandit Bhagwanlal Indraji, who died lately?" he asks. "He was a most remarkable man, combining the qualities of a European and an Asiatic scholar and acknowledged in a manner unexampled.

You will find an account of him in Oct. No. of the Indian Antiquary. I think it not be a fractious thing—and be more appreciated by good natives than a dozen democratic concessions of absurdity ---if the Governor of the State[700] could reflect it with respect and

696 MssEur F 216/2 Address: 13 Windsor Terraces, Plymouth; Date: 21 September [? Early 1880's]. Writer's Signature illegible.

697 MssEur F216/2: Address: 54 Hogarth Road, Cromwell Road, Date: 11 September 1880; Edmund Eastwick.

698 Later Sir Henry Yule of 'Hobson-Jobson' fame: It is a Glossary of colloquial Anglo-Indian words and phrases [new ed. London, J. Murray 1903.].

699 MssEur F 216/8; Date: 11 Dec. 1888; Signed: H. Yule.

700 The Governor of Bombay in 1888 was Lord Reay.

appreciation in a short despatch a paragraph. Do you see how this could be done? Speak to Sir James Peile[701]—as a Bombay man perhaps he would sympathize."

The same kind of trust is displayed in Mary Frere's letter to Birdwood.[702] She talks about the publication of *Old Deccan Days.* Being the fourth edition, she would like a "Review in the *Times*—not merely a notice but a Review....There is nobody (suited?) I should so much like to write it as you—*Could you possibly?*" she entreats Birdwood.

Old Deccan Days or *Hindoo Fairy Legends* has an interesting background.

In the cold months of 1865, young Mary Frere and her father, Bartle Frere,[703] British Governor of Bombay, set out in a caravan across the Deccan Province of South Central India. During their journey, Mary transcribed 24 popular Hindu folktales told to her by Anna Liberata De Souza her nursemaid about the Lingayat caste. That collection of tales, which she called *Old Deccan Days,* not only became the first Indian folklore to be published in English, but still holds interest today, and is a subject of enthusiastic curiosity.

Mary Frere continues her entreaty by asking Birdwood, "If you cannot do, you think Mr. Boulger[704] would? If so could you and would you use your influence and get him to do it?"

She wants the Review to appear before Parliament meets to get a hearing—as afterwards it will be lost and "crowded out" and Parliament news will naturally take the upper hand.

She has already sent a copy to the Editor of the *Times,* "Can you attack the Editor on the subject?" she asks. She again harps upon her request to Birdwood, "If I hear it's impossible for you to do it—I'll send Mr. D. Boulger a copy—but will not trouble him unless I hear that it is vain for me to hope for your magic pen. I know also that you know so much on the subject, that you will throw many side lights on the matter....showing the Poetry and romance of Indian life."[705]

As a postscript, which is of consequence, she writes, "Perhaps you've seen Sir W. Hunter today. My mother had a helpful little interview with him yesterday."[706]

This last remark refers to the Biography of Sir Bartle Frere's Life, which Hunter[707] undertook initially. He obviously had second thoughts about this project and confided in Birdwood.

701 14 Sir James Braithwaite Peile (1833-1906) administrator in India; was Acting Governor of Bombay during the British Raj from 27 March to 30 March 1885. Wikipedia, http//www.education.nic ....

702 MssEur F 216/9; Address: Wressil Lodge, Wimbledon Common, S.W. Date: 5 February 1889; Signed: Mary Frere

703 Henry Bartle Frere (1815-1884).

704 Demetrium Charles Bougler wrote 3 volumes of the History of China in 1886, published in London by W.H. Allen & Co.

705 Mss Eur F 216/9; Letter of Mary Frere.

706 MssEur F 216/9; Letter of Mary Frere.

707 William Wilson Hunter KCSI C.I.E. (July 1840 to February 1900) was a Scottish historian, statistician, a compiler and member of the Indian civil service. He was responsible for the *Imperial Gazetteer* to appear in 9 volumes in 1881.

William Wilson Hunter writes to Birdwood:

"I thank you heartily for your generous approval of my action in regard to Sir B.F.'s Life. My one desire is to act kindly by those good and devoted women, but to save them, the publisher and myself from the consequences of their too blind admiration of their idol. Thanks, dear friend, for your letter. It makes me feel stronger in what I am convinced is the only safe course."....[708]

In November 1889, Sir Bartle Frere's other daughter wrote to Sir George Birdwood immediately after receiving his letter. For she writes that his letter "has followed me, so I only received it this morning."[709]

She writes that her mother is in Wimbledon, and she knows that, her mother has "heard nothing at all up to last nights post" for otherwise she would have told her. She writes that she has been wondering about "this prolonged silence and if things are decided in the way you mention, I wonder still more that we have had no communication on the subject."[710]

It is certain, that she is alluding to Sir Bartle Frere's biography and William Hunter's silence regarding the matter. She is thankful nevertheless for she continues, "Whatever happens we are always most deeply grateful for all your most kind and unflagging exertions in the matter."

"I feel certain neither you nor we can blame ourselves whatever 'the issue,' on the score of having spared ourselves trouble."

"Your kindness has been a very real comfort to my mother in what has been a most trying time to her and it may be that such times are sent to us to test true friendships and make one see its full value."[711]

This letter celebrating the true friendship between the Freres and Birdwood is followed by a letter from William Hunter to Birdwood.[712]

The letter expresses his feelings, which in a sense seem diametrically opposite to those expressed earlier. For here he acknowledges his dissatisfaction in not having been able to complete his project.

William Hunter writes to Birdwood on 28 December 1889.

"I suppose you have heard from Lady Frere. She has decided, and however much I regret the event, I think she has decided wisely, to make her own arrangements for the continuation and completion of the biography. With so much literary talent in her family and with the

708 MssEur F 216/9; Address: Cherwell Edge, Oxford, Date: 5 August 1889, Signed: W.W. Hunter.

709 MssEur F 216/9; Address: Manor Down, Lamberthurst, Date: 19 November 1889, Signed: C.F. Frere

710 *Ibid.*

711 *Ibid.*

712 MssEur F 216/9; Address: Cherwell Edge, Oxford, Date: 28 December 1889, Signed: W. W. Hunter.

admirable knowledge which she and the young ladies possess regarding all events of Sir Bartle's Life after the period where I leave off, I feel sure that the work will be a success in their hands whether actually done by themselves or by some one under their direction."

"I hope Chapman and Hall pay me 200 pounds for the chapters written by me, covering the first 29 years of Sir Bartle's Life and ending with his marriage. From that point Lady Frere is really the best authority in regard to the career of her noble husband. I have asked Chapman and Hall to send the following announcement for the Column of Literary Intelligence in the *Athenaeum* and *Academy.*

'Owing to difficulties which have arisen in connection with the biography of Sir Bartle Frere, its preparation is, with the consent of the family, postponed for the present.'

So ends what has been to me a great disappointment. But under the circumstances which have arisen, and over which I have had no control, it seems the best conclusion of the matter now open to us. I thank you for all the trouble which you have taken, and remain,[713]

Sincerely Yours,
W.W. Hunter"

In the earlier letter to Birdwood,[714] William Wilson Hunter seems anxious to extricate himself from a difficult situation of penning Sir Bartle Frere's Life. In the second letter he is definitely sorry for himself.[715]

It was left to John Martineau to write *The Life and Correspondence of Sir Bartle Frere.* This was published in 1895 and John Murray was the publisher.[716]

The Freres had the highest degree of confidence in Birdwood's genuine friendship with them. They shared thoughts with him with complete nonchalance.

In 1890, Mary Frere's book entitled *England: A Valediction* was published. Writing to Sir George Birdwood on 22 October 1890,[717] she thanks Birdwood for his kindness about 'England' and for what he has done. Reading between the lines, one would imagine that he helped in promoting the book.

713 *Ibid.*

714 MssEur F 216/9, Date: 5 August 1889.

715 MssEur F 216/9, Date: 28 December 1889.

716 The book is entitled *His Life and Correspondence,* by John Martineau; Publisher: John Murray, 1895 http://en.wikipedia.org/wiki/Henry_Bartle_Frere p. 4 of 6.

717 MssEur F 216/24 1890; Address: Wessil Lodge, Wimbledon, Date: 22 October 1890; Signed: Mary Frere.

She then asks Birdwood in an informal manner, "Did I tell you the Empress Frederick[718] sent to thank me for a little copy[719] I send her—I am glad she has it—for she is so partial to what is English, isn't she?"

She refers to Sir Bartle Frere familiarly and informs Birdwood that 'Bartie' has written a short mention of Burmah[720] in its peaceful aspects which is to be published in Murray's Magazine (without his name but signed B.C.F. only) –Probably in the No. 5 number. She believes that Birdwood will like it, as she does, and be amused and interested with it.

The friendliness, trust and camaraderie are again displayed in Lady Catherine Frere's letter to Birdwood.[721]

Here she speaks about *The Book of Bombay* (by James Douglas). She supposes that the book must have been published towards the end of 1883 or beginning of 1884.[722] She comes to this conclusion as she is sure that they never saw it. She adds rather plaintively, "How it would have interested him—there were few who knew of Bombay and round about Bombay better than he did---I think had it been earlier than that some one would have sent it to my dear husband."[723]

She is curious about the reprint of the book and writes on, "There I see the Prospectus says it is to be republished in England! Who is arranging it? But the plates are I believe to be sent out to Bombay to Mr. Douglas. If it is to be republished in England who is going to publish it? But I see they say it would require 500 subscribers each taking a copy of 35 books---before it can be done. Is this number secured already?"[724]

---

718 The Princess Victoria, Princess Royal [Victoria Adelaide Mary Lousia] (b. 21 Nov. 1840 d. 5 Aug. 1901) was the eldest child and daughter of Queen Victoria of U.K. and Prince Albert. She was created Princess Royal of the United Kingdom in 1841. She became German Empress and Queen of Prussia by marriage to German Emperor Frederick III. After her husband's death, she became widely known as Empress Frederick (or in German: "Kaiser in Friedrich"). The Crown Prince Frederick and Princess were politically isolated because of their liberal and Anglophile views which clashed with the authoritarian rule of the Prussian minister-president, Otto von Bismarck. In fact their son Wilhelm favoured his German tutors in aspiring to autocratic rule and thus became alienated from his parents, suspecting them to put Britain's interests first. As a talented and gifted artist in her own right, she was patron of arts and learning, becoming one of the organizers of the 1872 Industrial Art Exhibition. http://en.wikipedia.org/wiki/Victoria_Princess_Royal

719 MssEur F 216/24 1890; The book is 16 pages.

720 Burma was annexed by Britain on 24 Feb. 1826. It was a province of India till 1937, when a separate Government was created. The Japanese occupied Burma from1942-45. It became independent in 1948.

721 MssEur F 216/24 1891; Address:Wessil Lodge, Wimbledon; Date: 3.3.91; Signed: Catherine Frere

722 *The Book of Bombay* by James Douglas was published in 1883.

723 *Ibid.*

724 *Ibid.*

To make it easier for Birdwood to answer her questions, she writes:

"Perhaps it may save trouble if you would kindly write answers of questions on enclosed sheet. Please also give me Mr. Douglas' address..."

She then asks if he has read any interesting Memoir of "our dear friend Colonel Yule," as somebody sent her a copy.

As a postscript she writes:

"Some kind friend always sends me regularly the Bombay Gazette Budget—and regularly I read it." She quotes page 8, dated Feb. 14 1891, "In an account of the annual meeting of the BBRAS with mention of the Dante's *Divinia Commedia*—surely it was there in our time? I may be wrong but I fancy I remember something."[725]

As a matter of fact, Lady Catherine Frere's hunch that Dante's *Divinia Commedia* was there in her time was quite correct, that is 1862-67 when her husband Sir Bartle Frere was Governor of Bombay and Sir George Birdwood was Honorary Secretary of the Bombay Branch of the Royal Asiatic Society from 1862-1868.

Coincidentally, at a meeting of the Bombay Branch of the Royal Asiatic Society, held on 25 August 1890,[726] the Honorary Secretary, Mr. Javerilal Umashankar Yajnik told the Managing Committee that he had received a letter dated 22 August 1890, from Sir George Birdwood, inquiring if the copy of the *Divinia Commedia* was still all right. This inquiry had prompted Mr. Yajnik to lay on the table an illuminated MS.Copy in parchment of Dante's *Divinia Commedia* that was in the possession of the Society. Mr. Yajnik had examined the copy very carefully. He had also shown it to the Hon'ble Mr. Justice Candy, Mr. Macdonell of Messrs. Wallace & Co; Mr. W. E. Hart and Mr. Westlake, who were probably not aware of the existence of this highly valuable literary piece being in the possession of the Society. They all thought that the MS., which was more than five hundred years old, was preserved in good order and condition. There were indeed some holes here and there, but the bulk of the copy was remarkably neat, clean and free of the ravages of white ants. Powdered camphor was constantly put into the body of the leaves.

Mr. Yajnik also revealed to the members a very interesting and important piece of information. He drew the attention of the Members to the July number (1890) of the *Journal of Indian Art,* where Dr. Birdwood had published a valuable Report on the *Old Records and Relics of the East India Company,* and his discovery of a copy of D'Kerhelob's *Bibliotheque Orientale* in a Parsee godown in Bombay. In this Journal, he had also made a reference to the MS. Copy of the *Divinia Commedia.* This would be most significantly brought out in his own words.

725 MssEur F 216/24 1891,Letter signed : Catherine Frere.

726 *Journal of the Royal Asiatic Society: 1890-94, XLVIII,* PROCEEDINGS OF THE B.B.R.A.S. (August 1889—May1891), *"AN ILLUMINATED M.S. COPY OF DANTE DIVINIA COMMEDIA,* pp. vii-viii.

"On becoming Secretary to the Bombay Branch of the Royal Asiatic Society, I went up under the roof of the Town Hall and began kicking up my heels among the heaps of rubbish lying all about the place, just on the chance of stumbling on some 'hid treasure,' when I presently struck 'thud' against a large vellum quarto. It turned out to be an illuminated MS. of Dante's poems, with a miniature of the poet, all painted within thirty years of his death, and certified by the Secretary of the Ambrosia Library at Milan to be one of the noblest M.S.S. of Dante extant. There was no record of the volume to be traced anywhere until going back for years in the minute-books of my predecessors I found that it has been presented to the Society in, if I remember rightly, 1827, by the Hon'ble Mountstuart Elphinstone. It is worth a lakh of rupees and I made a regular shrine of it, showing it to distinguish strangers. Every learned Jesuit that passed through Bombay used to be shown it; and I recollect one of them saying that it was absolutely priceless, and that 10,000 pounds would be given for it at once in Italy."[727]

This then is the invaluable contribution that Birdwood made to the Society, for as Yajnik read in his Report,

"The inside of the leather binding has on it an inscription in Italian, of which Dr. DaCuhna has kindly furnished the following translation: "Magnificent book in parchment of the *Divinia Commedia* of Dante Alighieri which equals in preservation and beauty those existing in the leading libraries of Europe, especially that existing in the Ambrosian Library of Milan, with which it has been compared. The form of characters shows that its date is near the middle of the XIV Century—that is, thirty years after the death of Dante, which took place in 1321 at the age of 56. The miniatures at the head of each canto allude to the contents of each canto, and indicate the style of art of the XIV Century in a way that renders this book highly precious."[728]

On 5 March 1891, W.R. Macdonell formerly scholar of Balliol College, Oxford read a paper on this MSS.[729]

Getting back to the Frere Ladies, they were literarily inclined. For instance, the Girton College Library[730] has rare or special collections of published materials that complement the manuscript holdings in their (Girton's) archives. These provide insights into the lives and

727 *Ibid.,* It is reported that in 1930, the Italian government under Benito Mussolini offered the Society one million pounds, calling the book a national treasure. Mussolini believed that the offer could not be refused, but to his shock, the Society turned down his request stating that it was donated by an ex-member of the Society and hence their property. Wikipedia, Asiatic Society of Mumbai. http://www.enotes.com/topic/Asiatic_Society_of_Mumbai

728 Proceedings B.B.R.A.S. 1889-1891, pp. vii-viii.

729 *JBBRAS,* 1890-94, pp. 56-70.

730 Girton College Library, Huntingdon Road, Cambridge CB3 OJG. Girton College Library:The Special Collections. http://www-lib.girton.cam.ac.uk/special/index.html

scholarship of their previous owners, in addition to their intrinsic values as scholarly texts. Of particular note is Mary Frere's collection of Hebrew and Samaritan texts and manuscripts. *The Girton Review,* Lent Term, 1913, notes, "An interesting collection of about 200 Hebrew books (including some Samaritan MSS.) was made to the College Library last summer under the will of Mary Frere. Several volumes are valuable editions ... [The bequest also includes] some Jewish marriage certificates of mediaeval times having borders in symbolic illumination."[731]

With these scholarly inclinations, it is but natural that the Frere ladies should correspond with Sir George Birdwood fairly regularly. What is more, they had a common bond. Their love for India, and particularly Bombay is seen in their letters. This is apparent in Mary Frere's Title page of her book *Old Deccan Days or Hindoo Legends current in Southern India.* It reads:

THESE STORIES,
ORIGINALLY DEDICATED TO
THE LITTLE SISTER
FOR WHOM THEY WERE WRITTEN
I Dedicate
TO THOSE IN ENGLAND WHO LOVE INDIA
AND TO THOSE IN INDIA WHO LOVE ENGLAND[732]

Many persons of renown sought Sir George Birdwood's advice, at the same time recognizing his service to India.

On 2 January 1891, the Hon. Javerilal Umashankar Yajnik had written to Birdwood with concern regarding his "weak state of health;" and yet he had worked with all the vigour of mind in producing a monograph in two issues of the *Journal of Indian Art* for October and January, copies of which he sent to him.[733] Birdwood writes,

"As one reads the monogram(sic)[734] one can not help thinking that you have done a real service towards connecting the cordial relations between the Paramount Power and our (?benign) and loyal feudatories of India by this permanent record of the very beautiful objects of Indian Art, which out of the fullness(?) of their hearts and the overflow of their loyal feelings they presented to H.R.H. the Prince of Wales regardless of the cost and trouble."[735]

---

731 *Ibid.*

732 Title Page, *Old Deccan Days or, Hindoo Fairy Legends current in Southern India;* London, J. Murray, 1868.

733 MssEur F 216/44; Address BBRAS's Society Rooms, Town Hall; Date: 2 January 1891; Signed: Javerilal U. Yajnik.

734 Should read as monograph. Where I have put ?-question marks, the word is indecipherable and could be interpreted as the possible word that I have given the text.

735 MssEur F 216/44, *Ibid.*

Yajnik hopes that these unique specimens of Art Treasures of India will remind His Royal Highness and members of his Royal Household about their visit to India, which occasioned jubilation among the 250 million people.

He goes on to commend Birdwood on his Introduction in the Journal about the Art Collection, especially in presenting the most charming reading about the Gold Inlay from Mysore which is a piece of exquisite workmanship, so also the Madura screen and Art work from Ahmedabad.

He requests Birdwood to send if possible, a complete set of Jaipur portfolios of architecture. He admits rather modestly that the cost of the portfolio is too big for the resources of the Society; then adds what encouraged him to ask for this favour, "The deep and abiding interest you have in the welfare of our Society emboldens me to make this request to you."[736]

Doubtless, Mr. Yajnik knew Dr. Birdwood well enough, for in his next paragraph he broaches the subject of presents of books sent to scholars in India by the India Office. He writes that he would be specially obliged if his name could be entered in the list of those to whom such presents are sent.[737]

On 26 March 1892[738] Yajnik wrote to Birdwood again to thank him for two favours of the 12 and 26 February. Birdwood's writing to Col. S.S. Jacob at Jaipur asking him to get H.H. Maharaja to present a copy of the family's Jaipur Portfolio and also for putting his name on the List of Scholars in India and Europe enabling him to procure publications by the India Office.

In the same letter he expresses his happiness that his brother Mr. Justice Birdwood has succeeded Sir Raymond West as Judicial Member of the Government of Bombay. He then states that the President of the Asiatic Society has generally been a member of the Executive Government. He gives the examples of Mr. Erskine, Mr. Frere and Mr. Gibbs, who were Presidents while they were members of the Executive Government. He has accordingly requested his brother to accept the President's place on Sir Raymond West's retirement; but his brother continues to hesitate.

Here is an example of one scholar, Dr. Birdwood, recognizing another and helping him with utmost sincerity.

---

736 *Ibid.*

737 *Ibid.*

738 MssEur F 216/44; Address: BBRASociety's Rooms, Town Hall, Date: 26 March 1892; Signed: Javerilal U. Yajnik.

JOURNALISM

Recognizing his literary skills *The Graphic* wrote to Birdwood on 3 October 1889,[739] conveying their new proposal in Journalism.[740]

They had worked out a scheme whereby instead of the ordinary anonymous letters that had hitherto appeared in their daily papers, they now intended having short articles written by people of such eminence that their words would at once command public attention and respect.

The Manager of the paper writes:

"I suggest that you should occasionally write giving your opinions on matters concerning which you possess a special knowledge to be published in our paper with your name attached."

She continues humbly, "Having originated *The Graphic* and been its active Manager since its foundation I trust you may consider my services have been of some value to the advancement of art and industry and on this ground I venture to enlist your sympathy and support."

This no doubt was an explicit recognition of Birdwood's immense knowledge of Industrial Arts.

On 20 November of the same year (1889), the editor of *The Daily Graphic* wrote to him.[741]

The editor suggested, "When any subject of public interest with which you are especially conversant, or in which you are particularly interested, comes to the front, we will communicate with you, or you with us, with regard to writing a signed article or letter on question."

"What we prefer from you would be some communication on an Indian subject, say on Indian art or literature, with which your name is so closely connected."

These letters themselves are proof of the tremendous respect that he commanded from the world of Journalism.

---

739 MssEur F 216/13; Address: The Graphic, 190 STRAND, LONDON; Date: 3 October 1889, Signed: Miriam L. Thomas.

740 About the same time the Director ofThe Graphic , William L. Thomas had sent the history of the paper. The paper had undergone constant enlargement and improvement. In 1869, it consisted of 24 pages produced at an annual cost of 54,000 pounds; now (1889) there were 36 pages at 74,000 pounds. Their proposal was to publish a daily newspaper distant from "THE GRAPHIC" with independent literary, artistic and engraving staff of its own , printed and published in a separate building. Special articles would be signed by the writers, who would be persons of well-known social or political distinction and would be prominent features.Mss.Eur F 216/13 Oct-Nov.1889.

741 MssEur F 216/13; Address: The Daily Graphic, Milford House, Milford Lane, Strand, London, W.C., Date: 20 November 1889; Signed: Heath Joyce; Editorial Department.

Earlier he in his own right had helped India. In order to understand this, we have to trace briefly the history of Indian Journalism. This can be traced back to 1780, when during the first three decades, it remained confined to the English language. Around 1785, an English weekly, *The Calcutta Gazette,* introduced a column in Persian devoted to news from Delhi and the Royal Court at the Red Fort.

The first Urdu paper, the *Jam-i-Jahan, Numa* was launched in Calcutta. This launch made it possible for the Urdu language press to play a dominant role for many years to come. The delay in its introduction is blamed on the repressive policy of the East India Company, especially against such English weeklies that ventured to criticise it.

Before the 1857 War of Independence, interest in politics was casual. Later the *Lahore Chronicle* (11 July 1857) speaks of Indian language papers engaging themselves in treasonable and subversive activity.

In June 1857, the Governor-General imposed an Act No. XV of 1857 to regulate the establishment of printing presses and to restrain circulation of printed books and papers. However, Urdu newspapers adopted an anti-British and pro-1857 attitude throughout the struggle. The pattern for the nationalist press was thus set in 1857.

This resulted in *The Pioneer* and a few other Anglo-Indian papers becoming extremely apprehensive of the Indian language papers, so much so, that they launched a campaign for curbing them. Their outcries led to the enactment of the Vernacular Press Act in 1878, which virtually gagged the politically conscious newspapers.

In 1877, Sir George Birdwood was in a position to certify that the "Native Press" of India, was commendably loyal. The criticism then became so feeble that the Duke of Buckingham, Governor of Madras, remarked that the "Offences complained of were statements of unpalatable truths in strong language." But the bureaucracy was not expected to tolerate truths that were not only unpalatable, but also expressed in strong language. The Indian press remained suspect despite its subdued tone. The Vernacular Press Act was repealed in 1882.[742]

Perhaps the action of repealing the Act was in no small measure due to Sir George Birdwood's intervention.

Birdwood might indeed have helped the Indian press, nevertheless, his old Bombay friend Robert Knight (1825-1890), who replaced George Buist in 1857 as editor of the *Bombay Times and Journal of Commerce,*[743] was a fearless critic of the Raj. He was a pioneer editor who wrote for the Indian cause. He exposed the falsehood of the so-called omniscience and omnipotence of the empire. He levelled his criticism through the papers that he created—the *Times of India* in Bombay and the *Statesman* in Calcutta. He was chiefly responsible for making the press a

742 Journalism, pp.1-7, http://www.education.nic.in/cd50years/u/47/3y/473Y0701.htm

743 Hirschmann, Edwin, *Robert Knight Reforming Editor in Victorian India,* Oxford University Press, New Delhi, 2008; pp.22-23.

'fourth estate' in India, a part of the political process. He provoked the Raj and thereby his countrymen by spreading ideas and the English-educated Indians lapped these up. This led to the emerging dissent of the British Raj and promoted Indian nationalism.

Birdwood shared Robert Knight's views on a number of key principles. This can be ascertained by studying and making a comparison of their opinions through their actions and writing.

- Knight's view after the War of Independence of 1857 was that Britain's mission in India 'is to civilize and not destroy her',[744] and "The best way for a foreign power to seek the reformation of a people is to teach them to reform themselves...."[745] Again in the *Bombay Times* issue of 19 May 1857, Knight denounced 'the cowardly massacre of defenceless women and children' but concluded 'Let the thought of bloody retaliation, which invariably arises in one's mind, give place to the memory that these men know not what they do.'[746] The same sort of thoughts are reflected in Birdwood's writings in *Sva* when he condemns the dastardly act of the killing of a defenceless Afzal Khan by Shivaji—but at the same time he sympathises with the great Mahratta warrior and justifies the act as the only recourse that he had in the circumstances at that time. "The deed was damnable; but Sivaji in truth and sincerity, deemed it high and worthy, and the last sacrifice of his devout patriotism to the welfare of his sacrosanct country."[747]
- Like Knight, Birdwood had a soft spot for the Maharajas. While Knight defended the Maharajas' cases through his writings,[748] Birdwood befriended the Maharajas and stood to gain especially in the International Industrial Exhibitions. The Maharajas contributed through native artists in their states, to add to the glamour of the exhibitions through the artistic representations.
- Both were interested in the Indigo Planters of Bengal.[749] While Knight assailed the Indigo planters for gross abuses against the peasants or *ryots* who were at the mercy of the planters,

744 *Bombay Times,* 12 and 15 May 1857 (as reprinted in *Bombay Times Overland Summary* of 27 May; cited in Hirschmann, Edwin, *op.cit.,* p.33.

745 *Bombay Times,* 10 August 1857, cited in Hirschmann, Edwin, *op.cit.,* p. 33.

746 *Ibid.,* p. 33.

747 *Sva; The Mahratta Plough,* p. 52.

748 The Raj was a conglomerate of about six hundred Indian states, some small others large with their traditional princes; called 'native states' or 'princely states'; they covered about two-fifths of India and held about one third of its people. The princes of a little more than forty states unwittingly signed 'alliances' with the British, little knowing that they had signed away their independence. Knight was against Governor-General Dalhousie's Doctrine of Lapse, his annexation of Oudh in 1856 and Policy towards Hyderabad. He was a defender of princes, a champion of justice. Hirschmann, Edwin, *op. cit.,*pp. 32-45.

749 Hirschmann, *op.cit.,* pp. 45-50 for Knight: Champion of Peasants and Rural Development.

Birdwood was interested in promoting the Indigo product for commercial reasons;[750] nor did he dismiss the peasants lightly, in fact he admired their simple life-style as is seen in his 'Mahratta Plough.'

- As Sheriff of Bombay, Birdwood played an active part in the civic affairs of Bombay—a city which he loved and revered. Knight also played an active role in Bombay's commercial and civic affairs.[751]

Though Knight and Birdwood were friends, they did not always see eye to eye on some issues. This came to light in 1914, when S.K. Ratcliff, a retired editor of the *Statesman* was speaking to the East India Association of London on 'The Press in India.' During this speech, he praised Knight as 'the ablest Englishman who has so far devoted himself to a career of journalism in India.' In the audience that day, was the eighty-two year old Dr. George Birdwood, who after Ratcliff's talk recalled how he had filled in as *Bombay Times* editor for three weeks while Knight was ill with fever. But he mischievously changed the paper's policy with an editorial favouring the politics of Pope Pius IX, where Knight had supported Garibaldi and the Italian nationalists. His editorship ended abruptly.

"When, on the paper being read to Knight, he at once sprang out of his bed in Colaba, and sending for a buggy while he dressed, galloped of in it to the Fort, and presently had literally emptied me out of the editorial chair, and all but literally kicked me downstairs—a very steep, dark flight—into Medows Street,"[752] Birdwood confided.

Knight gave up the editorial control of the *Times of India* on 1 March 1864. During his seven years as editor, he had built a vigorous, thoughtful and conscientious newspaper that had roused Bombay and its governing authorities.[753] Seventeen years after he had landed in Bombay as a non-descript shop manager, he transformed into a person of importance, an influential editor and co-owner of the city's outstanding newspaper.

However, in 1875, Knight fell out with Lord Northbrook's Council. On 8 July 1875, Northbrook's Council issued a government resolution forbidding ownership or management of the press by government officers, to end any ambiguity or this matter.[754]

Much to Knight's relief, in September 1875 Northbrook told Lord Salisbury, Secretary of State, that he wished to be replaced by the end of the year, due to health and family concerns.

750 *GD,* vol. 38 of 1859, pp. 75-77.

751 Hirschmann,*op.cit.,*pp. 77-78. Knight claimed credit for preventing a split in the Bombay Chamber of Commerce in 1861. He founded a 'Strangers' Home' for destitute Europeans and organized and served as first Secretary of a 'Strangers' Friend Society' to extinguish loaferism in Bombay altogether. This he did by winning over half a dozen merchants from whom he received endowments.

752 *Asiatic Review,* New Series, vol. 5 (July 1914), pp. 199-215; cited in Hirschmann, *op.cit.,* pp. 78-79.

753 Hirschmann, *op. cit.,* pp. 79-80.

754 *India, Home Dept. Public Proceedings,* August 1875, entry No. 6, Res. Entry nos.19-1134; cited in Hirschmann, *op.cit.,* pp.146-148.

The Conservatives appointed Lord Robert Lytton, who was socially and diplomatically superior to his predecessor, and also possessing a literary background.[755]

Two months after Lytton became viceroy, his private secretary Owen Tudor Burne, sent a letter to nine leading European editors expressing for better government-press relations.

Knight urged for a critical press within the British Raj. He proposed an official press bureau to review the press and provide the needed information. It would be headed by a sympathetic man, not an official monitor, and certainly not a censor, but more of a go-between.

Hirschmann believes that Knight was perhaps angling for the job himself. His long-lived Bombay friend Dr. George Birdwood proposed Knight as director. Although, when questioned about the intention, he is said to have coyly responded 'We intended nothing of the kind.'[756]

Ironically, though both Birdwood and Knight were pro-Indian, Knight sadly became a prophet without Honour. Although Indians will ever remain grateful to him, Knight was omitted from all histories of British India and all biographical dictionaries. This is because Knight's provocative editorial views brought upon him the enmity of his Anglo-Indian countrymen, including three consecutive Viceroys;[757] Earl of Dalhousie, (12 January 1848 to 28 February 1856)[758]; The Viscount Canning (28 February 1856 to 1 November 1858 and again as Viceroy 1 November 1858 to 21 March 1862)[759] and Lord Northbrook (13 May 1872 to 12 April 1876).[760]

Birdwood on the other hand was highly respected in India and later in England both by Indians and his countrymen. Obviously Birdwood was more skilled at building human relations, both with Englishmen and Indians.

755 *Ibid.*,p. 147.

756 *Statesman,* 3 February, 1877; cited in Hirshmann, *op.cit.,* p. 148.

757 Hirschmann, *op. cit.,* preface, p. ix. After the Proclamation of Queen Victoria, Governor-Generals were known as Viceroys of India.

758 Knight disapproved of the arbitrary annexation of Jhansi,and the rejection by Lord Dalhousie of the Hindu practice of adoption of an heir by the childless royal couple.*B.T.,* 15 January 1858, cited in Hirshmann, *op. cit.,* p. 35. Similarly, Dalhousie's annexation of Bhonsle Raja's Nagpur in 1853, (p. 41). Knight wrote about Dalhousie's Doctrine of Lapse (p. 42). His policy in Hyderabad (1853) of occupying the richest districts (p. 43-44) and 1856—annexation of Oudh (p. 43).

759 Knight was troubled that despite the Queen's Proclamation and promises, Lord Canning did nothing for the Bhonsle family of Nagpur (Hirshmannn, *op. cit.,* p. 43). He could not have approved of Lord Canning declaring Britain as the 'paramount power' in India, heir to the collapsed Mughal empire and to its claims of allegiance (p. 151). The British flaunting their power could not have appealed to a critical Knight.

760 Lord Northbrook's Council was responsible for the ouster of Knight from the government with a resolution on 8 July 1875 forbidding ownership or management of the press by government officers (*Ibid.,* p. 146).

Continuing Birdwood's association with journalism, it may be noted that Birdwood's writings were widely read, mused and mulled over. This is particularly noticeable in two letters from William Digby of the Indian Political Agency.[761] In the first letter he encloses a cutting of that day's *Times*, underlined with a blue pencil so as to delight Birdwood. After reading Birdwood's description of the Maharattas, he comments that it seems to have made an impact on "the first military people of the day." (Germans).

In the second letter Digby makes it clear that *The Times* (Berlin suggestion) which entailed the proposal to enlist the Maharattas for service in East Africa had resulted after the Germans had read Birdwood's article (A.2.R.) on the Mahrattas. It is obvious that Birdwood had praised the Mahrattas, for Digby writes in the first letter, "After what you have written about the Mahratta it should be gratifying to you to see his prowess recognised in such an unmistakable manner by the first military people."

"But is such a project as the Germans Desire feasible? Will the law of India allow foreign recruitment of the kind aimed at?"

Regarding Digby's feeling that Birdwood's article had incited the idea amongst the Germans is even more reassuring as he states, "I am glad to have my idea confirmed by your own shrewd supposition......"[762]

Although the thoughts expressed by the Germans seem far-fetched and impractical; the letter to Birdwood by Alfred Knott[763] of the India Office, bears a note of genuine appreciation about the Mahratta country. He writes that he has just read Birdwood's defence of "The Mahratta Plough" and he believes it is admirable. He is pleased beyond measure with Birdwood's intimate knowledge of the country and the charming way in which he describes it. He calls him a poet.

761 Letter 1. Mss Eur F216/8; Address: Indian Political Agency, 25 Graven Street, Strand, London. Date: 9.xi.1888; Signed Digby.

Letter 2. Mss Eur F/8; Address: Coromandel, Woodville Gardens, Ealing W. Date: 11/xi.1888;Signed:Digby.

William Digby (1849-1904) was a British author, journalist and humanitarian. He came to India in 1871. Digby witnessed the Great Famine of 1876-78. He was an outspoken critic of the British Government's India policy regarding failure to provide effective famine relief. He advocated full economic and racial equality, and eventually Self-Government for the Indians. He became a strong advocate of constitutional reform and acted as an unofficial guide to Indian National Congress Leaders visiting London. He was able to get Charles Bradlaugh (1833-1891), a political activist who took a strong interest in India, to attend the Fifth INC Conference held in Bombay in 1889. Digby died in 1904. Gandhiji wrote an obituary in the *Indian Opinion* on 29 October 1904; "By the death of William Digby CIE, India has lost a champion, whom it will be difficult to replace. His advocacy of the Indian cause was strenuous and well-informed....By his voluminous writings, the late Mr. Digby ever kept the different Indian questions before the public." http://en.wikipedia.org/wiki/WilliamDigby(writer) pp. 1-4

762 *Ibid.*

763 Mss Eur F 216/8 23-106 Address: India Office, Whitehall S.W. Date: 24/10/88; Signed : Alfred Knott.

Likewise in India, Jehangeer Dosabhoy Framjee was another admirer of Birdwood's "The Mahratta Plough," which appeared in the *Asiatic Quarterly Review.* He admits that he read it with great pleasure and interest. M.M. Bhownugree has suggested to Rakhamabai to translate it in Marathi, he writes.[764]

Birdwood would always lend a receptive hearing to the problems of friends. Jehangeer Dosabhoy Framjee writes in the same letter, "My father sends you his affectionate regards. Though retired from service, he still takes the same active part in the Municipal Government of the City—and in other public affairs. The question of a grant of land to him as a reward for his services is still hanging fire on account of the official red-tapeism."[765]

Take again Alfred Knott's letter.[766] He writes that he feels somewhat 'afraid' to submit his own verses for Birdwood's perusal. He then talks about his large accumulation of poems that he fears might be lost to oblivion, as he has no literary influence. He recognises that he really needs to know an editor of a magazine to give him a foothold. Unfortunately, he admits, that he has no means of introduction to either a publisher or editor who would help him. He realizes at the same time that it is futile for an unknown poet to send contributions, as he knows that these poems will be cast aside unread.

The gratifying part of this melancholy story is that Alfred Knott's poems were not lost in oblivion. His poems were finally published. They are called *The Three Spirits and other Poems* by Alfred Knott. This 100-page book is available even today and is published under the scheme of reviving meritorious literature of the past centuries. The Publisher is BiblioLife. Birdwood undoubtedly helped in getting the poems published at that time. Birdwood seemed to have discreetly assisted in this case as he did with his other friends.

Another case of a person benefitting from Birdwood's friendship is revealed in a telegram by Sir Philip Owen to Birdwood at the India Office, Whitehall. Philip Owen's genuine interest in India is shared with Birdwood, as is revealed cryptically in the telegram. It reads:

"Very many thanks for persistent interest and anxious desire for accomplishment of your wishes that services you and others consider important to India should be officially and permanently recognized."

764 Mss Eur F 216/8; Address: Peddar Road, Bombay, Date: 23 November 1888. Signed : Jehangeer Dosabhoy Framjee.

765 *Ibid.,* "Jehangeer's father Dosabhoy Framjee Karaka, who rose to become Chairman of the Bombay Municipal Corporation, was in the second half of the nineteenth century a distinguished exponent of the intellectual trend. In what was to become an influential text, he averred that the 'effect of English education upon the Parsis generally will be to raise them still higher in the scale of civilization.'(Karaka, 1884, repr. 2002/303) ; Wadia Rusheed, *IN THE EIGHTEENTH AND NINETEENTH CENTURIES: Bombay Parsi Merchants,* pp. 120-121 IN *"PARSIS IN INDIA AND DIASPORA,"* By John R. Hinnells, Allan Williams.

766 Mss Eur F 216/8 23-106 Address: India Office, Whitehall S.W. Date: 24/10/88; Signed: Alfred Knott.

Here Philip Owen is thanking Birdwood for supporting his work for India, for the next page reads:

"G [George] was the means of getting the C.I.E."—Companion of the Order of the Indian Empire, which honour he received from the British Empire.[767]

While William Digby's two letters regarding the Maharattas record an unexpected curious effect; yet together with the letters of Alfred Knott and Jehangeer Dosabhoy Framjee they exemplify a true respect for Birdwood's writings. Yet another interesting letter written by Ivor Newton (?) to Sir George Birdwood[768] makes an in depth study of the article "The Mahratta Plough." While expressing his deepest interest in the article "The Mahratta Plough", because of its analogy with then Arts of India, he would have liked to have read more about Shivaji, as his knowledge of Indian History and its heroes is 'very alright.' He candidly writes, "The plea for Indian Agriculture I am afraid will fall on ears that are equally deaf to the true intentions and accomplishments of Indian Art. We Westerners will insist upon answering all things by the standard that seems to fit the best. We will forget the differences of race and of climate and the surroundings that to build up the genius of a people in our insane desire to better a people in its Art (for that is the subject with which I am best acquainted) we only propagate a bastard mixture of the worst phases of both peoples when I think of the impertinence of our attempting to improve Indian Art which is complete and perfect from its own stand point, it makes me extremely angry, at the same time extremely sorrowful from the fact that a dominant race such as ours bringing with it many beneficial influences at the same time brings many (I may say all) of the evils of our modern civilization. But we have much to be thankful for when such as yourself who have great knowledge and personal experience (which always carries weight) protest against our impolitic and disastrous influence. I am quite sure that all (those) who read your article even if unacquainted with the subject will be influenced by the conviction of truth it carries with it."

He goes on to suggest, "Why don't you write an article on Indian Art from the same point of view and not let it be taken under the wing of weak kneed doctrinaires who will only excite contempt by their feverish shrieking (this private). I have formed the Committee of which Mr. F. Shields is a member, but I fear I shall not be able to give the matter the attention it deserves. I do not know what knowledge they possess of the subject, it may do some good if it only

767 The date of the Telegram is not clear. It was sent when Birdwood was in the India Office—1871-1902. (After 1879).

768 Mss Eur F 216/9; Address: Ettrick House, Steele's Road N.W. Date:23 November 1888; Signed Ivor Newton (not very legible). Ivor Newton was probably a British Officer who was in India; for in the very first line of his letter he says that, "The moving from the country and getting settled here have prevented me from writing to you about the Article on 'The Plough'." From his letter wherein he says he is best acquainted with Art, we may deduce that he probably belonged to 'The Royal Academy of Arts (1769-1904).

prevents India from becoming the Tom Tiddlers ground[769] of South Kensington certificated mastery as the worst who are the result of another form of competitive examination."[770]

He then speaks of Lock, who tells him that Birdwood is likely to call on him soon. He says he may be there. He adds that he is writing to Schellendorf to ask him to meet him when he has time for he shall ask him if he can get any information as to the 'Order'[771] as he does not intend to let it drop.

This letter candidly portrays that there were two groups—one genuinely interested and recognizing the Art of India, another trying to impose British norms on Indian Art.[772]

In the article on "The Mahratta Plough", which was originally written to vindicate the criticism of the Indigenous plough, Birdwood cleverly builds up a convincing defence for his theory justifying the use of the native plough. He proves that it is perfectly adapted to the conditions of the land, life and labour in basaltic Maharashtra. He believes that in all probability, in the course of secular trade between the East and West, the characteristic Maharatta drill ploughs, the *moghar* and *pabhar,* were introduced into Western India from Chaldea.[773]

The Mahratta *rayat* or cultivator adapted himself to his surrounding conditions—of jagged *Ghats* (mountains), rivers and sylvan streams, the furious monsoons and the historical black soil of the Deccan.

Slowly but gradually, he perfected his plough—the product of three thousand years' experience and managed to harness the soil to yield magical results, not once but twice in each year.

He then talks about his own practical experience "in flower, fruit and field cultivation" all the time that he was in Bombay.[774]

He is convinced that "the doctrinaire outcry against native agriculture from the days of Tennant[775] and James Mill downwards as unscientific and wasteful, is as ignorant and insular

769 Tom Tiddlers Ground is an ancient children's game in which "Tom Tiddler" stands on a heap of stones,gravel etc. other players rush to the heap crying "Here I am on Tom Tiddler's ground" while Tom tries to capture the invaders or keep them off. By extension the phrase has come to mean one who is easily taken advantage of. In modern English it is used as a euphemism for having an uncertain status; e.g. "I asked her why her performance review was late and I could tell she was on Tom Tiddler's Ground." Wikipedia http://en.wikipediaorg/wiki/Tom_Tidler's_Ground

770 Mss Eur F 216/9; Date: 23 November 1888; Signed: Ivor Newton (?).*Ibid.*

771 'Companion of the Order of the Indian Empire"

772 For Birdwood's view on the Art of India, refer to Chapter VI.

773 *Sva, "The Mahratta Plough,* p. 37.

774 *Ibid.,* p. 64.

775 He is probably referring to Rev. William Tennant.

as is the stereotyped depreciation of the Industrial arts of India, by the same writers and in the reports on the earlier International Exhibitions held in Europe."[776]

He feels that the introduction of the machinery of western agriculture into India is quite impossible in the present economic condition of the country.[777] At present simple agricultural life without the restless, hustling spirit of unhealthy competition is best suited to the Indians. It is the beneficent co-operative rural life whereon the whole system of the Hindus has been immemorially based.

Change will come with the economic advancement of the twentieth century but these will be gradual, through self-evolved changes of internal consciousness of the race of Brahmanical Hindus.[778]

"As of now," Birdwood writes, "the Indian plough is part and parcel of a fixed crystallised life."[779]

These are the facts that prompt Ivor Newton to say that he read the essay "with the deepest interest because of its analogy with the Art of India."[780]

British values of Art cannot be forced or imposed on Indian Art, nor can Indian Art be appreciated through biased western eyes. This is the very reason that urges Newton to say, "Why don't you write an article on Indian Art from the same point of view?"[781] (as the article on the Indian plough).

While speaking of the Indian plough, one might add that in the realm of agriculture, Sir George Birdwood wrote an important article on the carrot seed. This is entitled *"Memorandum of the purchase in Europe of Carrot Seed for the purposes of famine relief in Northern India: 1896."* This was written in London from the India Office in 1897.[782] It may be noted that William Digby, a good friend of Birdwood, witnessed the Great Famine of 1876-78 and involved himself as the Honorary Secretary of the Executive Committee of the Famine Relief Fund. In 1878 he wrote an extensive book about the famine titled "*The Famine Campaign in Southern India,* Vol. I & Vol. II. We have already seen that he had written to Birdwood in 1888.[783]

776 *Ibid., art.cit.,* p. 64.

777 *Ibid.,* pp. 74-75.

778 *Ibid.,* p. 74.

779 *Ibid.,* pp. 75-76.

780 Mss Eur F 216/9; Address: Ettrick House, Steele's Road, N.W. Date: 23 Nov. 1888; Signed: Ivor Newton (not legible).

781 *Ibid.*

782 *IOR/V/27/516/1 1897.* Part of Agriculture Fruit and Vegetables *IOR/V/27/516 1888-1952.*

783 Mss Eur F 216/8; Dates: 9.xi.1888 and 11/xi/1888.

BIRDWOOD AND ROYALTY

Dr. George Birdwood with his charismatic personality had garnered so much respect in society that even the Royalty looked upon him with awe.

Some of the "certificates" granted to Dr. George Birdwood speak eloquently of his immense capability. Take for instance the certificate from the Duke of Argll (Secretary of State for India) dated 21 June 1870. This was when Dr. Birdwood was seeking the office of Registrar to the London University.[784] Here His Grace says:

"I have much pleasure in stating that the service of Dr. Birdwood in India (where the last appointment which he held was that of Registrar of the Bombay University) were of a highly distinguished character, and have recently been acknowledged by the Secretary of State in Council."

The Letter from the Prince of Wales regarding the "Handbook to the Indian Court," Paris 1878, is worth recording:

Sandringham, Norfolk
January 27, 1879

My dear Birdwood,

The Paris Exhibition being now on end, I am anxious to convey to you the expression of my warm thanks for the valuable services which you have been so good as to render to the Royal Commission in connection with the Indian Section. These services were of the greatest assistance to the members of that Committee in enabling them to overcome the difficulties which they encountered and in lightening their labours.

I wish to take this opportunity of saying that I cannot speak in too high a sense of the Handbook which you brought out on India. It is universally acknowledged to be a work of importance and utility, and bears witness not only to the vast knowledge of art and correct judgment of the just means of promoting the highest development of the Industries of India which you possess, but it contains also some very valuable and novel contributions to the

784 There are likewise certificates of the highest order from Sir H.B.E. Frere and Sir Alexander Grant, Principal of the University of Edinburgh. The well-known Mr. Hunter of Bombay, also bore testimony to the great ability and thorough earnestness with which Dr. Birdwood carried on his professional duties.
William, F.B. (William Fergusson Beatson Laurie), 'Sketches of some distinguished Anglo-Indians,' pp. 36-39. APPENDICES 393-394.

history of Indian and Eastern Commerce and, as such, it is much appreciated by learned foreigners and by the best judges at home.

Although but a slight return for the care and industry you have bestowed on the work, I propose to place the copy-right of the Handbook at you disposal, and it will give me much pleasure to hear you accept my offer.

In conclusion, I have great satisfaction in sending you a print of myself, with my autograph attached to it.

Believe me, my dear Dr. Birdwood,

Very Sincerely Yours,

ALBERT EDWARD, P.
Dr. Birdwood C.S.I.[785]

It is obvious that Dr. George Birdwood was considered well-spoken by the members of the royal family, particularly by Prince Albert and his consort Queen Victoria. Likewise important people in society recognized his position with the royalty. Therefore, it is not surprising to find that George James Sheridan Lock,[786] who belonged to the Society of Arts, write to Birdwood in a rather euphoric tone.

While regretting his inability to be at the Society of Arts gathering that night and supporting his friend Linton[787] he writes that he thought that the latter's paper was very good, to the point and knowledgeable.

In the next paragraph, he talks about a letter that he received from Schellendorf[788] telling

785 *Ibid.*, APPENDICES:392.

786 Mss Eur F216/8; Tuesday 1888/9; Address:76 to 80 Oxford Street W. London. Signed:George J. S. Lock

787 Sir James Dromgole Linton, painter of historical figure subjects in watercolour, Illustrated at an early age for *The Graphic*. Attained success as a painter, being elected A.R.I. in 1867; R.I. 1870 and P.R.I. 1884-98, was knighted in 1885.
A.R.I. Associate of the Royal Institute of Painters in Watercolours.
R.I. Member of the Royal Institute of Painters in Watercolours.
P.R.I. President of the Royal Institute of Painters in Watercolours.

788 The name occurs several times in various letters. The spelling in unclear: Schellendorf (?) or Scehendorff (?). The institution of Aide-de-Camp was introduced by Queen Victoria. Admiral Henry Craven St. John held the office of Naval-Aide-de Camp to H.M. Queen Victoria between1887-89. This letter was written in 1888-9(?). As for the Queen's Private Secretary, this was held after the death of her husband Price Albert by General the Honourable Sir Charles Grey 1861-1870; for before this her husband Prince Albert had been effectively her Secretary. From 1870-95 it was Major General Rt. Hon. Sir Henry Ponsonby, G.C.B.; then Lieutenant Hon. Sir Arthur Bigg, KCB CMG 1895-1901; later Lord Stamfordham. Therefore Scehendorff(?) may have been the Queen's Aide for sometime.

Birdwood that Her Majesty the Empress wished him to call on her at Buckingham Palace at 9.30 a.m. that morning. He continues, "I was delighted to go and find her as full of interest in me as ever and anxious to chat on several matters she wishes me to later be back for her. Amongst other things I am to design and make her some crystal and silver claret jugs and vases for flowers. She also wished to tell me that she made the Prince of Wales promise to pay me a visit."

"Schellendorf is coming up in a fortnight and wishes to dine with *me* and to meet you and me one time more. I should like to ask Cunliff-Owen then—Will you broach the subject to him tonight and ask him whether he was present when the Empress spoke about me? I shall come and see you in a day or two."[789]

George James Sheridan Lock is an elated person who wants to share his experience with Dr. Birdwood, while also asking for a favour from him. Here again the trust and recognition of Birdwood's capacity to do something for a friend is displayed in this letter.

The other letter is a 'Confidential' letter from T.S. Townend[790] to Birdwood.

Townend, no doubt, realized Birdwood's savoir-faire---his ability to act appropriately in social situations. This fact is suitably brought out in Townend's own words of caution entrusting Birdwood with a delicate task of warning His Royal Highness The Prince of Wales against taking certain steps.

T.S. Townend's letter[791] was written on 12 April 1888 to Birdwood. In this confidential letter he writes:

My Dear Birdwood,

An effort is being made by the Promoters of a Ruby mine Co. through Mr. Marcus Beresford to induce the Prince of Wales to receive a deputation at Marlborough H.O. in order to show H.R.H. some samples of Colonial precious stones.

I believe the majority of these stones are from the MacDonald ranges in South Australia, and they are being pushed in England by a young man named Pearson. Very grave doubts are expressed about the *bonafides* of this project.

789 *Ibid.,* Mss Eur F 216/8; Date: 1888/9—Tuesday, Address: 76 to 80 Oxford Street W. London; Signed: George J.S. Lock.

790 Mr. T.S. Townend (1839-1927) was a veteran journalist who was well-known to many who visited England. He was editor and manager of the Australian Press Association. He died in London on 30 October 1927 at the age of 88. Several papers such as 'The Sidney Morning Herald' and 'The Brisbane Courier' reported his death.

791 Mss Eur F 216/8; Address: The Aigus and The Australasian, Melbourne Australia, Branch Office 80 Fleet Street, London. Tel. No. 2619. Date: 12 April 1888; Signed: T.S. Townend.

Some of the promoters will not bear very close scrutiny[792] and it is known to those who are behind the scenes that this proposed interview with the Prince is intended indirectly to help in floating what would prove a bad venture—or worse.

I think you know some of the Princes' entourage if you do, use your influence to stop this thing, for while the interview may profit the Company promoters, it may bring the Prince into discredit.

My letters from Australia show that this movement to float ruby companies is viewed there with great suspicion.

Truly yours,

T.S. Townend

Sir Geo Birdwood, C.I.E.

This letter clearly reveals the trust and respect that Birdwood commanded not only with important Journalists but also with the Royalty.

BIRDWOOD'S ARTISTIC INCLINATIONS

Birdwood's predilection for artistic works and his ability to procure these for others, made many people eager to share their opinions with him.

Lord Landsdowne[793] writing to Birdwood on 14 November 1888, shares his thoughts with him. Lord Landsdowne is particularly pleased with the illustration of the Jaipur enamels. He lauds Mr. Griggs' invaluable volume. This and the Manual of Art—8 India, will accompany Lady Landsdowne and himself to India. He also asks Birdwood to convey his thanks to Mr.

792 Scrutiny (sig) scrutinities (plural) [sometimes].

793 Mss Eur F 216/8; Address:Landsdowne House, Berkeley Square; Date: 14 November 1888, Signed: Landsdowne.
Lord Landsdowne was appointed Viceroy of India in 1888, finally returning to England in 1894. Lord Landsdowne entered the House of Lords as a member of the Liberal party in 1866. He served in William Gladstone's Government as Lord of Treasury from 1869-1872, and as Under Secretary of State from 1872-1874. He was appointed Under-Secretary of State for India in 1880 and having gained experience in overseas administration, was appointed Governor-General of Canada in 1883. The present day town of Landsdowne, Garhwal in Uttarakhand, India, was established in 1887 and named after him.

Griggs[794] and express his great admiration for his work.

The other letter of significance is from John Griffths,[795] thanking Birdwood for promptly despatching the box of Ajanta drawings, which he received that week.

Obviously, he had probably sent these to Birdwood for his perusal.

Griffths talks about the festive atmosphere in Bombay during the last fortnight doing honours to the incoming and outgoing Viceroy—into which Griffths "has been dragged much against his will." He writes that "Lord Reay kindly brought Lord Landsdowne to see the School of Art. Lord Landsdowne was greatly interested in all he saw, and he made before leaving "a capital speech" to the students. "Indeed he has evoked golden opinions all round during the short stay in Bombay." He then writes about the honour done to Lord Dufferin[796] at the Byculla Club, and the lusty cheering that greeted his speech.

He adds that he is sorry that "India is to take no part officially in the Paris Exhibition" although he writes, "I am glad to see that you are moving to get some representation made."[797]

Here Birdwood's significant contribution to the World of Art is lucidly brought out.

BIRDWOOD AND THE INTERNATIONAL EXHIBITIONS

Birdwood's name was identified with the representation of India at all principal International Exhibitions from 1857 to 1901.[798]

Different writers have viewed these Exhibitions also called World Fairs in varying ways. John M. MacKenzie[799] calls it the rise of "demotic Orientalism" which "occurred in precisely

794 Frederick Landseer Maur Griggs R.A., R.E.(1876-1938) was a distinguished English etcher, architectural draughtsman, illustrator and early conservationist, associated with the late flowering of the Arts and Crafts movement in Cotswolds.

795 Mss Eur F 216/8; Address: Bombay(Government of Bombay Seal); Date: 14 December 1888, Signed:Griffths.
John Griffths (1837-1918) was an artist and Principal of the Bombay School of Art. He was trained at the Royal College of Art. He was called by the Colonial Service to design the decoration of many of Bombay's new public buildings.He used his students to record frescoes in Buddhist cave temples at Ajanta, published in 1896-1897. He retired in 1895 returning to live in Montgomeryshire, later moving to Dorset. He died in Sherbourne on 1 December 1918. (John Griffths [Bombay] Papers).

796 Lord Dufferin (1826-1902) Governor-General and Viceroy of India (1884-1888).

797 In order to support this statement please refer to Appendix II.

798 *Journal of Indian Art*, vol. viii. *The Life and Work of Sir George Birdwood.*

799 MacKenzie, John M. *Orientalism: history, theory and the arts,* Manchester University Press, 1995, p. 86. John M. MacKenzie, Professor Emeritus of Imperial History at Lancaster University, England. He

those areas, the great exhibitions, places of recreation and instruction like the Crystal Palace at Sydenham, the theatre, seaside piers and other buildings."

All these developments took place at a time when the 'new imperialism was developing into a powerful ideology.'

"Exhibitions were important showcases of oriental crafts and products, but they were also housed in buildings that were well-adapted to the creation of specific geographical courts."

He supported his statements by giving examples of:

(1) The Crystal Palace of 1851 which contained such courts, of which the Indian was the most celebrated. This idea, he continues, was further developed when the Crystal Palace was shifted to Sydenham from Hyde Park in 1854

(2) The 1862 London Exhibition displayed Indian classical crafts

(3) A large Indian Pavilion by Sir Caspar Purdon Clarke was built for the Paris Exhibition of 1878

(4) Again at the Colonial and Indian Exhibition of 1886 held in London.

He goes on to say, "Indian pavilions reappeared with signs of Orientalism at the Paris Exhibition of 1889 and 1900 but it was in Glasgow in 1888, that a major international exhibition was housed in unashamedly oriental buildings."[800]

Carol Breckenridge[801] while speaking about objects from India assembled for display at International Exhibitions or World Fairs, comments that their "transience and ephemerality set world fairs apart as extraordinary phenomena in the world of collecting." She says that world fairs are "special because, despite the permanence they imply, they do not last; they come and go. Their buildings are constructed, and then, by international charter, they are deconstructed. They are also special because they place objects in the service of commerce and in the service of the modern nation—state, with the inevitable imperial encounters that these two forces promote. In doing so, they yoke cultural material with aesthetics, politics and pragmatics."[802]

Such views about International Exhibitions in general and the Indian participation in particular, bring out the influence of Oriental Art and Craft on the minds of the European visitors to Exhibitions, in the late 19th century.

---

also holds honorary professorships at Aberdeen, St. Andrews, Stirling and Edinburgh Universities in Scotland , and is a fellow of the Royal Society of Edinburgh.

800 *Ibid.*

801 Breckenridge, Carol A. *The Aesthetics and Politics of Colonial Collecting:India at World Fairs;* Comparitive Studies in Society and History, Cambridge Journal vol. 31, Issue 02, pp. 195-216, 1989. Carol A. Breckenridge, University of Pennsylvania. DoI: 10. 1017/SOO10417500015796 (About DOI) Published online:03 June 2009

802 *Ibid.*

Dr. George Birdwood had played a very significant role in promoting the Indian culture and products at many of the International Exhibitions. His intimate knowledge of India, his love for Indian people and their way of life and his visionary approach to projecting India on the world scene made him the guiding light of Indian Committees at such Exhibitions. His task of leading the Indian contingent could not have been easy as we can see from some letters written at the time of the Paris Universal Exhibition of 1889 among the Committee members. These letters bring out a rather intriguing story of the internal politics among them. Although each person involved may have contributed his might, they had sharp differences amongst themselves. Some of the players involved were Caspar Purdon Clarke, the architect of the Indian courts, Sir Philip Cunliff-Owen, earlier Curator of the South Kensington Museum and an intimate friend of Sir George Birdwood, Henry Trueman Wright Wood, Editor of the *Society of Arts Journal* and Secretary to the Society of Arts and Vincent Robinson, member of the Indian Committee.

The bone of contention, in all these letters, was two issues.

One was the role of Vincent Robinson and his participation;[803] and the other was the award of the Gold medal or Diploma awarded to the Indian Palace.[804]

Vincent Robinson was induced to accept the office by Sir Philip and Sir George on the condition that there should be no expense on his part.[805] However, Robinson had paid all his expenses from his own pocket;[806] this, presumably "when it was put to Robinson that no other members of the Committee were refunded their expenses, he gave way and has paid at least 150 pounds out of his own pocket."[807]

In a letter to Sir Philip Owen[808] Robinson complained that "I have very many grievances with Sir Polydore and Mr. Wood; they have systematically left me out whenever anything was going on. No whisper of any function in connection with the awards ever reached me and as usual no invitation to attend."

803 Mss Eur F 216/19; Address: Reform Club, Pall Mall, S.W. Date: 8 October 1889, Signed : Vincent (Robinson) to Sir Philip Owen.

804 Mss Eur F 216/19; Paris Universal Exhibition; Date: 1889; Signed: H.T. Wood to Sir George Birdwood.

805 Mss Eur F 216/19; Address: India Museum, South Kensington; Date: 8 October 1889; Signed: Caspar Purdon Clarke to Sir Philip.

806 Mss Eur F 216/19; Address: Reform Club, Pall Mall S.W. Date: 8 October 1889, Signed: Vincent (Robinson) to Sir Philip Owen.

807 Mss Eur F 216/19: Address: India Museum, South Kensington, Date: 8 October 1889; Signed: Caspar Clarke to Sir Philip.

808 Mss Eur F 216/19; Address: Reform Club, Pall Mall S.W. Date: 8 October 1889; Signed: Vincent (Robinson) to Sir Philip Owen.

"I only heard of the business when it had practically finished and then by accident."

In fact, he said in the same letter, "I have just received a note from Sir George Birdwood asking me why I did not go to Paris when you (Sir Philip Owen) went."[809]

Apparently Robinson did go to Paris on the advice of Sir George Birdwood.[810] That there was much distrust that Sir Philip had for Robinson is revealed in his 'Personal' letter[811] to Sir George Birdwood, where it is said that:

"Yesterday I heard from V.R. that he was crossing yesterday. I telegraphed and wrote hoping to stop him."

I have done all in my power for him—Wood also—that I am witness of –But all was to no avail. He made no position except that miserable one of rubbing up everybody. He is known for this all over the place. He has done nothing to [console] the authorities—He has neglected to be the Benefactor and friend of the Indians with whom he is obnoxious; all our efforts have led us to the one conclusion that he cannot hope for any consideration."[812]

With reference to the second issue related to the Gold Medal Diploma, in a letter written on 2 October 1889 by H.T. Wood to Sir George Birdwood, he says:

"A gold medal diploma had been awarded to the British Section for the Indian Palace. It was suggested that the award should be made to the Indian Tea Districts Association, who provided the guarantee and the suggestion seems to me to be an entirely reasonable one. Of course the idea of giving it to the Tower Tea Co. is out of the question. However, there is no reason why the matter should not be recovered for the consideration of your Committee.

Purdon Clarke will get a diploma for the design of the building.

As regards Griggs, his exhibit is really an unimportant one, though interesting to those who understand its technical value."[813]

A few days later, on 9 October 1889, Caspar Purdon Clarke writing to Sir George Birdwood says, "I have to protest against the new move, i.e., sending the gold medal to Lord Landsdowne! Probably for not interfering—I am sorry that V.R. (Vincent Robinson) proposed that it should be given to me and yesterday we both agreed that as Chairman of the Indian Committee you were more fairly entitled to it than anyone else. This I wrote to Sir

809 *Ibid.*

810 Mss Eur F 216/19; Address: India Museum, South Kensington, Date:9.x.89; Signed: Caspar Purdon Clarke to Sir George Birdwood.

811 Mss Eur F 216/19; *Personal* Date: 10 October 1889. Signed: P.O. (Philip Owen) addressed to 'My dear Friend (George Birdwood).

812 Mss Eur F 216/19; Personal; Signed P.O. (Philip Owen) to 'My dear Friend' (George Birdwood); Date: 10 October 1889.

813 Mss Eur F 216/19; Address: Paris Universal Exhibition 1889, Section Britannique, Exposition Universelle, Paris, Date: 2 October 1889; Signed: H.T. Wood to Sir George Birdwood.

Philip and I hope he will make Wood see it. The Viceroy did nothing but you did and without your name we would have never formed a Committee nor raised the money.

Griggs is very angry, he considers his exhibits have been kept in the background by enemies and I think he is right in one quarter. If Sir Philip had been in Paris Griggs would have received a gold medal."[814]

However, Sir Philip Owen, writing a 'Personal' letter to Sir George Birdwood says inter alia, "The Gold medal or Diploma with much trouble will be sent by the English Commission as given to India ---will be sent to the India Office—and you will send it to India for Governor General."[815]

That people like Caspar Purdon Clarke held a different view is evident from his letter to Sir Philip Owen written on 8 October 1889[816] wherein, besides other matters, he says:

In the matter of the Gold Medal award, neither Wood nor (Keyser?) had a right to dispose of it without reference to Sir George and Robinson. I am getting my guns ready for a fight and if they send the needed to Lord Landsdowne I shall take certain steps to make the Viceroy return the medal to Sir Polydore with thanks regretting.... They owe the Indian Section to Sir George, Robinson and myself and we ought to close it, not them.

Signed

C. Clarke

P.S. Both Robinson and myself wish to secure the gold medal for Sir George whose energy has pulled India through.

This correspondence clearly indicates the trust that many Indian Committee members had in Sir George and the esteemed respect that they held for him. He was indeed the Champion of the Indian cause.

Sir George's help was again sought for the Exhibition in 1892 by none other than H.T. Wood, the Secretary of the Society of Arts.

In his letter written on 18 January 1892 he says, "As you know I take no action on Indian matters without consulting Sir Owen and yourself."[817]

---

814 Mss Eur F 216/19; Address:India Museum, South Kensington, Date: 9.x.89; Signed:C.Clarke.

815 Mss Eur F 216/19; Address: None: Personal, addressed to'My dear Friend'; Date: 10 October 1889; Signed:P.O. (Philip Owen).

816 Mss Eur F 216/19; Address: India Museum, South Kensington, Date; 8 October 1889, Signed: Caspar Clarke to Sir Philip Owen.

817 Mss Eur F 216/44; Address: Society of Arts; Date: 18 January 1892; Signed: H.T. Wood.

Again, on 26 March 1892, H.T. Wood writing to Sir George says:

"Do you think there is a possibility of getting the very small grant of 3000 pounds from the Indian Government if they can be assured that India will be as well represented...."[818]

P.S. The matter must be decided at once or it will be no use at all."

Thus did Sir George enjoy the confidence of many in matters related to India.

BIRDWOOD AND HIS INDIAN FRIENDS IN THE BRITISH PARLIAMENT

Sir George Birdwood was a prominent person in the India Office in London during the late 19th and early 20th centuries. Among his close friends and associates were the first and the second Indian Members of British Parliament namely Dadabhai Naoroji (1825-1917) who represented Finsbury Central as a Liberal MP from 1892-1895[819] and Mancherjee Merwanjee Bhownagree, KCIE (1851-1933) who was a British Conservative Party politician of Indian Parsi heritage and represented the constituency of Bethnal Green North East in the British Parliament between 1895 and 1906.[820]

Dadabhai Naoroji referred to in his youth as "the promise of India" and in later years as "The Grand Old Man of India" was the acclaimed leader of the Indian National Congress (established in 1885) in the years 1886, 1893 and 1906. Although a businessman who lived in England for many years, Dadabhai was a true Indian nationalist. His economic critique of British rule in India, the drain of wealth theory and his active participation in the Indian National Congress Movement must have resulted in creating a number of opponents in England. This fact is borne out when his candidature for election to the British Parliament attracted negative publicity and Lord Salisbury, the Conservative Prime-Minister, raised the 'race card,' questioning the suitability of 'a black man' to stand for Parliament in Britain. In spite of this smear tactics, Dadabhai Naoroji won the seat.

It is important to note that correspondence between Sir William Wilson Hunter KCSI, CIE (1840-1900),[821] a Scottish historian, Statistician, a compiler and a member of the Indian Civil Service (1862-1887) and Sir George Birdwood reveals Hunter's opinion about Dadabhai Naoroji. Sir William Hunter was undoubtedly a scholar and an able administrator of Indian

818 Mss Eur F 216/44; Address: Society of Arts, John St. Adelphi, London W.C. Date: 26 March 1892, Signed: H.T. Wood, Secretary.

819 Migration Histories>South Asian>Politics Dadabhai Naoroji (1825-1917) http://www.movinghere.org.uk/galleries/histories/asian/politics/dadabhai_naoroji

820 http:en.wikipedia.org/wiki/Mancherjee_Bhownagree

821 Wikipedia, http://en.wikipedia.org/wiki/William_Wilson_Hunter

affairs. In his letter to Dr. Birdwood,[822] he writes: "If you reply to your native friend about your and my views: please take care to make it clear that while I cordially support the claims of the responsible leaders for cautious progress and well-considered development of political institutions I do not express any opinion in favour of Mr. Dadabhai's economic theories of the poverty of India."

"That I have treated this grave question from evidence collected at first hand in every province of India, and have shown the true causes alike of India's poverty and wealth in my book *England's Work in India.* This little book has been republished by loyal and patriotic natives of India by my permission at the nominal rate three pence (3 annas) a copy-5000 copies for the Madras Presidency alone."[823]

Both Dr. George Birdwood and Sir William Hunter were staunch supporters of the Indian cause. However, Sir Hunter was clearly disturbed about certain developments and utterances of the Indian leaders particularly in view of his own allegiance to the British and his concern for India. Thus in his letter to his friend and counsel Dr. George Birdwood, written on 23 December 1888 he writes, "What you say about some of the extreme doings of our India friends is most true. I have gone into the matter not because I expect gratitude, but because I think I can do a little good both for India and England. But I confess that there is a limit beyond which I cannot go with any man—and that limit is marked by the line between loyal representation and seditious appeals.

Deeply as I deplore some recent utterances I am not prepared to say that that limit has yet been reached. But I am as anxious as you, and as watchful as you could wish me to be."

He goes on to say, "I should like even at some personal inconvenience to myself, to support Mr. Dadabhai. I think, too, I could show that the cause of the peoples of India is one which is a better cause, and which rests on surer foundations than the overstatements of one side or the misrepresentations of another, I would do this delicately yet firmly not caring whether I got gratitude or not."

"But I shall act as you advise me, for this is essentially of the nature of 'public conduct' and for three full months from the beginning of November of which I literally can time (?) to the 1 March. I have placed myself in your hands."[824]

Dr. Birdwood must have played an important role in giving sagacious advice to Sir Hunter, as can be interpreted from the latter's next letter to Dr. Birdwood written on 16 March 1889, for he writes:

822 Mss Eur F 216/8; Address: Oxford; Date: Oct 10/88; Signed: W W Hunter.

823 *Ibid.*

824 Mss Eur F 216/8; Address: Cherwell Edge, Oxford; Date: 23 December 1888, Signed: W.W. Hunter.

"Your last letter was a great comfort to me, for I was anxious that what I had done should meet with you approval."[825]

It is evident from the contents of this letter that Sir Hunter helped in easing the complicated situation between England and India. He continues in this letter to Sir George, inter alia:

"No attempt will be made to press on matters in India, and Lord Landsdowne's [826] decision will be patiently awaited."

And, "The Black man incident is forgotten, and Sir John Forst (?) has kindly seen Mr. Dadabhai and had an interview with him, very soothing to Mr. Dadabhai."

So inspire of the disturbing elements of Hume's[827] writings, Norton's[828]speeches, Lord Dufferin's[829] after dinner eloquence, and the Black Man slip of the tongue, we are in quiet waters again."

Indeed, Dr. George Birdwood and Dadabhai Naoroji were close friends, both concerned for the cause of India. Birdwood was keen and anxious about the election of Dadabhai Naoroji to the Parliament in 1892. In fact, he addressed a letter to Charles T. Bruce of India Office in this context and received a reply on 26 July 1892:

"With reference to your letter about the scrutiny of votes in Mr. Dadabhai Naoroji's election, I placed your views before Lord Cross and he wishes me to say that neither the Government nor the Secretary of State have anything to do with the matter which is entirely in the hands of the local candidate and his local supporters." [830]

During his tenure as a member of the British Parliament between 1892 and 1895, Dadabhai Naoroji often corresponded with his friend Sir George Birdwood, soliciting his help in matters related to seeking information about certain British officials in India.[831]

825 Mss Eur F 216/9; Address: Cherwell Edge, Oxford, Date: 16 March 1889; Signed:W.W.H. (Private).

826 The then Viceroy of India.

827 Allan Octavian Hume set up the British Committee of "Indian National Congress" to oversee the Indian Agency's work.

828 John Eardley Norton (1852-1931) was a Madras barrister, judge and politician of British origin. In 1879, he set sail to India. He was appointed member of the committee which drafted the constitution of the Indian National Congress. He participated in the tenth session of the Indian National Congress in 1903. He was instrumental in enlisting the support of Charles Bradlaugh, MP, British Parliament for Northhampton, for the creation of an UK chapter of the Indian National Congress. He was frequently accused of sedition by his fellow countrymen. http://en.wikipedia.org/wiki/Eardley_Norton

829 Lord Dufferin (1826-1902) Governor-General and Viceroy of India (1884-1888).

830 Mss Eur F 216/33 Private. Address: India Office, Whitehall S.W. Date: 26 July 1892; Signed: Charles T. Bruce to Sir George Birdwood K.C.I.E.

831 (i) Mss Eur F 216/57; HOUSE OF COMMONS, Date: 1 June 1893, Signed: Dadabhai Naoroji.
(ii) Mss Eur F 216/57 ; HOUSE OF COMMONS, Date: 5 June 1893; Signed: Dadabhai Naoroji.
(iii)Mss Eur F 216/57; Address: National Liberal Club, Whitehall Place S.W. Date: 14 June 1893;

The personal bond between Dadabhai Naoroji and Birdwood is seen from the former's letter to the latter dated 17 October 1893.

"How sincerely thankful I am to Lady Birdwood and yourself for your deep sympathy in my grievous affliction."

"It is like you to remember and express all the kind words you have written to me."[832]

Birdwood on his part, was close to Dadabhai, and shared his personal thoughts with him. This is specially seen in a letter that Birdwood wrote to Dadabhai on 18 June 1889.[833]

It is regarding a young boy, Kaikhuskroo Edulji Gamut whom Dadabhai knew well. Though an "honourable youth" he came to consult Birdwood "on a question of conscience" the real crux of which was unknown to Birdwood, except that "he was at variance with his father and mother."

It seems that the young man was in disagreement with his father, in respect of his ancestral faith (Zoroastrian religion). Birdwood advised him "to surrender to his father as a duty he owes the author of his being; and have insisted that he while under his father's care (?) has no right to differ from him and that even when an independent man he'd wait until his parents' death before professing any disagreement with his ancestral faith."

Birdwood then advised the young man to see Dadabhai to take advice. Birdwood adds, "I have the deepest rooted horror of young men causing their parents grief and sorrow through religious differences with them."

This shows Birdwood's traditional thoughts of respecting the elders in matters of religion.

Dr. George Birdwood continued his cordial relations with persons of Indian origin who became members of the British Parliament. Although Dadabhai Naoroji lost the elections in 1895, Mancherjee Merwanjee Bhownagree (1851-1933), a Parsi gentleman, originally from Bombay and a British Conservative party politician, was elected to the Parliament in 1895, representing the constituency of Bethnal Green North East. He continued to be MP till 1906.[834]

During his ten years in Parliament, Bhownagree was a supporter of British rule in India and opposed the campaign of home rule.[835]

Signed: Dadabhai Naoroji.

(iv) Mss Eur F 216/57; Address: National Liberal Club, Whitehall Place S.W. Date: 6 Oct. 1893, Signed: Dadabhai Naoroji.

832 Mss Eur F 216/57; Address: Saltwood House, Hounslow; Date: 17 October 1893; Signed: Dadabhai Naoroji to Sir George Birdwood.

833 Mss Eur F 216/16; Date: 18 June 1889; No Address; Signed: GeoBirdwood.

834 http://en.wikipedia.org/wiki/Mancherjee_Bhownagree

835 *Ibid.*

Bhownagree had the highest regard for Sir George Birdwood as a highly respected person and dear friend. Prior to Bhownagree's entry into the British political circles, on being called to the bar at Lincoln's Inn 1885, he was appointed the judicial councillor by the Maharaja of Bhavnagar State in Kathiawar in India, the very next year.[836]

Bhownagree had extensive correspondence with Sir George Birdwood on several issues.

Addressing a letter to his 'dear and kind friend' from Bombay on 14 December 1888[837] Bhownagree candidly expressed his personal affliction and sought solace from Sir George. Sending Sir George belated good wishes for his birthday, Bhownagree writes:

"I had prepared for your birthday which passed—I trust happily and cheerfully with your family—last Saturday a pair of silver cutchwork serviette rings encased in an inlaid Surat work sandal and ivory box with your crest. Also a pair of gold broaches with your portraits of Delhi painting on ivory. The broaches you will see have your crest engraved on the framework. These also are in the same sort of cases—These are intended for both your charming daughters...It may be a sentiment of fond memory to your daughters to know that my Ave had greatly been pleased both with the pictures, the designs of the broaches and that her dear friends were to have them."[838]

The contents of the letter make it evident that Sir George Birdwood's family and the Bhownagree family were very close to each other.

The letter also throws light on the fact that the Birdwood family had a crest of their own.

Bhownagree in his next letter to Sir George written from Bombay on 28 December 1888[839] expresses his gratitude to Sir George and Lady Birdwood for the letters of condolence for his bereavement on the loss of his sister. Further he appreciates Sir George's thoughts and plans for his future well-being and elevation. He goes on to inform Sir George that he wishes to curtail his activities in India; but continue his duties as Judicial Counsellor for Bhavnagar State, as there is nobody in the Maharaja's confidence to whom the work could be transferred. However, he is determined to stay in India for sometime to see the completion of a Memorial Hall in the name of his mother. He has also set apart Rs 25,000 in memory of his sister. Then he says his "work in this life will be over and I shall be free to leave this land to settle down in some quiet way in England."[840]

In a later letter written from Bhavnagar on 5 January 1892, he talks of the need of securing help (financial) for the completion of the large rooms of the Imperial Institute.[841]

---

836 *Ibid.*

837 Mss Eur F 216/8; Address: 3 Churchgate St. Bombay; Date: 14 Dec. 1888; Signed: M.M. Bhownaggree

838 *Ibid.*

839 Mss Eur F 216/8; Address: 3 Churchgate St. Bombay; Date: 28 Dec.'88, Signed: M.M. Bhownaggree.

840 *Ibid.*

841 Mss Eur F 216/33; Address: Naku Bag, Bhownagar, Date: 5 January 1892, Signed: M.M. Bhownaggree.

This Institute was first established in 1887 as a result of the Colonial and Indian Exhibition of 1886, by the governments of the United Kingdom and several countries of the British Empire to promote research which would benefit the Empire. The Institute has since been renamed as the Commonwealth Institute by an Act—"The Commonwealth Institute Act of 1958," with a change of mission from research to education.[842]

Bhownagree suggested to Dr. Birdwood in this letter of 5 January 1892, that the Maharaja of Bhavnagar was keen to attend the opening ceremony of the Imperial Institute and if he were to get recognition, he will give a good deal of help. Bhownagree clearly indicates that the chief (i.e. Maharaja) should receive some mark (honour).[843]

Bhownagree seems to have proceeded to England immediately thereafter as he writes to Sir George on 20 January 1892 addressing him as "My dear and kind Friend," from Chiswick W., informing him that "I had a very Good reception at the *Times* last night, and you see the result in this morning's paper."

"Other papers have also mentioned about the wealth and it is quite enough for the purpose."[844] (Imperial Institute).

In a subsequent letter written on 23 February 1892[845] Bhownagree informed Sir George that he had secured the approval from India (Bhavnagar) for his proposals in toto. He suggests that Sir George should convey the good news to Sir Frederick Abel.[846]

Bhownagree then wrote to Sir Frederick Abel on 9 March 1892[847] stating, "Now I shall proceed definitely to get an immediate decision from the two bodies in Bombay in reference to the donation with whom I have been in communication, and in a few weeks time hope to place my offer with the conditions to be attached thereat before you in writing."

Bhownagree continued his efforts to find financial help for the Imperial Institute. In his letter dated 16 April 1892[848] to Sir George Birdwood, Bhownagree mentions three important points. Firstly he states, "Yes, it will be a great pleasure to me to accompany you in the

842 http://en.wikipedia.org/wiki/Common_Institute

843 Mss Eur F 216/33; Address: Naku Bag, Bhownagar; Date: 5 January 1892; Signed: M.M. Bhownaggree.

844 Mss Eur F 216/33; Address: Jessville, Priory Road, Chiswick W. Date: 20 January 1892; Signed: M.M. Bhownaggree.

845 Mss Eur F 216/33; Address: Jessville, Priory Road, Chiswick W. Date: 23 February 1892 (in Postscript), Signed: M.M. Bhownaggree.

846 Sir Frederick Abel (1827-1902) was an eminent chemist, a Fellow of the Royal Society (FRS), an Ordinance chemist at the Royal Arsenal at Woolwich from 1854 to 1888; became the organizing Secretary and first director of the Imperial Institute from 1887-1902.

847 Mss Eur F 216/33; Address: 5 Lisbourne Crescent, Torquay; Date: 9 March 1892; Signed: M.M. Bhownaggree.

848 Mss Eur F 216/33; Address: Jessville, Priory Road, Chiswick W. Date: 16 April 1892; Signed: M.M. Bhownagree.

capacity of squire when you go to be enrolled a knight." This clearly shows the camaraderie between two friends.

The second point concerns Sir Frederick Abel, when Bhownagree says that he will hand over a letter to Sir Frederick personally at his home and enclose the cheque so that he (Sir Frederick) might feel sure that there is no hesitation or delay regarding the money.

Thirdly Bhownagree alludes to the Birthday of the Queen which "is approaching and if the thing is to be accomplished now, I think we might try hard now within the next fortnight."[849]

It obviously refers to the honour expected to be conferred on the Maharaja of Bhavnagar.[850]

THE BUST OF SIR GEORGE BIRDWOOD IN THE LIBRARY OF THE UNIVERSITY OF MUMBAI, FORT CAMPUS

Sir George Birdwood's contribution to the social, cultural, literary and educational aspects of Bombay's evolution as a premier city of India is truly memorable. In honour of his work and in memory of his contributions, a bust has been installed in the Library of the University of Mumbai.

The bust was sculpted by Mr. Alfred Gilbert R.A. 16, Maida Vale in England, in 1893.[851]

849 *Ibid.*

850 It may be observed that donations to the cause of the Imperial Institute from the Princes of India were not always appreciated. An article in the Indian newspaper *The Indu Prask* or 'Moonlight' dated 25 September 1893 was wired by Reuter. The article reported the news that Mr. Jehanghier C.J. Readymoney had given a donation of two lacs of rupees towards the funds of the Imperial Institute. The article decried this act by saying, "a great part of the funds have been subscribed for by the Princes of India, and no doubt those who have plenty of money and do not know what to do with it, may be induced by hopes of titles and decorations to contribute their quota towards this aristocratic Institution." Mss Eur F 216/47 Newspaper cutting dated 25 September 1893.

851 Sir Alfred Gilbert (1854-1934) was an English sculptor and goldsmith who enthusiastically experimented with metallurgical innovations. He was a central—if idiosyncratic—participant in the New Sculpture movement that invigorated sculpture in Britain at the end of the 19th century.
Gilbert's sense of decoration was paramount in all he did. He produced busts of extraordinary excellence, and among many of Sir George Birdwood.
Gilbert was chosen associate of the Royal Academy in 1887, full member in 1892 (resigned in 1909), and professor of sculpture (afterwards resigned) in 1900. In 1889 he won the Grand Prix at the Paris International Exhibition. He was created a member of the Victorian Order in1897.
http://en.wikipedia.org/wiki/Alfred_Gilbert
http://glueideas.com/Encyclopedia-Britannica-Volume-10-Part-1-Game-Gun-Metal/...

Mr. M.M. Bhownagree had a prominent role in getting the bust completed by Mr. Gilbert and his correspondence with Sir George and Mr. Gilbert regarding the bust brings out an interesting background of the sculpture.

In a letter to Mr. Gilbert, dated 2 November 1893, Mr Bhownagree says:

It is I think about two months since I wrote you regarding the bust of Sir George Birdwood, then a gentleman replied on your behalf that you were out of town but that he knew the bust was near completion. Since then, not hearing from you I wrote to Mr. Lock[852] asking him to get the work completed as it was through him I thought the commission (was given for?) due execution of work. The delay impairs my credit with them[853] and imposes on me a lot of correspondence and worry.

You promised to let me have the bust last November. This has not only been not done but no reasons have been given for the delay which I could send on to Bombay and in the absence of which they think it is all my neglect.

The Convocation of the University comes off in January and if I can send the bust out almost immediately it would arrive in time for the unveiling on the occasion. Will you kindly oblige me by enabling me to send it out in time?

Yours sincerely,
M.M. Bhownaggree
Sir Alfred Gilbert R.A.
16, Maida Vale[854]

Mr. Bhownagree continued his efforts by writing to Sir George on 11 November 1893[855] saying:

"My last letter to Gilbert after all fetched him. He wired me yesterday saying he would be in whenever I should call to inspect the bust. So I have named Saturday at 2p.m. Sir Owen Burne[856] is coming too, in fact we both go together after lunching.... If you come also, it will be such a pleasure. Gilbert's address is 16, Maida Vale."[857]

852 Mr. Lock belonged to the Society of Arts.

853 Presumably concerned people of India.

854 Mss Eur F 216/47; Date: 2 Nov.1893; Signed:M.M .Bhownaggree to Mr. Gilbert.

855 Mss Eur F 216/47; Address Jasmine Lodge, Chiswick, Lord Mayors Day [11 Nov.] 1893; Signed: M.M. Bhownaggree to Birdwood.

856 Sir Owen Burne worked with Sir George Birdwood on the London Committee of the Tasmanian International Exhibition. *Launceston Examiner (Tas: 1842-1899)* Monday 4 Dec. 1893, p. 6. http://nla.gov.au/nla.news-article39494007

857 Mss Eur F 216/47 1893; *Ibid.*

Thus it appears that the bust was ready.

A few days later on 1 December 1893, Bhownagree addressed a letter to Sir George saying, "The enclosed is the finally settled inscription, as I had sent it to Gilbert. I send it for your definite information. The Swastika will have to be done in proper form if you think Gilbert's workmen can't follow it out."

"The archaic characters Gilbert will of course see properly cut. I have left him choice of putting the archaic characters either below or above the inscription in English and over or under the Swastika, as he may think best. I hope I have done right."

"We meet next Tuesday. I have not heard from Gilbert yet: but we will go to him and I shall be with you about 2 or 2.30 p.m."[858]

Enclosed with the letter was the proposed inscription, as follows:

AIENARISTEVEIN

卐

Sir George Birdwood
M.D., L.L.D., K.C.I.E., C.S.I., etc

In communication of his momentous service to the city of Bombay
and in grateful appreciation of his enlightened and life-long
devotion to the study and exposition of the Industrial Arts of India

卐

The inscription under the bust of Sir George Birdwood installed in the Library of the University of Mumbai matches with the one which Bhownagree had sent to Sir George

858 Mss Eur F 216/47; Address: Jasmine Lodge, Spencer Road, Chiswick; Date: 1 December 1893; Signed: M.M. Bhownaggree.

Birdwood for his approval, with the exception that the archaic letters are placed below the text and the Swastika at the bottom is reversed to look like:

Thus it is that Bhownagree pursued the task of getting Sir George Birdwood's bust ready to be shipped to Bombay so that it could be installed in the campus of the University of Mumbai.

It is indeed fitting that the bust of this scholar and former Registrar had been installed in the Library of a seat of learning.

Sir George Birdwood's bust is cast in metal and is of extraordinary excellence; it is on his goldsmithery that Sir Alfred Gilbert, the artist, enjoys his reputation. In the bust, Birdwood is shown to hold a delicate rendering of a *Tara,* which in Tibetan Buddhism is regarded as a Bodhisattva of compassion and action. She is the female aspect of *Avalokitesvara.* A quiet smile of compassion emanates from Birdwood's face reflecting the qualities symbolized by the *Tara.* The *Tara* itself is a piece of decorative art, of which Birdwood was a champion. In a sense, therefore, the sculpture is also allegorical exuding the love and affection that Birdwood had for art, and for his Indian friends and compatriots, for whose interests Birdwood strived all his life.

Bhownagree seems to have tried to help in various ways, many of his fellow country-men, especially Parsis, by seeking Birdwood's wise counsel.[859] Many of the letters show Bhownagree's intimate association with Sir George Birdwood with whom he regularly corresponded both on personal and official matters.

CORRESPONDENCE BETWEEN BIRDWOOD AND HIS FAMILY

The Birdwoods include Sir George's brother Herbert Mills Birdwood, Judge of the Bombay High Court, and his son Frank Birdwood[860]

859 (i) Mss Eur F 216/47; Address: 46, Queen's Gate S.W., Date: 15 May 1893; Signed: M.M. Bhownaggree.
(ii) Mss Eur F 216/47; Address: 46, Queen's Gate S.W. Date: 17 May 1893; Signed: M.M. Bhownaggree.
(iii) Mss Eur F 216/47; Address: Jasmine Lodge, Chiswick. Date: 4 August 1893; Signed: M.M. Bhownaggree.
(iv) Mss Eur F 216/47; Date 28 August 1893, Address: Jasmine Lodge, Signed: M.M. Bhownaggree.

860 Mss Eur F 216/47; Date 21 November 1893, Signed: Frank Birdwood.

In a letter dated 28 August 1892 by Herbert Mills Birdwood from Poona, he writes to Sir George, about Justice K.T. Telang (1850-1893)[861]

"But on Telang, succeeding Governor, allowed me to mention to Jardine and there can of course be no question as to Telang's fitness and he has served the University well as Syndic. In the Senate, the Syndicate will lose the advantage of his debating power, which was his strong point."[862]

Referring to the Family he writes:

"Are you going anywhere for the holidays? And how are Fanny and the girls?" He also asks after Sir George's son Frank.[863]

He goes on to candidly say, "I am getting on as well as I'd wish with Lord Harris.[864] He has strong common sense. We don't always agree. But I am not always sure he is not right when we differ. He is liberal and continues Lord Reay's[865] policy in most matters—and he is thoroughly straight and just and will if not disturbed in office by any machinations end by being fairly popular with the natives, with Englishmen of course he is most popular."[866]

Correspondence between persons from all walks of life and Sir George Birdwood, bring to the fore his versatility, his sagacity and level-headed persona. With his knowledge and persuasive nature, he often acted as an arbiter in sorting out issues which could potentially lead to conflicts. This is obviously the reason why his wise counsel was sought on so many occasions.

---

861 Mr. Justice Kashinath TrimbakTelang, M.A., LL.B. was unquestionably the most versatile and brilliant Judge of the Bombay High Court. He was appointed Judge of the High Court at the remarkable age of 38 (1889). He was also an educationist and a staunch champion of English and liberal education. He was appointed as the Vice-Chancellor at the age of 36 (1886) and was the first and youngest Indian Vice-Chancellor of Bombay University. His untimely death caused universal regret.
http://bombayhighcourt.nic.in/libweb/judges/Telang%20K.T..html
Also see Kosambi, Meera, *Intersections:Socio-cultural Trends in Maharashtra,* edited by Meera Kosambi, Orient Longman Ltd. New Delhi, 2000; K.T. Telang by Toshio Yamazaki, p. 84. mentions his year of demise as 1893.

862 MSS Eur F 216/33; Address: Poona; Date: 28 August 1892; Signed : Affectionately, H. Birdwood.

863 *Ibid.*

864 Harris served as Governor of the Presidency of Bombay in British India from 1890 to 1895.
http://en.wikipedia.org/wiki/George_Harris_4th Baron_Harris

865 Lord Reay was the Governor of Bombay immediately preceeding Lord Harris. As a matter of interest, it may be noted that a statue of great beauty, at once novel in treatment and fine in design was that of Lord Reay sculpted by Sir Alfred Gilbert and set up in Bombay.
http://glueideas.com/Encyclopedia-Britannia-Volume-10-Part-1-Game-Gun-Metal/...

866 *Ibid.*

Epilogue

Many epithets can be used to describe Dr. George Birdwood's character. Yet just one word is not sufficient to encompass all he did for India, particularly Bombay and England. To many he was like an 'epiphany' –a sudden and inspiring revelation that guided them to clear waters.

Though a Doctor of Medicine and credited with holding the chairs of Anatomy and Physiology, and Botany and Materia Medica at the Grant Medical College, it is not in connection with these medical and scientific appointments alone that his name is best remembered in Bombay. His reputation depends rather upon his rapport with the Indian peoples, and the uses to which he shrewdly put it. He genuinely felt a warmth towards them. He mixed freely with their leaders and learned men, and their co-operation and wealth were readily available to him for any objective that was beneficial to the community. Never was trust more loyally met and used.

Indeed "there was not a member of the Bombay community, European or Indian who did not believe implicitly in the integrity, enthusiasm and intensity of purpose of George Birdwood."[867] It was Birdwood who was responsible for establishing an 'entente cordial' between India and England.

He devoted his life to building a brotherhood between English and Indian peoples. This he did "through efforts of his pen and deed which were aimed at teaching the subjects of the Queen, East and West, to understand each other, and to realise the enormous benefits to both which flow from their connection."[868]

As in several other fields, Birdwood excelled in the field of science, particularly with his deeply researched paper "*On the Genus Boswellia*."[869] Birdwood carried out detailed research on the scientific writings of several predecessors on the subject of the 'frankincense tree.'

Tristram in his '*Natural History of the Bible,* London, 1867' had written, "Frankincense is the fragrant gum of an Indian tree procured through Arabia...... yet we have no reason to believe that the frankincense tree grew in Arabia."

867 William Fergusson Beatson Laurie, *Sketches of some distinguished Anglo-Indians*, pp. 36-39, Appendices 389.

868 *Ibid.*

869 Birdwood, George, *On the Genus Boswellia,* pp. 136-148, Transactions of the Linnean Society, vol. xxvii; Reprinted by India Office.

Birdwood's research doubted the view of Tristram as he referred to the work of the Assistant Surgeon Carter, who had travelled in the south-east coast of Arabia and also in India. To a question from Birdwood, Carter wrote on 28 January 1869, "On the 25th December 1844, I made my first excursion in the south-east coast of Arabia. It was to see the frankincense-trees growing at the foot of the great limestone cliffs, near the village of Merbat. They were then leafless; but the odour of the gum-resin was convincing, even before they were touched. The same was the case with *Boswellia serrata,* which covers the sides of the Ajunta range, which I traversed with Bhau Daji. The whole air was redolent with their fragrance. On 21st of April 1846, I found the frankincense-tree growing on the *detritus* of the great white limestone cliffs of Ras Fartak, within a few feet of the sea. It was then in full foliage, without flowers. On 22nd of May following, a little further to the north-east, I got a Bedoo to go up into the limestone mountains, close to the shore, and bring me some branches in flower. He brought them with some rooted stems also, which I brought to Bombay, and from which the plant in the Old Gardens at Bombay was obtained. Having specimens of the branches and leaves, which I myself gathered just a month before, from the trees under Ras Fartak, I compared all, and found all to belong to the same species, and forthwith made the drawings on board, of which you have the lithograph."[870]

Carter says, "Ibn Batuta calls the tree *al Kundoroo.* The gum is called by the Arabs *Laban.* The Maharas call the tree *Maghrayt d'sheehaz,* the gum *sheehaz.".*[871]

Carter also explains, "The gum is procured by making longitudinal incisions through the bark, in the months of May and December.... On its first appearance, the gum comes forth white as milk, and, according to its degree of fluidity, finds its way to the ground, or concretes on the branch ... from whence it is collected by men and boys employed to look after the trees by different families who possess the land in which they grow."[872]

Birdwood persisted with his studies by requesting Colonel (then Captain) Playfair, at Aden, to procure cuttings of the African frankincense-tree.[873] Birdwood received from Colonel Playfair several varieties of dried leaves and of cuttings, accurately labelled with their native names; these were of three kinds:- *Yegaar* yielding *Luban maitee*, an undoubtedly new species, and *Mohr Add* and *Mohr Madow*, yielding *Luban sheheri*, the bulk of olibanum exported from Soumali country.

After much observation regarding the flowering and leafing in Aden and in India, Birdwood rearranged the genus and stated, "I have with Dr. Thomson and Professor Oliver's kind assistance prepared the descriptions and Mr. Fitch has drawn the figures of the three

870 *Ibid.,* p. 136.
871 *Ibid.,* p. 136.
872 *Ibid.,* p. 137.
873 *Ibid.,* p. 138.

species which I have named:-

Boswellia Carterii (Mohr Madow).

Boswellia Bhau-Dajiana (Mohr Add).

Boswellia Frereana (Yegaar)."[874]

In his paper, Birdwood provides the following descriptions:

Mohr Madow –identified first by Carter—therefore named after him—same species as his Arabian plant.

Mohr Add –named after Dr. Bhau Daji, Hindu physician of Bombay, well known in Europe as an oriental scholar, and whose eminent services to his countrymen and city, Sir Seymour Fitzgerald recognised in making him Sheriff of Bombay.

Yegaar –named after Mr. W.E. Frere.

Birdwood believed "that *Mohr Madow—Boswellia Carterii* along with *Mohr Add – Boswellia Bhau Dajiana* were the source of the bulk of olibanum of commerce exported from the Soumali country, and is the same species as the plant *Maghrayt d'sheehaz* which Carter found produced the frankincense of the Hadramut –and also that the *Boswellia thurifera* (including *B. Glabra*) of India, and *B. Papyrifera* of Abyssinia whilst thuriferous species are not known to yield the olibanum of commerce."[875]

Therefore, when so much evidence of its origin from Arabia and Soumali was known, it is surprising, says Birdwood that India should have been fancied to be the source of olibanum of commerce. This error he feels is due to the change in trade routes between Europe and the East.[876]

He concludes his findings by saying that the practice of using sweet odours, in religious rites (such as sacrifices), originated in sanitary precautions. They not merely mask bad smells, but correct them. They also drive out vermin. The beautiful rite of burning frankincense before a pot of holy basil (*tulsi*) placed before every Hindu home and invoking the blessings of heaven heightens the meaning of the ritual and enhances the clean air around the house.

On his return to England in 1868, due to reasons of ill-health, he did not lead a life of quiet retirement, but pursued a vigorous regime, wherein he kept up his connection with Indian cultural affairs, especially in the form of international exhibitions and the museological display of Indian arts and crafts. He was Keeper of the Indian Museum at South Kensington (now incorporated into the Victoria and Albert Museum collections).

In 1880, his reputation as an authority of Indian art and manufacture grew to the highest stature with the publication of *The Industrial Arts of India.* This book greatly appreciated the

874 *Ibid.,* p. 138.
875 *Ibid.,* pp. 139-140.
876 *Ibid.,* p. 141.

production of Indian arts and crafts in overly paternalistic tones and praised and admired the small-scale village organizations and traditions involved in the production of crafts. What is important is the outcome of this tome, for it influenced a large number of British designers and craftsmen, including William Morris and Owen Jones.[877]

Dr. George Birdwood's authority and knowledge in the field of Art led many to seek his views. It is in this light that he was sought out to pen the Preface, Introduction or the Advertisement to no less than a dozen books. Among these, his Introduction to *The Dawn of British Trade in the East, as recorded in the Court Minutes of the East India Company, 1599-1603,* published in 1886,[878] stressed on the value of these contemporary annals, for the Court Books, Factory Diaries, Consultations and general correspondence constitute a continuous narrative, to the student of history.

The other Introduction was to the English translation of Count Goblet D'Alviella's book *The Migration of Symbols* written by Dr. Birdwood on 7 July 1894. Here Birdwood calls the Count the greatest living exponent on the subject of the study of symbolism and on the decorative designs of the artistic industries of the West.

The importance of this alluring book is that with its English translation, it is now within the reach of the Schools of Art throughout the United Kingdom; and as widely accessible to archaeological students in India, where so much symbolism of antiquity still survives, permeating the entire mass of Hindu populations.[879]

Goblet D'Aleviella's view that the religious symbols common to different historical races of mankind have not originated independently among them, but have, for the most part, been carried from one to the other, in the course of their migrations, conquests and commerce, is more or less similar to that held by Birdwood.

Dr. George Birdwood was no insular academic. It is obvious that he was present when the British elite met at social functions and events. Along with Birdwood, his friend Lockwood Kipling and his wife Alice Kipling, were also present on these occasions. For Birdwood is credited to have recalled a couple of spicy incidents. Lockwood Kipling, the

877 William Morris (1834-1896) was an English textile designer, artist, writer, and socialist associated with the Pre-Raphaelite Brotherhood and English Arts and Crafts Movement. http://en.wikipedia.org/wiki/William_Morris
Owen Jones (1809-1874) was a London-born architect and designer of Welsh descent. His theories on flat patterning and ornament still resonate with contemporary designers today. He rose to prominence with his studies of Islamic decoration at Alhambra in Granada. He was responsible for the interior decoration and layout of exhibits for the Great Exhibition building of 1851 and for its later incarnation at Sydenham. Jones advised on the foundation collections of the South Kensington Musuem through his close association with Henry Cole, the Museum's first director and another key figure in nineteenth century design. http://en.wikipedia.org/wiki/Owen_Jones (architect)

878 Published by H. Stevens and Son, 115 Martin's Lane, London, 1886. Reprinted in 1970, Printed in U.S.A.

879 D'Alviella, Goblet, *The Migration of Symbols,* Introduction, p. viii.

learned[880] artist and Curator of the Lahore Museum and George Birdwood were friends. Alice Kipling's boldness caught the attention of the then Viceroy Dufferin. Thereafter he 'took such opportunities as offered of conversing with her, leading to 'heartburning among the ladies.'

Lord Dufferin's declaration that 'dullness and Mrs. Kipling cannot exist in the same room'[881] spread like wild fire in the Simla salons. So also did Alice's response when accosted by an irksome female acquaintance, demanding an explanation over the length of her conversation with the Viceroy; Alice is reported to have retorted tersely, "Yes, my dear, and it was as broad as it was long."[882]

It is thus clear that Dr. George Birdwood enjoyed and remembered pithy remarks and possessed a sprightly humour.

On his return to England in 1868, he joined the India Office Revenue and Statistics Department. While he was at the India Office, he compiled a *Report on the Records of the India Office: with Supplementary Note and Appendices.* (1891)[883]

He was knighted in 1881 and made KCIE in 1887.[884]

He kept up a close correspondence with Indian friends like Dadabhai Naoroji and M.M. Bhownagree and helped them with their queries when they were elected to the British Parliament.

His reputation as a champion of Indian art was somewhat challenged when he chaired a meeting of the Indian Section of the Royal Society of Arts on 13 January 1910. After the speech of the Principal Speaker, E.B. Havell, Birdwood made the claim that India possessed no 'fine art' which he had come across in all his years in India.

Being a thorough scholar and knowing so much about history, particularly Mughal history and more especially the history of Akbar the Great, as is evidenced in his book *Sva,* it is truly surprising that Dr. Birdwood chose to ignore the sensitivity to natural beauty so eloquently captured in numerous graphic descriptions in the sophisticated biography of Babur—the *Baburnama.*[885]

880 His son Rudyard Kipling, himself acknowledged his great debt to his father, Lockwood Kipling, for accurate details of Indian folklore and caste practices and customs; cited in Field-Marshall Lord Birdwood of Anzac and Totnes—*Khaki and Gown:* An Autobiography, U.K. 1941, p. 71.

881 Allen, Charles, *Kipling Sahib,* India and the Making of Rudyard Kipling, Little Brown, Great Britain, 2007, p. 188; ATK to Stanley Baldwin, Edinburgh, 27 March, 1945, Rudyard Kipling Papers, Sussex.

882 Allen, Charles, *op.cit.,* p. 188. This and the earlier remark about 'heart-burning' were recollected by Sir George Birdwood. Quoted in a note in the *Kipling Journal;* December, 1941.

883 http://en.wikipedia.org./wiki/George_Christopher_Molesworth_Birdwood p. 1 of 2.

884 http://www8.open.ac.uk/researchprojects/makingbritain/content/george-birdwood

885 Rogers, J.M. *Mughal Miniatures;* The British Museum Press, 1993; pp. 28-29. Also Mascarenhas, Aruna, *Akbar and the Making of Mughal Miniature,* unpublished article written for *Jnanapravaha*—3rd Assignment for Post Graduate Diploma on 'Indian Aesthetics.'

The founder of the Mughal Dynasty –Babur (1526- 1530) was himself a connoisseur of painting and inherited his taste from his Timurid predecessors in the fifteenth century Herat. Herat was famous for its painters, illuminators, calligraphers and binders.[886]

Babur's son Humayun was likewise interested in art and took the initiative of bringing with him two of the most talented artists —Mir Sayyid Ali and Khwaja Abd-al-Samad— from the studio of Safavid Shah Tahmasp when he returned to India from exile in 1555. Humayun's deep love for art must truly have prevailed over his uncertain situation when he took the decision to bring the artists to India.

However, it was during the reign of Akbar the Great (1556-1605) that Mughal Miniature painting ---the art of the book —a move from palm-leaf to paper which was cut to size and polished to make it impermeable to ink or other colouring, that came into being. He established the royal atelier and the first major work was the *Hamzanama.* His growing kingdom was replete with skilled artists and architects. In 1590 his atelier had more than a hundred painters, predominantly Hindus who were said to be 'famous masters' with many others 'approaching perfection.'[887]

Mughal Miniature Painting portrayed nature, trees bearing fruit, fish, deer, tigers, elephants—animals in forested scenes, flowers and grassy bowers—fine art par excellence!

Indian painting –Jain, Buddhist and Hindu which consisted of cave and palm-leaf paintings were now moved to paper imported from Persia and probably Italy.

Instead of primary colours (red, blue, yellow) Mughal painting ventured to a more varied palette, using partly opaque pigments loosely termed as gouache: orpiment for yellow, cinnabar for red, copper salts for viridian and lapis lazuli for deep blue—partly organic materials such as saffron, lake crimson from the lac insect—100,000 i.e. a lakh of which were said to be needed to produce the dye; indigo for blue and peori, a vivid yellow produced from the urine of cows which had been fed on mango leaves.[888] Colours to please the eye and titillate the senses.

---

886 Rogers, J.M. *op.cit.,* p. 27.

887 Stronge, Susan, *Painting for the Mughal Emperor. The Art of the Book 1560-1660.* V. & A. Publication, London, 2002. It is not that Sir George was unaware that 'Akbar took a great delight in painting' and that 'he had in his service a large number of artists,' *(Industrial Arts of India,* p. 141). He chose not to study 'Miniature painting 'and look at it as 'fine art.'

888 J.M. Rogers, *op.cit.,* p. 21. It may be noted that Sir George Birdwood who was keenly aware and knowledgable about Indian dyes talks about the "beauty and brilliance" of Indian natural dyes. He remarks, "One of the greatest improvements in English textile manufactures would be the substitution of the rich deep-rooted Indian dyes for the harsh flaring chemicals especially the Magenta series, at present in use. *Handbook to the British Section , Paris Exhibition of 1878,* p. 92. Birdwood also dicusses 'lac'. 'Gum Lac –Lake is the resinous exudation produced on certain Indian trees by the *Coccus Lacca* or Lac insect, and Lake , the dye soaked out of the resin, that is, soaked out of the female insect imbedded in it. The name *Lac* has been given to it by the Hindus because of the hundred thousand—the multitude of these small insects found in it....'pp.20-21.

Mughal painting left behind a legacy of authorship with names of well-known artists like Basawan and Manohar to live for posterity.[889]

As an art form, it percolated to the princely states of Rajasthan in varying degrees depending upon their interaction with the Mughals and then on, through the Thakurs, to the hill-states of the Punjab and eventually to the Deccan Sultanate.[890]

Why then did Birdwood make that enigmatic remark about no fine art existing in India and comparing the *Dyani Buddha* to 'a suet pudding?'

Having made the remark with such fortitude, he could not perhaps retract from an awkward situation. To some it seemed like an unwise statement, but it certainly proved somewhat of a blotch on his otherwise accepted alacrity for art, recognised particularly by Indian and British gentry.

Dr. Birdwood's deep knowledge of literature and keen interest in literary pursuits is evident as he was invited to pen the biographical sketches of eminent Indians for the Encyclopaedia Britannica. He wrote these in 1901, with his characteristic sense of taking care of details and correcting proofs in his own hand. (Originals found in the British Library). Thus he contributed to the life sketches of:

1) Framjee Nasarwanjee Patel (1804-1894)
2) Kursondas Mulji (1832-1875) written by Birdwood entirely and bearing his name.
3) Kashinath Trimbak Telang C.I.E. (1850-1893)
4) Kristo Das Pal (1838-1884)
5) Bankim Chandra Chatterji (1838-1894)
6) Bhau Daji (Ramkrisna Vithal) [1822-1874] Corrected with Birdwood's writing visible.
7) Gaurishanker Udayshanker (1805-1892)
8) Iswar Chandra Vidyasagar (1820-1891) Proof-read by Birdwood. Evident from note from the Editor with the request that article be proof-read.
9) Jagannath Shankersett (1800-1865) Revised and proof-read by Birdwood.
10) Mangaldas Nathoobhai Sir (1832-1890) Written by Birdwood.
11) Vurjeevandas Madhowdas (1832-1890) Revised and proof-read by Birdwood.
12) Mahadev Govind Ranade C.I.E. (1842-1901) Written by Birdwood.
13) Pratap Singh, Sir (1844--) Proof-read article.

While in India, Dr. George Birdwood had helped convert the newspaper *The Standard* into the *Times of India* with Robert Knight. In Bombay he also edited the *Saturday Review,* and after his return to London he wrote for the *Pall Mall, Athenaeum, Academy* and *The*

889 Mascarenhas, *art.cit.*

890 *Ibid.*

Times. Thomas Chenery, the editor of *The Times,* helped Birdwood, as did Sir George Yule[891] who incidentally was the principal instrument in enabling Dr. George Birdwood to establish the celebration of Primose Day.

Primrose Day is the anniversary of the death of British statesman and prime- minister Benjamin Disraeli, Ist Earl of Beaconsfield, on 19 April 1881. The primrose was his favourite flower and Queen Victoria would often send him bunches of them from Windsor and Osborne House. She sent a wreath of primroses to his funeral. On Primrose Day, Beaconfield's statue in Parliament Square, London, is decorated with primroses, as is his grave in Hughenden, Buckinghamshire.[892]

Dr. George Birdwood himself had a great admiration for Disraeli and with a profound knowledge and love of flowers was the real originator of the Primrose League.[893]

Dr. George Birdwood died at Ealing on 28 June 1917. He was a remarkable man who had a distinguished career both in India and at the India Office in London. He was learned, accomplished, generous and genial. His nephew, Field Marshall Lord William Birdwood, who himself served in the armed forces in India for 56 years,[894] recalls that Lord Curzon, who had a great thirst for knowledge, once told him that whenever he wanted information about any abstruse point of Indian mythology, folklore, or theology, his uncle could always be relied upon to give the required details.[895] In fact, at the India Office, it became a maxim that when a puzzling question of fact or custom arose, the answer was to "ask Birdwood."[896] There were two advantages in asking Birdwood: the first was that nine times out of ten he knew, and the second that if he did not he said so frankly.[897]

An interesting observation that his nephew William makes is that Sir George was "himself so steeped in Hindu mythology that he always used to prophesy that he would live to what the Hindus regard as the 'age of beatitude'---namely eighty-four."

Coincidentally, Dr. George Birdwood, who was born in Belgaum on 8 December 1832, died on 28 June 1917; which would make him 84 ½ years old when he died.

To continue with what William Birdwood had to say: "This number (84) is obtained from its factors, 12x7, i.e. the (twelve) signs of the Zodiac multiplied by the (seven) number of Planets. Sure enough, the old gentleman died at the age of 84.[898] I have often wondered

891 http—www.education.nic....
892 http://en.wikipedia.org/wiki/Primrose_Day
893 Birdwood, William, *Khaki and Gown,* p. 310.
894 *Ibid.,* p. 440.
895 *Ibid.,* p. 310.
896 *British Medical Journal,* 7 July 1917, p.30.
897 *Ibid.*
898 William quotes the year of Sir George's death as 1916; however, Sir George died on 28 June 1917, but it still makes him 84 ½ years old.

whether this was an instance of will-power, or at least genuine prescience."[899]

Sir George Birdwood received the C.S.I. when Queen Victoria was proclaimed Empress of India (1 January 1877), the K.C.I.E. in 1881; the Honorary degree of LL.D. from Cambridge in 1886. He was also made an officer of the Legion D'Honneur and a Laureate of the French Academy. This extraordinary man fully deserved all these honours and credits.

One must wonder how a single person could master the intricacies of a wide variety of subjects, be thorough in his studies, display administrative and organisational skills, be capable of being a leader and a statesman, influence decision-makers—both English and Indian with sound judgment and be an ever popular individual. **Truly Divine!**

899 Birdwood, William, *Khaki and Gown,* p. 310.

Appendix I*

BOOKS, REPORTS, PAPERS, LECTURES, AND MAGAZINE ARTICLES WRITTEN BY SIR GEORGE BIRDWOOD

Books.

Handbook to the British Indian Section of the Paris Exhibition of 1878. Published by the Royal Commission, both in English and French; and also republished as a Parliamentary Blue Book.

Handbook to the Industrial Arts of India. Published by Chapman & Hall for the Science and Art Dept., 1880.

The Arts of India (a Handbook to the Collection of His Royal Highness the Prince of Wales, compiled for the Yorkshire Fine Art and Industrial Institution, York). R. Clay, Sons, and Taylor, 1881.

Two Letters on the Industrial Arts of India. Whittingham & Co., 1879.

Ausstellung Indischer Kunst-Gegenstände zu Berlin. 1881. R. Clay, Sons, and Taylor.

Indiens Konstslöjd en Kortfattad Skildring. Stockholm, F. and G. Beijer, 1882.

Indiens Kunstindustrie, en Kortfattel Fremstilling. Kjobenhaven, G. E. C. Gad. 1882.

The Economic Vegetable Products of the Bombay Presidency. Published by the Bombay Government, 1862. Second edition, 1868.

Books of which he has written the Preface, Introduction, or the Advertisement.

Pandurang Hari, reprinted by H. S. King & Co., 1873; Preface by Sir Bartle Frere, and Advertisement by Sir G. Birdwood, being a letter written to the late H. S. King, Esq., recommending the republication of the work.

The Miracle Play of Hasan and Husain, by Sir Lewis Pelly. Allen & Co., 1879. Preface by Sir G. Birdwood.

Eastern Carpets, by Vincent Robinson. H. Sotheran & Co. 1882. The Introduction by Sir George Birdwood.

Oriental Carpets. Published by the Imperial Ministry of Commerce, Worship, and Education, Vienna. 1893. The Monograph on "The Timeless Antiquity, Historical Continuity, and Integral Identity, of the Oriental Manufacture of Sumptuary Carpets," by Sir George Birdwood.

Catalogue of a Loan Exhibition of Embroidery by Indian Women. 1893. Introduction by Sir Geo. Birdwood.

Catalogue of Indian Section of Edinburgh Forestry Exhibition, 1884. The Preface by Sir George Birdwood.

Truth about Opium, by H. Brereton. Allen & Co., 1882. Containing a reprint of Sir George Birdwood's Letters on Opium in "Times" of 6th December, 1881, and 20th February, 1882 : also

All about Opium, by Harlmann H. Sultzberger, 110, Cannon Street, 1884, containing a reprint of the same Letters.

The Dawn of British Trade in the East, as recorded in the Court Minutes of the East India Company, 1599-1603. H. Stevens and Son, 115, St. Martin's Lane, London. 1886. Introduction by Sir Geo. Birdwood.

The First Letter Book of the East India Company, edited by Sir George Birdwood and Mr. William Foster, B.A. Quaritch, 1893. The Introduction by Sir George Birdwood.

Biographies of Words, by F. Max Müller. Longmans, Green & Co. 1888. Appendix I. "The Aryan Fauna and Flora," by Sir George Birdwood.
The Migration of Symbols, by the Count Goblet D'Alviella. Archibald Constable & Co. 1894. The Introduction by Sir George Birdwood.

Reports, Papers, Letters, &c.
(Not including signed contributions to Times, Athenæum, Academv, Pall Mall Gazette, St. James's Gazette, Graphic, and Daily Graphic).
"The Genus Boswellia," Transactions of the Linnean Society, Vol. XXVII. Reprinted by the India Office.
The article " Incense" Encyclopaedia Britannica.
The article "The Perfumes of the Bible," Cassell's Bible Educator.
"On an Ancient Silver Patera," Transactions of the Royal Society of Literature.
"The Bed and Delta of the Nile," Transactions, Bombay Geographical Society, Vol. XV.
"Is the Habaiah of Bruce the Source of the White Nile?" Transactions, Bombay Geographical Soc, Vol. XVI.
"On recent Discovery in Eastern Africa and the Adventures of Captain Singleton (De Foe)," Journal of the Bombay Branch of the Royal Asiatic Society, Vol. VII.
"On Competition and the Indian Civil Service," Journal of the East India Association, 1872. See also Society of Arts Journal, 24th May, 1872. (See also in Journal of East India Association for Letter on Mr. Dady Seth's Lecture, and Remarks on a Lecture by Mr. Watherston).
"On Competition (and the Indian Civil Service)," Journal of the Society of Arts, 2nd June, 1876.
"On *the* Native Press of *India," Journal of the Society of Arts, 23rd March, 1877; and further* statistics, 26th October, *1883.*
"On the Quest and Invention of India," Journal *of the* Society of *Arts, 7th* February, *1879. This* is the Note in the Official "Report *on* the Miscellaneous *Old* Records *of the* India Office."
"Indian Pottery at the Paris Exhibition," *Journal of the Society of Arts, 28th* February, *1872.* Republished *in* Sir George *Birdwood's* " Industrial *Arts of India."*
NOTE.—See also in the same Journal, Letters and Remarks *on the* following subjects :—" The Wild Silks of India," 9th May 1879; "The Opium Trade," 20th January 1882; "Forest Conservancy in India," 17th March; "Domestic Architecture of India," 8th June 1883; " Eastern Carpets," 19th March 1886; "Condition of Applied Arts in England," 4th Feb. 1887; "Economic Resources of India," 1*8th* February; "Application of Gems *to* the Art of the Goldsmith [Aaron's Breastplate]," 18th March and 22nd April; "Principles of Design as applied *to* Bookbinding," *24th* February 1888; "Persian Textiles," 8th June; "Recent Movements in relation to *the* Applied Arts," 25th January and 1st February, 1889; "Ruby Mines of Burma," 22nd February; "Art of the Jeweller," 22nd March; "Indian Wheats," 14th June; "Egyptian Tapestry," 20th September; "Modern Indian Art," 18th April 1890; "Industrial Arts of Japan," 6th June; " Industrial Arts of India, in Code of Manu and other ancient writings," *25th* July and 1st August; "Hall Marking of Silver Plate," 30th January 1891 ; "History of *the* growing use of Tusser Silk," 12th June; *"The Tughra* of the Turks," *4th* and 25th September and 9th October; "From the Tian Shan to the Pamirs," 29th January 1892; "Woodcuts of Gothic Books," 12th February; "Artistic Treatment of Jewel and Address Caskets," 4th March; "Indian Sanitation," 11th March; "The Opium Question," 1st April; "English Brocades and Figured Silks," 22nd April; " Lustre Ware," 24th June; " Occupation and Caste in India as shewn in the last [J. A. Baines] Census," 31st March 1893; "Pattern Designs in Textiles," 21st April; "The Manufactures of India," 5th May; "Architecture and Advertisements," *1st* December; " Goldsmiths' Work," 9th March 1894; "Beauty in Ceramics," 6th April; "Evolution *in* Decorative Art," 27th April; "Etymology of 'Pewter,'" 8th June; "Native Sweetmeats of Bombay," 24th August; "Roman and British-Indian Systems of Government," 14th December; "Forestry,"

21st December; "Woman in India," *15th* February 1895; "Cyder," 8th March; "Improvements in British Silk since 1890," 31st May; "Etymology of 'Bleached,'" 14th February 1896; "Tobacco," 13th March and 3rd April; "Moral Advance of the People of India" [Slavery in India], 5th January and 26th March 1897; "Promotion of the Advanced Study of Physics in India," *26th* February; "Rhea," 2nd April; "Lead Work," 9th April; "Kerman and Persian Baluchistan," *4th* June; "The Life Work of the late Sir Henry Doulton," 26th November; "The Recreation of an Indian Official" [Native names of Indian plants], *4th* February 1898 ; " Stained Glass and Mosaic Work," 8th April; " Ancient and Modern Inks," *6th* May.
"The title of Kaiser-i-Hind," Journal of National *Indian* Association, *1887.*
"Are we despoiling India," by *"John Indigo,"* National *Review* for September 1883.
Review of "Hobson and Jobson," by Colonel H. Yule, C.B., Quarterly Review 1887.
"On the Christmas Tree," Asiatic Quarterly Review, *January 1886.*
"The *Empire* of *the* Hittites," *Asiatic* Quarterly *Review, January, 1888.*
"The Mahratta Plough," Asiatic Quarterly *Review, October 1888.*
"Leper in India," *Asiatic* Quarterly *Review, April 1890.*
Remarks on Sir *W. W.* Hunter*'s* Lecture *on* Indian *Trade before the* Colonial Institute. *See* their Transactions for *1888.*
"Carter's Geology *of* Western *India,." Bombay* Quarterly *Review, 1858. (His first review article).* Report on the Miscellaneous *Old* Records *of the India* Office. *India* Office, *1879.* Reprinted *1889, and again* [by Allen & Co.] *1891.*
Reports on the Cultivation of *the* Spanish Chestnut. *India Office, 1892.* Reprinted *1892.*
Memorandum on *the* Purchase *in Europe of Carrot Seed for the purposes of Famine Relief in* Northern *India.* India *Office, 1896.* Reprinted *[by Messrs. James Carter & Co.] 1898.*

SELECTED LIST OF SIGNED CONTRIBUTIONS TO "ATHENAEUM," "ACADEMY," "TIMES," &C.
N.B. -When the date on which a letter was published has not been verified, the date on which it was written is given instead, with the word *circa* before it.

THE ACADEMY.

Review of Bowdich's *Ashantee,* 10th January 1874. Review of Bell's *Naturalist in Nicaragua,* 21st February. Review of Schweinfurth's *Heart of Africa,* 21st and 28th March. Review of Rohlf's *Morocco,* 18th July. Review of Winwood Reade's *Ashantee Campaign* and Stanley's *Coomassie and Magdala,* 1st August. Review of Cooley's *Livingstone and the Royal Geographical Society,* 26th September. Review of Flückiger and Hanbury's *Pharmacographia,* 14th November. Review of Waller's *Last Journals of David Livingstone,* 13th February 1875. Note on Cooke's "Report on Gums, Resins, &c., in the India Museum," 6th March. Review of Rawlinson's *England and Russia,* 10th April. Review of Monteiro's *Angola and the River Congo,* 22nd January 1876. Note on "Double" in "Midsummer Night's Dream," 15th July. Review of Dutt's *Materia Medica of the Hindus,* 11th August 1877.

THE TIMES.

A Catalogue of Current Literature, *circa* 6th January, and 20th February 1874. Letter signed "Indian," The Royal Progress in India, 3rd February 1876, Letter signed "Anglo-Indian," Empress or Queen, 13th March. Letter signed "Anglo-Indian," The Royal Titles Bill, 16th March. The Indian Mahomedans, *circa* 12th June, and 25th June, 9th July, 10th, 15th and 18th October, 1877. Lahore Jail Carpets, 8th October, 1879. Letter signed "Indigo," The Indian Arms Act, 9th December. Letter signed " Indicopleustes," Candahar, *circa* 11th June, &c., and 24th September, 1880. The Industrial Arts of India [Mahratti *Kirtans,* i.e. ballads, denouncing use of European manufactures], 14th October. The Morality of Opium, 6th December 1881. The Opium Question, 20th January 1882. Letter signed "Out of the Hurly-Burly," The Late Lord Beaconsfield, 14th April. Letter signed "Hortus Siccus," Primrose Day [first use of this phrase], 29th March, 1883. Professor Sayce, the Aryans and the Birch Tree, 5th and 21st September, and 3rd and 15th October, *et caetera,* 1887. The Prickly Pear in the Deccan, 2nd February 1889. The Play of" Mahomet" in England, 9th and *circa* 15th October *1890. Approaching End of British Rule in India, 11th February 1891. Hindu Prejudices, 2nd September. Wroth Silver, 18th November 1892. Cyder ["How to help Agriculturists"], 19th September and 4th October. Etymology of "Sindh," "Hindustan," "India " ["The Indian Army"], 1st February 1895. Loan Exhibition of Relics and Memorials of the late H.E.I. Company, 5th February. The Evolution of a Show Place, 23rd October. The New Penny. 24th and 30th December. The Plane Trees by Spring Gardens, 17th January 1896. The Rule of Succession in Islam, 1st September. Arbor Day in Kent, 29th December. The Birthplace of Buddha, 28th January, 19th March, and 9th September 1897. The Victorian Era Exhibition, 18th March. Sea Power, 6th May. Etymology of "Gallant Soldier," 28th October.*

THE ATHENAEUM.

The so-called "Custard Apple" of the Ajanta Cave Paintings, 31st October 1874. The so-called "Pine Apple" on an Assyrian Monument [Rawlinson's "Ancient Monarchies," Vol. II. p. 212, ed. 1862], 6th March 1875. The Earliest Mention of "Guano," 29th May. Anachronisms in the introduction of flowers and fruits in the paintings at the Royal Academy, 3rd July. The Sea Level, 11th March 1876. Anachronisms at Royal Academy, 29th July. Bulgarian Horrors, 14th and 28th October. The Title of "Kaisar-i-Hind," 11th November, 2nd and 16th December. The Title of "Kaisar-i-Hind," 6th January 1876. Anachronisms at Royal Academy, 21st July. The so-called "Custard Apple" of the Ajanta Cave Paintings and Bharhut Sculptures, 17th January 1880. The Pine Apple in the Old World, 30th August. The Ajanta Cave Paintings, 11th June 1881. Letter signed "Christopher Molesworth," Bonaparte at Long wood, 23rd July. The Industrial Arts of India in the 17th Century, 11th March 1882. Mr. Gladstone's Jubilee, 16th December. Wordsworthiana, 2nd March 1889. Clothes and Conduct on board an Old Indiaman, 6th April. "Journal of Indian Art," 14th March 1891. Etymology of "Larboard" and "Lair-Cart," 8th and 22nd August. Etymology of "Alabaster," "Ivory," and "Elephant," 22nd June 1895. Etymology of "Patchouli," 22nd October 1898.

THE PALL MALL GAZETTE.

Letters signed "F.R.G.S." on Cameron's Expedition, 21st, 26th and 30th December 1874. An Odious Comparison, 7th June 1875. Leitner's Buddhistic Sculptures, 3rd June. The Turk, circa 16th December. Mr. Gladstone's Homeric Synchronisms, 24th March 1876. Russia in Asia Minor, 7th and 14th May 1877. The Euphrates Valley, 28th May. Sir Vernon Harcourt and the Question of Armenia, 19th June. Armenia and Afghanistan, 22nd June. The Old Afghan War, 27th June and 2nd July. The Muslim Khalifate, 26th July. Poetic Prophecy, 10th July. Letter signed "Anglo-Indian" on Our Afghan Frontier, circa 17th August. Letter signed "Anglo-Indian" on The Retention of the Candahar Garrison, circa 8th September. Letter signed "Iran," on Irresolution on the Indian Frontier, circa 30th September. Letter signed "Indigo," on The Indian Government and Shere Ali, 23rd October. Letter signed "Indigo" on Baluchistan and Afghanistan, 9th November. Letter signed "Anglo-Indian," on The Fall of Kars, 26th November. Midhat Pasha, 4th January 1878. Letter signed "Iran," on The Development of the " Perish India" Policy, 4th October. Letter signed "Iran" on Lord Napier of Magdala's Views about Afghanistan, 14th October. Letter signed "Iran," on Lord Lytton's Ultimatum, 5th November. Letter signed "Iran," on Lord Napier of Magdala on the Indian Frontier Question, 19th November. Letter signed "Nemesis," on The Moralities of Moral Statesmanship, 2nd December. The Miracle Play of Hasan and Husain, 4th and 8th August, 1879. Crisis in Central Asia, 12th September. The Bombay Riots [Etymology of Dashara], 17th and circa 22nd August, 1893. The Discovery of

Madagascar, 4th November. Wanted, Twelve Saints, circa 2nd October and 12th October. Etymology of Maundy-Thursday and maund 6th April 1896. Names of Wild Flowers, 24th November and 4th and 14th December 1897.

ST. JAMES' GAZETTE.

Letter, signed in error "G. P. B." *[for* " G.B."], *The Opinions of Lord Bolingbroke, circa 24th June 1880. Letters signed "Anglo-Indian," on General Burrows' Route, 31st July and 5th August. Letter signed "Anglo-Indian," on The Times on our Indian Empire, 3rd August. Does India Pay? [in reply to Grant Allen], 21st October. Letter signed "Durani," on The Annexation of Candahar, 1st February, 1881. The three following letters were published in St. James' Gazette between 1881 and 1888 inclusive:—Etymology of "Punch," circa 9th May; Etymology of "Gillyflowers," circa 6th August. Etymology of" Jerusalem Artichokes," circa 14th November. Curious Phrases, 16th October 1889. The Colossus of Rhodes, 19th May 1890. Holkar's Letter to the Baroness Burdett-Coutts [Etymology of "Open Sesame"], circa? 1891. A Letter signed "Mezzoramian," on Women of the Day, by Themselves, 6th April. The Saibis, 4th May. The Antiquity of the Pheasant-Eyed Narcissus, 1st June 1892. The Dawn of Astronomy, 27th March 1894. Another Gruesome Story, 29th March. Misquotations, 23 and 24th July. The Beasts of India, circa 28th November. The Seven Seas, 27th October 1897.*

Miss Manning's INDIAN MAGAZINE.

Article, The Title "Kaisar-i-Hind," June 1887. Review, Kipling's Beast and Man in India, January 1892. Reproduction of Introduction to the Catalogue of a Loan Collection of Embroidery by Indian Women, exhibited in 1894 *at Chesham House, Regent Street, by the Society for the Encouragement and Preservation of Indian Art, July 1893. Letter [to Mr. Frederick Moore] on The Ancient Sources of Silk, February 1895. Letter [to Mr. John Murray] on The Preservation of Indian Monuments, February 1895.*

THE GRAPHIC.

Etymology of "Curry," 15th October 1887. Article, St. Nicholas' Cakes, 6th December, 1890. Review, History of Persian Art [Perrot and Chipiez], 27th February 1892.

THE DAILY TELEGRAPH.

Etymology of "Dog-Watch," 20th March 1889.

THE BOMBAY GAZETTE.

Old Record, Bombay in 1682, "B.G. Summary " of 14th October 1889. Old Record, Transfer of Bombay to East India Co., "B.*G. Budget" of 12th November.*

THE SPEAKER.

Review, History of Persian Art [Perrot and Chipiez], 17th September 1892.

THE DAILY GRAPHIC.

Etymology of "Harrier," 27th September, 1895. Whittington's Cat, 12th and 20th December. Lancashire and India, 17th December. Etymology of "Oranges and Lemons," 8th April 1896.
The Journal of Indian Art. *Article, The Decoration of the Taj Mahal, Agra, July 1885. Articles, The Honourable East India Company, July 1890, January and April 1891. Article, Indian Art at Marlborough House and Sandringham, October 1891 and January 1802. To* the *Temple, January 1898.*

**Cited in The Journal of Indian Art and Industry Vol. VIII, pp. 48-50.*

Appendix II*

Address from Artists, on "Handbook to Indian Court," Paris, 1878.

TO GEORGE C. M. BIRDWOOD, ESQ., C.S.I., M.D., &C, &C.

1May, 1879.
Dear Sir,-We, the undersigned, wish to express the thanks we owe you for the manner in which you have performed an important duty in your report on the Articles of Indian Manufacture exhibited in Paris last year. In common with all who have given any attention to the subject, we have seen and lamented the rapid deterioration that has of late befallen the great historical arts of India. The independent and courageous criticism contained in your Handbook, founded on close observation and long experience, has shown us the causes that have been at work in bringing about this deterioration, and has given us a hope that something may yet be done to stay its further progress.

We do not doubt that all men of culture will agree with us in thinking that the welfare of the arts in question is important both to India and to Europe, and that the loss of them would be a serious blow to civilization, and an injury to the pleasure and dignity of life : and if this importance be at once admitted, together with the danger to them that comes of the manner in which they are now being dealt with by Europeans that are brought into contact with the Asiatic workmen, we cannot conceive that any thoughtful person will deny the responsibility of England in the matter, or the duty which a great country owes to the arts of exercising foresight and patience , lest, for an apparent commercial gain, she and the world in general should lose industries which have for ages made India famous, industries whose educational influence on the arts of the West is so universally acknowledged by all the students of art and history.

At a time when these productions are getting to be daily more and more valued in Europe, their sources are being dried up in Asia, and goods which ought to be common in the market at reasonable prices are now becoming rare treasures for museums or the cabinets of rich men. This result seems to us the reverse of what commerce ought to aim at, and we cannot help thinking that when the producers and the public wake up to a knowledge of the facts in the case, they will be eager to restore these industries to their due position. We think they will have a good chance of success if it be not then too late, and if no artificial obstacles be thrown in their way.

We therefore think that your remarks on these manufactures were both necessary and timely, and will be most useful in promoting a better understanding of the only conditions under which the so much admired art of the East can flourish, or, in the long run, exist; and we beg once more to tender you our hearty thanks, in the full belief that in doing so we express the feelings of all lovers of art who have read your excellent report.

(Signed)

GEORGE AITCHESON., RUTHERFORD ALCOCK., THOMAS ARMSTRONG., EDWIN ARNOLD., G. P. BOYCE., ANDREW CASSELS., T. CHENERY., C. PURDON CLARKE., WALTER CRANE., FRANK DILLON., HENRY DOULTON., M. E. GRANT DUFF., ARTHUR ELLIS., BARROW H. ELLIS., AUGUSTUS W. FRANKS., F. GARRARD., CARL HAAG., J. A. HEATON., W. HERTZ., GEO. HOWARD., W. STANLEY JEVONS., EDWARD BURNE JONES., FRED. LEIGHTON., COUTTS LINDSAY., JAMES D. LINTON., GEORGE J. S. LOCK., CLEMENTS R. MARKHAM., NEVIL STORY MASKELYNE., JOHN EVERETT MILLAIS., WILLIAM MORRIS., A. MORRISON., LEWIS PELLY., ROBERT PHILLIPS., VAL.PRINSEP.,H. RAWLINSON.,RICHARD REDGRAVE.,VINCENT ROBINSON.,R.ROST., T. L. SECCOMBE., R. NORMAN SHAW., R. H. SODEN SMITH., W. G. SPOTTISWOODE., W. STEBBING., E. ALMA TADEMA., W. T. THORNTON., WILLIAM S. W. VAUX., HORACE WALPOLE., THOMAS WARDLE., PHILIP WEBB., MONIER WILLIAMS., THOMAS WOOLNER., H. YULE.

TO WILLIAM MORRIS, ESQ., AND OTHERS

India Office, 1 June, 1879.

GENTLEMEN,- In acknowledging your letter of 1 May, 1879, I must begin by frankly confessing to a feeling of intense personal pleasure.

Not less sincere is my satisfaction in receiving so weighty a testimony to the excellence of the historical handicrafts and hereditary craftmasters of India. Your approbation will do more even than last year's Paris Exhibition to quicken the growing popular interest in Indian art, and in the self-contained and self-supporting Indian communal life of which the arts of that country are the bright emanation. The unity in variety of Indian, as of all Eastern life, must never be overlooked by those who would understand the traditional arts of India and the East. It has a vital lesson for us, among whom, owing to our system of land tenure, those political revolutions, which in the East rarely affect the democratic organization of society, have so often destroyed the continuity of popular progress, to the manifest injury of the indigenous domestic arts, and of the higher forms of art, such as painting and sculpture, for which the people of the West have a far greater natural ability than those of the East. Art in England has, therefore, rather expressed sectarian views than the catholic sentiments of a people at complete unity with themselves; and this is why it has hitherto failed both in homely use and epic grandeur. It is only in times of its decay that men begin to talk of Art as being its own end and aim. In reality, Art is the highest expression of the whole moral and material condition of a people, and their ever strengthening incentive to a higher life. To impart this incentive has always been the purpose of Art wherever it has sprung from the life of a people; and where it does not serve this end, where, through social disorganization, it is no longer rooted in national life, it fails in inborn vigour and originality, and ceases to exercise any elevating influence on national character.

The arts of India are indissolubly bound up with the popular institutions of the country; and however much the Hindu may have erred from the right way, and obscured the light that is in him, he yet, as regards all the thoughts and intents of his heart, lives in the unseen world of man's spiritual consciousness, by which he is influenced in every act of his life and in whatsoever he does to adorn life; and Art, the preservative of all the arts, is true to itself, and vindicates its participation in divineness only when it is inspired by the highest ideals of a people gathered together in natural and coordinated unity, as in the cooperative village communities of India.

In estimating the disturbing effect of European influences on the arts of India, we must avoid too exclusive and too indiscriminate blame of Schools of art. The influence of Europe on the East is inevitable, and the presence in India of cultivated English gentlemen at the head of Schools of Art cannot fail in end to correct the degrading effects of the necessary strain of European commerce on the village and sumptuary arts of India. After all, the chief offenders against Art in India are the official departments engaged in the manufacture of jail carpets, and the construction of public buildings; and it is particularly through the neglect of native architecture and the propagation of a bastard English style, blindly followed by the people themselves, that the Government threatens the slow destruction of the historical handicrafts of India. Art never long survives among a people who neglect architecture, the chief of the arts. All the minor arts in England suffered during the period of the decline of our national building style, and our painting and sculpture still suffer, as is shewn in their prevailing anecdotal character, from their long disassociation with architecture. But in many parts of India, such as Rajputana and Kattyawar, a spontaneous native architecture survives. The late ALEXANDER KINLOCH FORBES, the author of "Ras Mala," was always seeking to obtain the employment of the native workmasters (*maestries*) of Kattyawar on public buildings of their own designing; and it is not yet too late for the Government, by the encouragement of native hereditary architects, not only to arrest the decadence of the arts of India, but to promote their revival. Schools of Art might become effective agents in this *renaissance*, only it is absolutely essential that their work should begin, where that of the native draughtsman always begins, with the study of architecture.

There is nothing in what has been advanced to justify the charge sometimes made of a desire to Orientalise the decorative arts of other countries. But every European, artificer and artist alike, might well take the handicraftsmen of India for an example in the patience, perseverance, and thoroughness which are the ground of their excellency, and by which the inspirations of art are wrought into reality and life. The legerdemain which some would fain substitute for patient labour in the arts destroys all mastery in their methods, and at last dissipates the very sense of artistic imagery and invention. Labour is the probation of perfection. The innumerable ingenuities and subtle incommunicable graces of the arts can be obtained through labour alone: and their end and aim must, as is taught by all Eastern Art," By Nyle, or Gange, or Tygre, or Euphrate," be steadfastly set on the glory and enjoyment of the Most Highest, in whom is the Perfect Mastery and the Sum of Perfection.

I have, &c,

*G*EORGE *B*IRDWOOD.

Resolution approved by the Secretary of State for India in Council, the. 22nd of September, 1880.

In receiving from the Lords of the Committee of Council on Education, for the use of this office and for transmission to India, copies of the work on the Industrial Arts of India, which has been prepared by Dr. George Birdwood, C.S.I., special assistant in this office, to serve as a Handbook to the India Museum, as now reorganized under the Science and Art Department at South Kensington, the Secretary of State for India in Council takes the opportunity to record his high sense of the services which Dr. Birdwood has rendered to Indian industry by the preparation of this book, as well as by his Handbook to the Indian Department of the Paris Universal Exhibition of 1878. The value of the latter work has been noticed in warm terms by His Royal Highness the Prince of Wales, and the Royal Commissioners for the Representation of the Queen's

Dominions at that Exhibition, and the Secretary of State in Council is glad to add his own recognition of its importance in stimulating a wide public appreciation of Indian art manufactures, whilst it strives to maintain unimpaired their former beauty of design and execution.

True copy communicated to Dr. George Birdwood, C.S.I.

(Signed) Louis *MALLET*.

**Cited in The Journal of Indian Art and Industry Vol. VIII, pp. 51-53.*

Bibliography

Unpublished Primary Sources

Unpublished State Papers in the Maharashtra State Archives.

I.1. *General Department*

Volumes

94 of 1850/ 73 of 1856/ 74 of 1856/ 38 of 1859/ vii of 1861/ 21 of 1862-64/ 1 of 1866

I.2. *Judicial Department*

Volumes

64 of 1854/ 25 of 1863/ 25 of 1864/ 37 of 1865/ 77 of 1876

I.3. *Public Works Department*

Volumes

10 of 1861/ 38 of 1862

I.4. *Education Department*

Volumes

1 of 1859/ 15 of 1859/ 20 of 1859/ 31 of 1860/ 4 of 1861/ 3 of 1862/9 of 1864

I.5. **Unpublished Minutes/ Articles**

Bombay University Minute Book IV.

CD entitled *Minutes* (Asiatic Society) 1862-1865.

Minutes of the Bombay Branch of the Royal Asiatic Society, 1860-1865.

Minutes of the Bombay Branch of the Royal Asiatic Society, 1865-1868.

Mascarenhas, Aruna, *Akbar and the Making of Mughal Miniature,* Jnanaparvaha, Post Graduate Diploma on Indian Aesthetics, third assignment, 2011.(10th May 2011).

I.6. **Unpublished Primary Sources**

British Library

INDIA OFFICE SELECT MATERIALS

List for shelfmark Mss Eur F216

Papers of Sir George Birdwood, medical scientist, botanist, promoter of Arts and Crafts movement, and Indologist

Mss Eur F216/1 Letters to Birdwood - 1876-79

Mss Eur F216/2 Letters to Birdwood - 1880

Mss Eur F216/8 Letters to Birdwood including letters from M M Bhownagree, - 1888
William Digby of the Indian Political Agency, Sir William Hunter, George

James Sheridan Lock, and Col. H. Yule.
Mss Eur F216/9 Correspondence with Lady Frere, - Aug. 1888 – Dec. 1889
Sir William Hunter and others concerning the biography of Sir Bartle Frere
Mss Eur F216/13 Letters from the *Graphic* and the *Daily Graphic* - Oct-Nov. 1889
concerning their suggestion that Birdwood should write for them.
Mss Eur F216/16 Other letters: L-Y including Sir James Dromgole Linton, - 1889
Dadabhai Naoroji, Lord Northbrook, Thomas Wardle of Leek and Col.H.Yule
Mss Eur F216/ 19 Correspondence relating to the Indian Section at the - 1890
Paris Exhibition
Mss Eur F216/24 Letters to Birdwood: E-F including letters from Ernest - 1891
Ayscoghe Floyer, Dosabhai Framji of Bombay and the family of Sir Bartle Frere
Mss Eur F216/33: Letters to Birdwood: B including letters from - 1892
M M Bhownagree
Mss Eur F216/44 Letters to Birdwood: T-Y including letters from - 1892
Thomas Wardle, Stephen Wheeler, Henry Benjamin Wheatley, H.T. Wood,
And Javerilal Yagnik
Mss Eur F216/47 Other letters to Birdwood: B including letters from - 1893
M M Bhownagree
Mss Eur F216/57 Letters to Birdwood: N-O including letters from - 1893
Dadabhai Naoroji and Sir P. Cunliff Owen

Published Primary Sources

II.1 *Minutes, Reports and Others*

Birdwood, George, *Report of the Government Central Museum and on the Agricultural and Horticultural Society of Western India, 1864.*

Transactions of the Agricultural and Horticultural Society of India, Volume I, 1820.

Maharashtra State Universities Act, 1994.

Bombay University Calendar for the year 1864.

Report of the Superintendent of Police submitted with the report of the Senior Magistrate of Police, No. 493 of 1854, dated September, 22, 1854.

Journal of the Bombay Branch of the Royal Asiatic Society, The Centenary Memorial Volume.

Bombay Branch of the Royal Asiatic Society, Sardha Satabdi Celebrations.

Times of India cutting in *Minutes of the Royal Asiatic Society (1860-65),* November, 1864.

Transactions of the Literary Society of Bombay, Volume I.

Times of India, 30th July, 1863.

Bombay Saturday Review, 1st August 1863, on *Early Marriages of the Hindoos.*

Report of the Maharaja Libel Case and of the Bhatia Conspiracy Case, connected with it, Bombay, 1862.

Birdwood, George, *Handbook to the British Section of the Paris Exhibition of* 1878.

Official Catalogue to the 1886 *Colonial and Indian Exhibition in London.*

Journal of the Royal Society of Arts, February, 4, 1910.

Journal of Indian Art and Industry, Volume viii.

Journal of the Royal Asiatic Society: 1890-94, XLVIII, *Proceedings of the B.B.R.A.S.* (August 1889-May 1891), *"An illuminated M.S. Copy of Dante 'Divinia Commedia',"* pp.vii-viii.

II.2. *Periodicals and Records*

Bombay Government Gazette: January-June 1864.

Bombay Government Gazette: March 3, 1864.

Journal of Indian Art and Industry, Volume viii, pp.45-47.

Marg Publication, 1997, *Bombay to Mumbai.*

The Bombay Builder, Volume I. No. I. July 5, 1865.

The Bombay Builder, Volume I. No. 3, September 5, 1865.

The Bombay Builder, Volume I. No. 7, January 5, 1866.

The Bombay Builder, Volume II. No. 6, December 5, 1866.

Brochure of Dr. Bhau Daji Lad Museum, City Museum [available at the Museum].

Secondary Sources

I.1. *Gazetteers*

Gazetteer of Bombay City and Island, Volumes, I, II, III, Bombay 1909.

Maharashtra State Gazetteers Greater Bombay District.

I.2. *Literature*

Allen, Charles, *Kipling Sahib, India in the Making,* G.B. 2007.

Birdwood, George, *Sva,* edited by F.H. Brown, London:Philip Lee Warner, Humphrey Milford, Oxford University Press, Bombay, Melbourne, Toronto, MDCCCCXV.

Birdwood, George, *Catalogue of the Vegetable Productions of the Presidency of Bombay; Including a list of the Drugs sold in the Bazar of Western India,* 2nd edition, Bombay. Printed at the Education Society's Press, Byculla, 1865.

Birdwood, George, *Report on the Old Records of the India Office: With Supplement Note and Appendices,* Second Reprint, London, W.H. Allen & Co. Ltd. and at Calcutta, 1911.

Birdwood, G.C.M., *The Stree Bodhe and the Social Progress in India: A Jubilee Memorial, Together with the Account of Jubilee Celebrations and Lectures,* Bombay, 1908.

Birdwood, George, *Industrial Arts of India,* September, 1880.

Birdwood, George, *On the Genus Boswellia,* Transactions of the Linnean Society, Volume XXVII, Reprinted by the India Office.

Birdwood, Lord William Field-Marshall, *Field-Marshall Lord Birdwood of Anzac and Totnes—Khaki and Gown:* An Autobiography, U.K. 1941.

Buckland, C.E., *Dictionary of Indian Biography,* Reprint, Delhi, Varanasi, 1971.

Chodankar, Anant Atmaram, *Yugapurush—Namdar Jagannath tatha Nana Sunkersett,* Aapala Prakashan,

Goregoan (East), Mumbai 63, (Marathi), July 2010.

Cowasjee Jehanghier, J., *Life of Cowasjee Jehanghier Readymoney,* Bombay, 1890.

Cunningham, Alexander, *The Stupa of Bharhut,* Published by the Order of State for India in Council, London, 1879.

Dantawala, M.L., *A Hundred Years of Indian Cotton,* Bombay East India Association Ltd., Bombay, 1947.

Dongerkery, S.R., *A History of the University of Bombay, 1857-1957,* Bombay University, 1957.

Dwivedi, Sharada, *Premchand Roychand* (1831-1906), *His Life and Times,* Eminence Designs Pvt. Ltd., Bombay, 2006.

Govind, Narayan, *Mumbai-An Urban Biography from 1863,* Gyan Prakash, 1852.

Gupchup, Vijaya, *Bombay Social Change,* 1813-1857, Popular Book Depot, Bombay, 1993.

Gupchup, Vijaya, *St. Thomas' Cathedral, A Witness to History,* Eminence Designs Pvt. Ltd. Bombay, 2005.

Hirschmann, Edwin, *Robert Knight Reforming Editor in Victorian India,* Oxford University Press, Delhi, 2008.

Laurie, William F.B. (William Ferguson Beatson), *Sketches of some Distinguished Anglo-Indians with an account of Anglo-Indian periodical literature,* W.H. Allen, 1887, Also in Google Books, History, 420 pages, Appendices 388,389,390,391,392,393,394. VIII, Sir George Birdwood, K.C.S.L. LL.D.

Lipsey, Roger, *Coomaraswamy,* Volume 3, *His Life and Work,* Princeton University Press.

MacKenzie, John M., *Orientalism: History, Theory and the Arts,* Manchester University Press, 1995.

Mainkar, T.G., *Writings and Speeches of Dr. Bhau Daji,* University of Bombay, Bombay, 1974.

Priyolkar, A.K., *Dr. Bhau Daji: Vyakti, Kaal va Kartrutva,* Mumbai Marathi Sahitya Sangh, Mumbai, (Marathi).

Rogers, J.M., *Mughal Miniatures,* The British Museum Press, London WC IB 3QQ, 1993.

Sedgwick, Mark, *Against the Modern Traditionalism and Secret Intellectual History of the Twentieth Century,* Oxford University Press, 20D4, 2004.

Shirodkar, P.P., *Hon. Jagannath Shankershet Prophet of India's Resurgence and Maker of Modern Bombay,* Pradnya Darshan Prakashan, Goa, India,2005.

Smith, Vincent, *History of Fine Art in India and Ceylon,* London, 1911.

Stronge, Susan, *Painting For The Mughal Emperor: The Art of the Book 1560-1660,* V&A Publication, London, 2002.

Tikekar, Aroon, *The Cloister's Pale, A Biography of the University of Bombay,* Bombay, Second edition, 2006, Reprinted 2007.

Vedak, Gadadhar S., *A Life Sketch of the Hon. Mr. Jagannath Shankershet,* Bombay, 1937.

Wacha, D.E., *A Financial Chapter in the History of Bombay City,* Cambridge & Company, Bombay, 1910.

Wacha, D.E., *Premchund Roychund: His Early Life and Career,* The Times Press, Bombay, 1913.

Yule, Henry, *Hobson – Jobson: A Glossary of Colloquial Anglo-Indian Words and Phrases,* (New edition), London, John Murray, 1903.

Internet

Mitter Partha and Clunas Craig, *A Grand Design, A History of the Victoria and Albert Museum, pp. 1-14;* http://www.vam.ac.uk/vastatic/microsites//1159 grand design/ essay-the-empire-of-things new. html.

Web Hostings by Netfirms: 6/28/2009

<Roots Web:INDIA-L DOMESTIC OCCURENCES 1863> From "Sylvia Murphy"

Elephant Symbol and Meaning, Elephant in FengShui, in Chinese Culture

The Sacred Lotus, Nelumbo nucifera Nymphaeceae http://www.holisticaroma.co.uk/shp/The Sacred Lotus.htm

A Critical History of Architecture in a Post-Colonial World: A View from Indian History, Department of Architecture, University of California at Berkeley, Posthumus Destinies, POSTED BY DEBBANERJI, Published July 15, 2009.

Origin of the Kushanas, http://www.indianetzone.com/21/the origin early history kushanas.htm

http://www.monadarling.com/lifestyle/jawahar-lal-nehru.html

Girton College Library, The Special Collections,

http://www-lib.girton.cam.ac.uk/special/index.html

http://www.education.nic.in/cd50years/u/47/3y/473YO701.htm

IOR/V/27/516/1 1897 Part of Agriculture:Fruit and Vegetables IOR/V/27/516 1888-1952

Breckenridge Carol A. The Aesthetics and Politics of Colonial Collecting: India at World Fairs

Comparative Studies in Society and History, Cambridge Journal Vol.31 Issue02, 1989.

DOI:10.1017/SOO10417500015796 (About DOI)

Migration Histories>South Asian>Politics Dadabhai Naoroji (1825-1917)

http://www.movinghere.org.uk/galleries/histories/asian/politics/dadabhai_naoroji.htm

http://nla.gov.au/nla.news-article 39494007

http://bombayhighcourt.nic.in/lib web/judges/Telang% 20K.T..html

http://books.google.co.in/books?id=2oUBmVk032wC&pg=PA202&dq...

http://gluedideas.com/Encyclopedia-Britannica-Volume-10-Part-1-Game-Gun-Metal/...

http://www.racollection.org.uk/ixbin/indexplus?_IXACTION_=file&_IXFILE_=tem...

http://trove.nla.gov.au/ndp/del/printArticleJpg/39494007/3?printt=y

http://www.houseofnames.com/birdwood-family-crest?a=54323-224

http://www8.open.ac.uk/researchprojects/makingbritain/content/george-birdwood

http://www.fathom.com/feature/60964/index.html

http://www.enotes.com/topic/Asiatic_Society_of_Mumbai

http://www.indianetzone.com/3/lord_dufferin.htm

Dancewithshadows Bhau Daji Lad-Mumbai's Oldest Museum By Harpreet Kaur

Internet

http://www.loc.gov/pictures/resource/cph.3c02645/
http://www.loc.gov/pictures/resource/cph.3f03719/
http://www.tmoi.org.uk/about-john-forbes-watson.html
http://www.vam.ac.uk/content/people-pages/obituary-caspar-purdon-clarke/
http:www.houseofnames.com/product/Family+Crest+Image+%28jpg%29+Legacy+...
http://www.artmagick.com/pictures/artist.aspx?artist=j-d-linton

Index

A

Abel, Frederick, Sir 174
Afghans 115, 116, 117
Agri-Horticultural Society 3, 13, 16, 17, 41, 45, 54, 55, 57, 62
Alfred Knott 155, 156, 157
Ananda Kentish Coomaraswamy (AKC) 130, 135
Approbation of Indian Art in Britain 128
Arabs 115, 116
Arts and Craft movement 130

B

Babar 117
Bhau, Daji 3, 11, 17, 23, 25, 31, 32, 36, 121, 122, 181, 182, 186
Bhownagree, Merwanjee, Mancherjee 169, 172
Birdwood, Frank 178, 179
Birdwood, H.M. Justice 78, 149
Bombay Branch of the Royal Asiatic Society 28, 33, 37, 38, 40, 41, 42, 50, 51, 61, 146, 147
Bombay Castle 14, 15, 23, 67
Bombay City 141
Bombay Government 6, 13, 15, 55, 102
Bombay Times and Journal of Commerce 151
Bombay University 10, 85
Bopp, Prof 44
Breckenridge, Carol 165
Byculla Club 164

C

Cama, Rustomjee, Cursetjee 6
Carey, William Rev 17, 35, 52, 55, 56
Carter H.J. 32, 33, 35, 48, 49, 181, 182
Chancellor 69, 70, 71, 72, 75, 82, 83, 84, 86
Chandavarkar, N.G. Justice 123, 124
Chattopadhyay, Swati 98, 105
Chisholm, Robert 133, 134
Clarke, Purdon Caspar 98, 104, 105, 165, 166, 167, 168
Coomaraswamy, Kentish, Ananda 130, 132, 135, 137, 140
Crane, Walter 130, 132
Cunliff-Owen, Philip 104, 140, 162, 166
Cunningham, Alexander 103, 104
Curtsetjee, Maneckjee 31, 32

D

Decorative Art of India 95
Dhyani Buddha 132
Digby William 155, 157, 159
Director of Public Instructions' offices 10
Divinia Commedia 146, 147
Dongerkery, S.R. 70, 71
Douglas, James 145, 146
Dr. F. Giraud 17
Dufferin, Lord 164, 171, 184
Duke of Argll 160
Duncan, Jonathan, Governor of Bombay 28, 29, 30, 38

E

Eastwick, Backhouse, Edmund 141
Elphinstone College 10, 36, 85, 125
Elphinstone Institution 10
Elphinstone, Lord, Governor of Bombay 1, 14, 86
Erskine, William 28, 30, 32, 48, 149
Esplanade 10, 11, 12, 13, 14, 19, 120
Exhibitions, Crtical, Review 97

F

Factory Diaries and Consultations 92, 183
Fergusson, James 102, 105, 136
Finch, Captain 21, 22, 23, 24
Fitzgerald, Seymour, Sir, the Governor of Bombay 25, 77, 182
Forbes, Charles 28, 30
Fraser, Garden, Alex 2, 3
Frere, Bartle, Governor of Bombay 16, 25, 56, 70, 75, 76, 77, 81, 82, 86, 142, 143, 144, 145, 146
Frere, Edward, William 28, 31, 32, 37, 38, 39, 41, 182
Frere, Lady, Catherine 39, 56, 143, 144, 145, 146, 147, 148
Frere, Mary 142, 144, 148
Fry, Roger 130, 131, 135

G

Genus Boswellia 180
Gilbert, Alfred 175, 176, 177, 178
Giraud, F. Dr. 17, 55
Girton College Library 147
Gothic 11, 18, 19, 44
Government Central Museum 1, 2, 5, 6, 7, 9, 10, 11, 26, 56, 97
Grant, Alexander, Sir 34, 35, 36, 75, 81, 83
Grant Medical College 180
Griffths, John 164
Griggs, Maur, Landseer, Frederick 164, 167, 168

H

Handbook to the British Section of the Paris Exhibition of 1878 93, 98, 104
Havell, Ernest, Binfield 130, 131, 133, 134, 136, 138, 184
Heycock E. 10
Historical Retrospect of Indian Art 93
Hobson-Jobson 121
Hooper, Luther 134
Hunter, W.F. 2
Hunter, Wilson, William 142, 143, 144, 169, 170

I

Imperial Institute 173, 174
Impey Dr. 2
Indian plough 113, 159
India Office 13, 14, 88, 91, 92, 93, 131, 138, 141, 149, 155, 156, 159, 168, 169, 171, 184, 187
India Society 135
Indigo 5, 6, 89, 152, 153, 185
Indraji, Bhagwanlal, Pandit 141
Industrial Arts of India 93, 118, 127, 129, 159, 177, 182
INTACH, Indian National Trust for Art and Cultural Heritage 25

J

Jamnalal Bajaj Foundation 25
Jamsetjee Jeejeebhoy School of Art and Industry 10, 14, 17, 56, 137
Jehanghier, Cowasjee 7, 32, 38, 39, 46, 75, 76, 84
Johur 115, 116, 117
Journal of Indian Art 137, 146, 148
Jubilee Celebration 123, 124, 125

K

Kabraji, Kaikhushro N 123, 125
Karsondas, Mulji 124, 125
Karwar 60
Keith, James 105
Kensington Museum 132, 140, 141, 166, 182
Kipling, Lockwood, John 98, 105, 137, 183
Knight, Robert 151, 152, 153, 154, 186
Knott, Alfred 155, 156, 157

L

Landsdowne, Lord 163, 164, 167, 168, 171
Leprosy in India 121
Lethaby, W.R. 135
Literary Society of Bombay 29, 31, 38
Lock, Sheridan, James, George 161, 162
Lyall, Alfred, Sir 137

M

Macaulay, Lord 131
MacKenzie, John M 164
Maharashtra Universities Act 71, 73
Malcolm, John, Sir 30
Malet, A. 4, 14
Mandlik, Narayan, Vishvanath 36, 48
McClelland, Scott, Messrs 18, 21, 22, 23, 24
Mount Estate 11, 12, 13, 16, 17, 55, 57, 62
Mughal 117, 184, 185, 186
Muharram 119, 120, 121

N

Naidu, Sarojini, Mrs 124, 125, 126
Naoroji, Dadabhai 125, 169, 171, 172, 184
Nathoobhai, Mangaldas 186
Newton, Justice 37, 45, 47, 50, 61

O

Officers of the University 70, 72, 73
Old Deccan Days 142, 148
Opium 5, 7, 89

P

Palladian 18, 19
Pappe Dr 8
Piele, J.B. 15
Pioneer 151
Playfair, Captain 8, 181
Premchund Roychand 20, 41, 46, 76, 77, 84
Prince of Wales 61, 99, 104, 148, 160, 162
Pro-Vice-Chancellor 71, 72, 73
Public Works Department 21, 24, 25

Q

Quarterly Review 49, 131, 156

R

Rajputs 113, 114, 115, 116, 117, 118
Rast Goftar 123, 125
Registrar 63, 68, 70, 71, 72, 74, 75, 76, 77, 78, 79, 80, 81, 82, 83, 84, 85, 160, 178
Report on the Government Central Museum 26
Report on the Old Records of the India Office 88
Robinson, Vincent 166, 167, 168
Rothenstein, William 135
Royal Academy 133
Royal Society of Arts 131, 133, 134, 135, 138, 184
Ruskin, John 128, 129, 134

S

Sattara Native Library 6
Scott, Gilbert 77
Sedgwick, Mark 138
Senate 69, 70, 71, 73, 74, 76, 79, 81, 82, 83, 85, 179
Sewri Gardens 55

Sheriff 10, 63, 64, 66, 67, 68, 153, 182
Sinclair, Professor 2
Smith, Vincent 135
Social Reforms 123
Statesman 151, 153, 187, 188
Stovell, Dr 41
St. Thomas' Cathedral 18, 19
Sunkersett, Jugonnath 16, 32, 36, 38, 39, 46, 78, 81, 82, 85
Sva 107, 109, 152, 184
Svastika 109
Syndicate 70, 73, 77, 78, 79, 80, 81, 82, 85, 179

T

Taylor, James 42, 48, 49, 50, 71, 75
Tea 90, 91, 99, 167
Terry, Wilkins, George 17
The Book of Bombay 145
The Daily Graphic 150
The Graphic 105, 150
Times of India 106, 151, 153, 186
Townend, T.S. 162, 163
Tracey, William 17, 18, 35, 56
Turner, William, Mallord, Joseph 133
Tyreman, Mrs 58

U

University of Mumbai 71, 137, 175, 177, 178

V

Vice-Chancellor 69, 70, 71, 72, 73, 74, 75, 76, 81, 83, 85
Victoria and Albert Museum 13, 16, 18, 19, 20, 21, 23, 24, 25, 28, 35, 56, 140, 182
Victoria Gardens 13, 16, 17, 35, 45, 56, 57, 59, 60, 61, 62, 81

W

West, Raymond, Sir 149
Wilkins, Captain 10, 11, 12, 13, 14, 15, 17, 19
Wilson, John, Rev. Dr 31, 34, 36, 39, 40, 41, 43, 44, 48, 49, 50, 74, 83
Wood, Charles 13, 14, 16
Wood, H.T. 167, 168, 169
Wood's Education Despatch 68

Y

Yajnik, Umashankar, Yajnik 146, 148

Z

Zamorin 121

PHOTO CREDITS

Farooq Issa, Phillips Antiques, Mumbai
Chhatrapati Shivaji Maharaj Vastu Sangrahalaya, Mumbai
Neeta and Sushil Premchand, Family Archives
Sharada Dwivedi, Premchand Roychand (1831-1906), His Life and Times
Sir George Birdwood, SVA
Sir George Birdwood, The Industrial Arts of India
Sir George Birdwood, The Stree Bodhe And The Social Progress in India
Asiatic Society of Mumbai
University of Mumbai
Veermata Jijabai Bhosale Udyan, Municipal Corporation of Greater Mumbai
Library of University of North Florida, Jacksonville, Florida, USA
Swyrich Corporation, "houseofnames.com"
All other photographs from Wikipedia, Internet

NOTE FROM THE AUTHOR

Today, on the 8 December 2011, as I finish my book, I realize that this was the day when Sir George Birdwood was born. He has been in my thoughts for the last 3 years , but today hundreds of thousands of people on Facebook remember him on their 'Rare Books Society of India' section, where Sva, is featured along with the Introduction to Mrs. Murray-Aynsley's book Symbolism of the East and West, by George Birdwood, published in London by George Redway in 1900.

These examples of his writing are representative in a sense, of his deep-rooted beliefs, his expertise and his easy accessibility and availability to the people of India and England.